The Siren's Call and Second Chances

The Siren's Call
and Second Chances

A STORY OF PERSEVERANCE, SERVICE,
HEROIC COURAGE AND LOVE

⎯⥾⎯

Tom and Joan Kelley

Cover Art by John DuVal, www.duvalfineart.com
Copyright © 2017 by Tom and Joan Kelley
All rights reserved.
ISBN-13: 9781539979579
ISBN-10: 1539979571

To our children,
Liza, Kate, Jane, and Brian

Table of Contents

Foreword

ᰡ

by Judy Woodruff

I MET TOM AND JOAN Kelley at a Congressional Medal of Honor Society dinner in New York a few years ago. They are the kind of people you like instantly, friendly, outgoing and easy to laugh: Tom, the celebrated recipient of that Congressional Medal, and Joan, his bright, engaging partner. I knew there had to be more to his story than the paragraph in the dinner program, but it was only when they later sent me a galley copy of the book they'd written together that I began to appreciate who they are and what they represent.

As the daughter of a career Army father, I grew up surrounded by the sights, sounds and expectations of military life. In our family's travels to Germany, Taiwan and a half dozen Army bases in the United States, I saw the pull that service to country has on the men and women who sign up for duty. It's that same pull that drew Tom Kelley and Joan O'Connor to enlist in the Navy, at different times and different places, and that would ultimately draw them together.

Their story is, as the title says, one of courage, perseverance and love, in the face of relentless obstacles that would have defeated just about everyone else. Tom and Joan have written with bracing honesty about growing up in Boston — ten years, but less than ten miles apart — taking divergent paths through life, and repeatedly confronting large and small challenges that caused each to rethink what next step to take. With unusual candor, they share what they see as mistakes, embarrassments and moments of serious self-doubt. In other words, the very things that all of us can identify with.

I can't imagine reading this story by Tom and Joan Kelley, who don't meet until each has already led a full life, and follow their love for each other, for country, and for the men and women who serve it, without a sense of hope. Both turned moments that could have made them bitter, into a reason to give back. I was inspired, as will all of you who turn the page will be.

Introduction

—᧒

NOT LONG AFTER TOM AND I got together, some dozen years ago, we talked about writing our story. We wanted to leave a legacy concerning Tom's heroic actions that led to his receiving the Congressional Medal of Honor, and share the unique twists of fate that brought us together, giving us both a second chance at love and life. This is the only Medal of Honor recipient's memoir that includes his wife's complete story, including her own military career.

Although we're not experts on values, in telling others what we've discovered about perseverance, service, and courage, we hope to inspire our readers to overcome the obstacles life throws at all of us, and to move on from disappointment, while taking the high road.

We've tried to reflect honestly about what happened to us, while also pointing out the humorous side of our experiences. We hope you enjoy the journey!

All net proceeds of our book sales go to veterans' charities.

This is a true story, though some names and details have been changed. Characters who appear without last names are composites of individuals, and conversations are represented to the best of our recollection.

—Joan Kelley

Part One: Tom

C H A P T E R   1

The Tribute

~&~

BOSTON, MAY 2011

THE ORANGE AND RED STREAKS *of the setting sun filter through the windows of the large hallway at Boston's Hynes Convention Center, but I'm in a fog. The tinkle of ice in glasses and the hum of small talk build as the room fills with people. Six hundred seats have been sold for the Massachusetts Soldiers' Legacy Fund dinner, and I'm the main attraction. No pressure there.*

I swipe my sweaty palms against my suit coat pockets as first names, mostly Irish, fly through my head. Bob, John, Mary, Mae, or is it Margaret? I'm desperately hoping I'll remember their names—including those of our four children. I see more family, old friends and honored guests. That representatives from some of our major sponsors—people who've trusted their money to us—are here in person, only amps up the jitters.

I catch a glimpse of Joan, who's working the room from the other end. Her tight smile lets me know that she, too, is risking embarrassment with every handshake and hoping to avoid throwing up or passing out from nerves. We've worked hard for this—we've worked hard for this together. *She nods her head toward the doorway alerting me to a sea of uniforms that's just sailed into the room: Admiral Ann Rondeau, retired Navy Reserve Admiral Ray Couture, and retired army generals Jim Peake and Tom Sellers. And behind them, U.S. Senator Scott Brown has also just arrived along with several elected state officials.[1] As I walk toward*

---

1 Ann Rondeau, since retired from the navy, was then president of the National Defense University in Washington, D.C. Dr. Jim Peake was the former head of the U.S. Department of Veterans' Affairs, and Tom Sellers was then deputy commander of the Massachusetts National Guard.

them, my mind spins through the alphabet again, but then I look at Joan. We've got this, I can hear her say.

Organizing this fund-raiser might be the biggest public endeavor we've undertaken jointly, but separately and together, we've faced battles—literal and metaphorical—and we've usually won. Eventually. This is an especially tough moment for me, because although it's a party in honor of my forty-plus years of military and public service, my retirement was recently forced due to politics. Let's just say that some of the people walking into the room are not among my friends, but I've resolved to take the high road with them. Hopefully, they won't stay long.

Dinner and the main event of the evening are about to begin. I brush a piece of lint off the baby blue ribbon around my neck from which dangles my medal. Though it's been more than forty years since the day I earned this, the Congressional Medal of Honor will always be at the forefront of my mind. Not for the physical repercussions and the eye I lost in battle, but because it drew me into an elite club of outstanding military personnel—all of whom risked their lives for those of their people. All of whom embody the ideals and actions that Joan and I have dedicated our lives to upholding. That they're here to show their support doesn't surprise me, but will always touch me.

My fellow Medal of Honor recipients—Army Colonel (retired) Jack Jacobs, Navy Captain Tom Hudner (retired) and Paul Monti, father of posthumous recipient Sergeant First Class Jared Monti—take their seats among representatives from giant corporations such as General Dynamics, Raytheon, United Healthcare, and Granite Communications, hoteliers Nancy and Rick Kelleher, and more of the generous Boston philanthropists—Jack Connors, John Fish, and Marshall Carter.

Richard "Doc" Nelson—the man who saved my life some forty-two years ago, steps out of the crowd to congratulate me and wish me luck. After a strong embrace, he turns and moves to an honored place at our table. I flew him here from Georgia to be with me tonight, and I'm as happy to see him as I was on that blistering hot day when I was on death's doorstep.

The volume of chatter and laughter swells as our guests file into the ballroom. Familiar faces nod and hands reach out to shake mine as I make my way through the crowd with a smile plastered on my face.

I get to my seat and Joan is already there with Doc and her best friend, Linda. Just as I pull my chair out, the color guard appears—perfect timing! There's a hushed silence as we stand to attention. The guard marches to the stage followed by Pauline Wells, a uniformed police officer, whose lyrical alto voice lifts our spirits with the national anthem.

A relative calm ensues. For the first time all day, I'm exactly where I want to be—with Joan on one side and my old navy friend Dick Feinstein on the other. Dick's handiwork in writing the eye-witness accounts helped me earn the Medal of Honor.

Folks are conversing while happily digging into their salads, when the stage lights go down. The face of John Kerry, U.S. Senator from our state,[2] looms large on the twin screens over the stage:

"I want to thank you for honoring this important American, a great man of Massachusetts, Thomas Gunning Kelley. What a night to salute Tom and his wife, Joan. Not only is it Tom's birthday today, but tomorrow marks the forty-some years since President Nixon hung the Medal of Honor around Tom's neck for his courage and valor under enemy fire in Vietnam.

"I think it's clear to all of us that we got Tom back to Boston at the right time, before we launched Operation Iraqi Freedom and Operation Enduring Freedom. Under his leadership, Massachusetts has literally been second to no state in its service to returning soldiers and their families. We have Tom to thank for a lot of that. He championed the Welcome Home bonus, the SAVE program to help suicide-prone veterans, employment services, and he introduced a law allowing non-combat veterans to receive state benefits.

"Our very first commander-in-chief, George Washington, said 'The willingness in which our young people are likely to serve in any war, justified or not, is directly proportional to how they perceive veterans of earlier wars are treated and appreciated.' But there's also the special bond of veterans. We all feel a duty to show respect to our fellow veterans, to honor their sacrifice. In Tom's case, what they've achieved is one helluva lot!

---

2 At the time John Kerry, himself a Vietnam Veteran, was U.S. Senator from Massachusetts, but he later became America's Secretary of State under President Obama's administration.

"America demands sacrifice and sacrifice demands men like Tom Kelley—men of valor and courage to sustain this country. It makes us all very proud to thank you, Tom, for your courage, your devotion to this country and for the job you've done for the people of Massachusetts, for your never forgetting your fellow veterans and for all you've done to make us proud to be Americans. God bless you!"

"Wow," I whisper into Joan's ear, "I didn't expect that!"

"Neither did I," she murmurs back.

Next up, Senator Brown is telling the audience that he and I go back to when he was in the state legislature and we'd worked together on veterans' bills. There's more. His comments are similar to Senator Kerry's, and I appreciate them. It seems like my life is passing before me.

While dinner is being served, emcee Anne Aldred, an NBC affiliate newscaster, welcomes Peter Trovato to the podium. He's the founder and head of the Soldier's Legacy Fund, a charity that provides education for children of those killed in action in the War on Terror and our recipient of tonight's funds.

Joan and I can't sit still for long even though dinner's been served. I'm hopping up to greet more guests and Joan's visiting our family's tables. An eighteen-minute video produced by Joan with a team of professional filmmakers is highlighting my combined forty-two years of navy and public service. It's well done, but now I am literally watching my life pass before me on screen.

It's George Ford next, my Holy Cross classmate, approaching the podium, to deliver the coup de grâce, *by sharing tales out of school of my less than stellar achievements:*

"When one considers the background of someone who's risen to prominence, such as the one we honor tonight, we usually find great promise: academic achievement, a summa cum laude out of high school or college, Hollywood good looks, perhaps athletic success. But not so with our boy, Tommy Kelley. He has never been saddled with any of those attributes, never had to endure the anxiety of living up to those expectations.

"In our senior year, we had to take oral exams in philosophy. I still see that panel of eight Jesuits, walking out of the exam room, glassy-eyed trying to figure out what Tom's responses were to those questions. Because, no matter what questions were posed, and this may be indigenous to us Irishmen, Tom always had an

answer and a response: right field, left field, out of his left shoe, it didn't matter, but he had one. I daresay that his penchant for answers caused the recruiters, when he went down to Worcester to the navy recruiting office, to make the very fortunate mistake of bringing him into Officer Candidate School. Imagine how Tom's Medal of Honor redeemed and saved those recruiters from otherwise complete oblivion!"

Although I'm touched, I'm also slightly embarrassed when George compares me to Saint Thomas More who lost his life for upholding his principles and opposing King Henry VIII. My "upholding" only led to loss of my job, not my life.

George continues, "He's a man for all seasons and a friend for all reasons. A common man with a capital C. He has strength of character and embodies the Jesuits' creed of service to others. He is a fun-loving guy, but when push comes to shove, he produces."

Now my friend Ann Rondeau is telling the audience that the name, "Kelley" means bright-headed or shiny object and stubborn. She recalls the story of when I'd return the memos she'd worked on with red ink, stating it's "KELLEY WITH TWO Es!"

Then she moves into my Medal of Honor story: "The boat is disabled. The ramp won't go up. The rocket propelled grenade comes in. He circles the boats around the disabled craft and makes that boat stronger by making sure it can get its ramp up and get underway. That's a metaphor for him. He will encircle all of us who are in some way weak or disabled for the moment, having the belief that we can and will get stronger."

Ann wraps up her speech to cheers and applause and Joan's eyes tear up. I shift uneasily in my seat, smiling and nodding. My nerves are telling me my turn on stage is coming next.

The dais has been set up like a talk show with plush chairs and a coffee table for the mock interview of me by my colleague, Jack, whose day job is as a military commentator for MSNBC. He's done his homework, and is waiting for me in ambush with a series of questions about my navy career. Jack had served as an advisor to the Vietnamese 9th Infantry Division in the late 1960s, the same time I was there. I'm feeling a little self-conscious walking up to the stage, but then I kid Jack, who's very short, about whether there's a phone book for him to sit on.

Without missing a beat, he retorts, "Yeah, and it would have to be a Manhattan phonebook at that!" I chuckle and now I'm comfortable as we sit.

Jack begins, "Why did you volunteer to go from the navy's big, impregnable steel ships off the coast of Vietnam to those cardboard boats in the Mobile Riverine Force in the Mekong Delta, South Vietnam?"

I fire back, "Well, I knew that your outfit—the Vietnamese Army needed all the help they could get. And, being a good squid, I decided to do my bit for the army and go over there and bail them out."

When Jack got hit the first time over there, crossing a rice paddy, his reaction, as he then described it, was the same as mine.

"Yeah," Jack says, "you always think the tape is being run in the wrong direction. You're supposed to run it back, and it's supposed to happen to the other guy! And then I think you realize that it is happening to you and that's when you get really scared. I was always scared in combat. And I was convinced that anyone who said he wasn't scared was either lying, or a psycho, or a lying psycho."

I respond, "The one thing I feared more than combat was—not doing your job, not living up to what the men or women you led expected." Jack's nodding in agreement.

"How many times were you ambushed during your ten-month tour in the Mobile Riverine Force?"

"Eighteen to twenty times."

"Did you ever suspect why you were ambushed so frequently?"

"Sure, we were noisy and slow and they knew we were coming. We always went to very predictable places, and the canals were narrow, so you didn't have to be a marine sniper to land a round on us."

Jack notes that he experienced the same frequency of ambush and then muses aloud, with a healthy dose of irony, why the higher-ranking commanders insisted on repeating an unsuccessful tactic.

I add, "We used to have the colonels and commanders who would fly overhead in a helo and observe the action below. We'd be ducking incoming rounds; people would be getting injured and killed. We'd be calling for air support or artillery . . . 'No,' they'd reply, 'you don't need it; you're not in a firefight.'"

As our discussion turns to the dead and dying, I figure it's time to call Doc up to the stage.

"This is the navy corpsman who, at the risk of losing his own life, saved mine." Now I'm unable to hold back the tears. "Without him there would be no party tonight. He has my everlasting gratitude." The audience explodes in applause and stands for Doc.

We get around to my navy retirement and I explain that it was time to retire, because I knew I wasn't going any higher in the navy. No sooner do I get the words out of my mouth when I realize I'd given Jack the ammo—his cue to scold me for not following the rules and embarrass me further. He brings up the story of my tour commanding the USS Lang and bringing that destroyer into the Busan Harbor, South Korea, without tug boats, a pilot—or permission.

"I find it interesting that you did this with one eyeball, actually, and one propeller."

"Well, one eyeball and one screw equal luck, I guess."

Jack's got me pinned down. He kids me about being rejected by the navy, because of my nearsightedness the first time I tried to get in right after high school.

"I ate all those carrots, and I tried the Naval Academy, ROTC, the Coast Guard, and Massachusetts Maritime academy, but they didn't want me. Fortunately, Officer Candidate School took me four years later. Their standards were not quite as high, or maybe they were desperate."

"I think their standards were pretty high," Jack says. "We were very lucky to have you in the navy. But why did you stay in for thirty years?"

"I really loved what I was doing. There's nothing more rewarding, at least in my experience, than being around a military team, whether it's a platoon, or a company, or a ship, or an aircraft squadron. You form bonds. You rely on each other. In the end, it's all about the people."

CHAPTER 2
Another Attempt

——✂——

COLLEGE OF THE HOLY CROSS, MAY, 1960

BEFORE ME STOOD A MARINE recruiting poster come to life. Tall with an athletic build and a dozen medals pinned to his chest, Marine Corps Major Kelly oozed confidence. Even his firm handshake and the way his eyes locked onto mine conveyed a no-nonsense attitude.

I was about to graduate from the College of the Holy Cross, in Worcester, Massachusetts, with an economics degree and no clue how to use it. I was looking for the next step. Several of my classmates who had been in the Navy ROTC program spoke with such reverence about Major Kelly, I was sure they'd stake their lives on his ability to walk on water. One day I bumped into him on campus and decided to introduce myself.

My heart skipped a beat as Major Kelly uttered the words that would ultimately change the course of my life.

"It's a shame that you couldn't be one of us," he said, referring to my failed attempt to get into the ROTC program due to my poor eyesight.

Major Kelly congratulated me on my forthcoming graduation, wished me luck, and disappeared from my life. But his words stayed. They created a picture in my mind of a team that I knew I wanted to be a part of.

Had I gone to my other option, Boston College, this opportunity wouldn't have come my way, because there was no Navy ROTC program there and, consequently, no recruiter to goad me into following my dream. As mentioned, the U.S. Naval Academy, U.S. Coast Guard Academy, and the Massachusetts Maritime Academy had all rejected me.

Backing up a bit, while attending one of those schools had been my dream, I chose Holy Cross over B.C. partly because of what the school's symbol and nickname—the Crusader—meant to me. The Crusader's image is that of a knight mounted on an armored horse. Imagine having beliefs so strong—religious beliefs or otherwise—that you would sacrifice the daily comforts and security of ordinary life. Imagine having beliefs so strong that you would be willing to give your life to uphold them. Of course, the early Christian martyrs also gave their lives for their faith, but knights held a special pull on me. They drew strength and courage from their beliefs, but also from military service. *Would I ever have that kind of courage?* Becoming a modern-day knight appealed to me as a way to stand up for what I believed in, even if it was unpopular and resulted in personal sacrifice. Serving others and doing unto them as you would have done unto yourself seemed a good life motto.

In my first year at Holy Cross, I had trouble studying. I was used to the privacy and relative quiet of my own room at home. I was homesick, too. After a little while of trying to hit the books, I would get up and wander the halls of the dorm until I found some guys in a bull session that I would join. Living in close quarters with these students from varying economic and geographic backgrounds was part of my education. Though I didn't know it then, getting along with different people helped prepare me for a navy career in which I would work with men and women from even more diverse backgrounds and beliefs. Part-time jobs taught me the need to be honest and above board at all times. Most importantly, I tried never to take myself too seriously.

Eventually I developed good study habits. My classmates voted me business manager of our yearbook under the mistaken impression that fundraising and balancing the accounts were right up my alley, because I was an economics major. The yearbook was financed entirely by ads and subscriptions, and my job was a bit daunting at first, an eye-opener for me on the world of business. But with the help of the dedicated yearbook staff, we met our financial goals and published a book that still makes me proud.

My penchant for economics showed up in other ways too. I was perpetually short on funds, and always looking for ways more lucrative than waiting tables in the dining hall to increase my cash flow. One day I struck gold.

Uncle Bill, my mother's brother, was an executive at the Philip Morris Company in New York. The company had just come out with a new cigarette, Marlboro, symbolized by a rugged cowboy, the famous Marlboro Man. The company wanted to market the product on college campuses. Uncle Bill contacted me to ask if I would be interested in becoming the Marlboro Man on the Holy Cross campus. No-brainer! Of course I would!

In fact, I had been smoking since I was twelve years old, having been introduced to the naughty weed while serving as an altar boy at the West Roxbury Veterans' Administration Hospital. After Mass, old World War I veterans would approach me like they were treating me to an ice cream cone and say, "Hey kid, want a butt?" and then hand me a four-pack of Lucky Strikes. Thus began my days as a smoker that would last for forty-two years, until I quit when the studies linked it to cancer.

My new job gave me unlimited smokes and made me one of the most popular men on campus, especially when I could be found in the recreation area handing out free samples. The cigarettes would be shipped in huge boxes. Naturally, there was no shortage of volunteers to help me move them to my room.

A year later, Uncle Bill reluctantly gave me the bad news: the sales of Marlboros on campus had actually declined since I had become the Marlboro Man. The Phillip Morris Company of New York was pulling out of the Holy Cross campus and riding into the sunset. Well, of course, no one had been buying Marlboros, because good old Tom Kelley had been giving them away! *College Lesson Number 1*: You find out who your true friends are when you stop doing favors for them.

All of a sudden, I needed another source of revenue, if I wanted to be seen as a high roller in the eyes of girls I was trying to impress. Again, I struck gold. One of my pals headed the syndicate on campus for selling so called "football cards." I would sell you a card listing the odds on that week's college and pro football games and you would pick the winners of three or more games. The payoff would depend on how much you paid for the card and how many games you picked correctly. This job meant going room-to-room to sell the cards, collecting the cash, and then driving to Boston to deliver the proceeds of the sales. On Sunday evenings, after the weekend games, I would return to Boston for the cash to be paid out to my customers with the winning cards. This became particularly exciting work on one or two occasions when the money I handed in was short of what the record said I'd sold. The boss was not happy.

"Hey kid! Where's the rest of it?"

"That's all I collected."

"Well, the numbers don't add up. You sold fifty cards and you gave me the proceeds from forty-eight. Where are you hiding the rest?"

"I swear that's all I have. I must have screwed up."

"You sure did, college boy. I thought you kids were geniuses. Bring the rest of what you owe next week, or you may have trouble walking as well as counting."

I'm assuming the operators of the book in Boston liked me, because my legs were never broken, but I did have a few tense moments. At some point along the way it occurred to me that what I was doing was probably on the wrong side of the law, but I kept moving.

College Lesson Number 2: It's dangerous to step outside of your comfort zone, particularly when mobsters are involved.

My last financial endeavor occurred in the spring of my senior year when my buddy Tom McNaboe talked me into helping bankroll his book-making operation. The "six-hit" pool called for the customers—other students—to pick three major league baseball players and bet that among the three, they would collectively get six hits that day. This became really stressful when a couple of young rookies for the Giants, Willie McCovey and Orlando Cepeda, caught fire and were getting about three hits every day. Of course, everyone kept betting on them and Mac and I kept paying out until we went bust. I would like to say I got out of the gambling business because it was illegal, but it had more to do with the fact that I was losing my shirt.

College Lesson Number 3: If a deal sounds too good to be true, it probably is.

Weekends were spent hitchhiking back home to Boston, or hanging around the all-male campus.[1] The school arranged periodic "mixers" where

---

1 Holy Cross began admitting women in 1972.

busloads of girls from neighboring Catholic women's colleges were driven to campus and discharged into the field house for dances. Boys like me would be waiting there to ogle them. With high hopes that they'd accept, we would sometimes summon the courage to ask them to dance. The ultimate goal was to invite a girl to step outside to see the starry sky, but most of them were astute enough to reject the offer . . . at least in my case they were.

I dated in college, but I didn't have a serious girlfriend. Looking back, I realize that, until a few days before graduation, I had been in a quandary about what I was going to do after college. I didn't want to get involved with a girl and take on the added responsibility of an engagement as some of my classmates, who already had jobs, had done. Besides, I wasn't sure what kind of girl I was looking for. Nice, smart, pretty, and fun sounded right. I thought I had plenty of time to figure things out. I was among the youngest in my class, turning twenty-one just before graduation. My earlier dreams of a sea-going career were just dreams then. I had no idea what I'd do with my life.

Call it coincidence, fate, or luck, but on that very day when I met Major Kelly, my two roommates had signed up for the Navy Officers' Candidate School (OCS) program, a four-month course leading to a commission. When I asked them why, their response was a little bit of all the following: "It's a great life. You get to travel. You get a nice uniform. And there are a lot of pretty girls and stuff."

For obvious reasons, I was really curious about eyesight requirements. And, of course, when someone said, "Domenic wears glasses, and they took him," that was all I needed to hear. I had no job, and it was just days from graduation. I had nothing to lose.

The next day I went to the local recruiting office, feeling upbeat. The office was basically a small room in the post office. A nicely groomed petty officer wearing crisp white bell-bottoms greeted me with a firm handshake. At least I was in the right place.

"So what can I do for you?"

I pulled back my shoulders, stared him straight in the eye and tried to sound supremely confident. "I'd like to join the navy."

"Well, lots of people want to join the navy. Why do you think we'd want *you*?"

"I'm comfortable around the sea. I can swim and sail. And I'm about to graduate from college."

"Oh, are you a buddy of the two guys who were in here yesterday?"

"Yes, Sir. They spent last night trying to recruit me to join them."

"I notice you're wearing glasses." My heart fluttered. *Was this yet another door being closed?*

"Yes, Sir, but otherwise I'm in good shape."

"We'll see about that."

Handing me an application form, he directed me to a small desk in the corner. When I turned in the paperwork, he sent me to the next room, where a physician—or some guy wearing a white coat—listened to my heart and lungs, banged my knees with a hammer, looked at my teeth, and asked me to read the eye chart. I couldn't read the letters without my glasses, so I whispered a prayer.

They re-tested me with my glasses, and I passed!

Next he handed me an aptitude test that didn't have much in it about the navy. But it didn't seem too difficult and I felt confident after completing it.

"Okay, Mr. Kelley, everything looks good. We'll send this package to Boston, and you should be hearing from us in a few days."

I thanked the sailor and walked out with mixed emotions. *What had I gotten myself into? Was my dream of being a sailor and my desire for naval service, after many setbacks along the way, finally going to be realized?* I could now tell my parents I had an opportunity to serve my country, and they'd be proud of me. I was ecstatic.

Finally, a week or so before graduation, the door opened for me, and a path lay ahead. Life gave me a second chance, and I took it.

It may sound as though I joined the navy on a whim because I didn't have any other career options, and that wouldn't be entirely false, but it's not entirely true either. My love of the sea began in early childhood, and a sense of adventure had pushed me to join the sea service even before college. I'd been imbued with the importance of service by my parents and church my entire life. This was simply the inevitable coming to fruition.

CHAPTER 3

When the Siren First Called

⎯᷑⎯

BAR HARBOR, SUMMER OF 1946

IT WAS BLAZING HOT, EVEN for Maine. I was seven. My uncle took me to
see the visiting battleship, USS Missouri (BB-63). Her nickname was the
"Mighty Mo" because of her superior gun power. Just a year earlier, at the end
of World War II, she had been the site of the Japanese surrender in Tokyo Bay
and was now on tour.

I climbed the gangway and stood on the main deck, eyes wide. I drew in a
deep breath as I scanned every detail, from the newly scrubbed wooden decks
with neat coils of thick rope in the corners to the powerful sixteen-inch guns.
The navy men looked jaunty in their dress white bell-bottom uniforms with
their Dixie cup hats sitting back on their heads, as they went about their duties, joking with one another. Patriotism, and the sheer joy that World War II
was over, buoyed most Americans. It was a time of optimism and hope. This
was my first exposure to a real U.S. Navy ship and those sailors were my first
exposure to real life heroes. They remain among the navy's finest in its long
history.

From that day onward and throughout my boyhood, thoughts about life
aboard that massive hulking ship and sailing the seven seas had a hypnotic
pull on me. I dreamed of faraway shores with exotic landscapes and different
people speaking their own languages. Some of my childhood books incited
my wanderlust for adventure. Just from that one visit, I could sense the cama-
raderie among the sailors as they went about their duties. This meant something to me.

Playing team sports was like fresh air and sunshine. I needed it. I associated sports with teamwork. In spring and summer we (the kids who showed up on the playground that day) would play baseball and stick ball. Fall activities included two-on-two football, and in the winter we played ice hockey. I imagined that on a ship like that I'd be part of a great team. We'd work and live together. Plus, I would be helping others by protecting my country. That single visit to the battleship sparked a deep interest in a sea-services career. My young, impressionable eyes had seen the glory. The navy was a noble thing.

Maine is where I first encountered the sea herself. Every summer, as soon as he finished teaching the school year, my father would drive my mother, my older brother, John, and me from our home in Boston, to Northeast Harbor where my father managed a summer hotel—the hundred-room Kimball House.

John and I spent our days playing in the shallows, or in one of the inlets where the smooth, sun-heated rocks warmed the otherwise frigid water. At the Kimball House, I learned to swim and, as soon as I was old enough, I learned the responsibility of working. By eight or nine I was diving into small jobs around the hotel, which included scrubbing pots and pans. My father took advantage of our summers at the hotel to teach me the value of earning and saving my own money. More importantly, he showed me the worth of every individual by the way he treated waiters and waitresses with the same respect he showed the hotel's owners and its wealthy guests. He fostered teamwork and taught me leadership. Later I would realize that my father ran that hotel like a well-functioning ship.

My brother John taught me the fundamentals of sailing and nurtured my confidence in and around the water, and before too long I was teaching younger kids. With a slight turn of the rudder in my hand or a quick loosening of the sails, I controlled my speed and direction. I loved the soft "glug, glug" sound the boat made when the sails were trimmed and the boat cut through the water picking up speed. On the sea, in my Herreshoff Bull's-Eye, I was master of the elements.

That irresistible call to the ocean came every summer through my college years, until I overcame the eyesight obstacle and made my dream a reality.

Even today, I return to Northeast Harbor at least once every summer to re-connect with friends in this place that holds so many wonderful childhood memories, and from where I set out on a path towards sea service.

My desire to serve others came partly from family tradition and partly from my education by Jesuit priests. At forty-three years of age, my father was too old to be drafted in World War II, but he helped his country as a volunteer air-raid warden. His job was to march up and down our street at night wear-ing his helmet and making sure the blackout curtains in our homes shut in the light so that the enemy couldn't find targets and drop bombs. I would kneel on the big armchair in the living room window and watch him, my little chest bursting with pride.

From the time I attended Boston College (B.C.) High, a private school, through my college years at Holy Cross, I learned the value and satisfaction of living a life for God and others. [1] One afternoon when I was about twelve, I went to my brother John's room, where he was working at his desk with his beloved jazz music playing softly in the background. I asked him what he wanted to be when he grew up.

"I don't know," he said, chewing on his pencil and staring out the window, "Probably a teacher, like dad."

"Would you ever consider becoming a priest?" I asked thoughtfully.

"God, no! Why! Would you?"

The thought had entered my mind. I admired the priest's role in caring for souls and looking after people who are less fortunate, but my brother's response overwhelmed me and forced me to reveal what was really on my mind.

---

1 The school had, and still has today, an excellent reputation as a college preparatory school. A private boys' school, it was founded by the Jesuit priests in 1863 to educate the burgeoning popu-lation of Irish immigrants. The Jesuits are known as "God's Marines," because in the 1500s when they were founded, they had to accept orders to go anywhere in the world and live in extreme con-ditions. Similar to the military, the Jesuit order is highly organized with a hierarchy. Both demand personal sacrifice—sometimes the ultimate—conformity and obedience to a higher authority. This may be the reason some prominent military leaders graduated from B.C. High. Among them are four-star (the highest) generals: Army General George Casey and Marine Corps generals Joe Dunford, (presently chairman of the joint chiefs of staff) Jack Sheehan, and Joe Hoar.

"I like helping other people," I said digging in. "Uh—I was voted the most polite boy in third grade, remember? But—what I really want to do is find a girl and have a family, like mom and dad. "

"Well then," John said, looking slightly amused, "I guess that leaves out the priesthood!" He waved me off and turned back to his homework. "Don't feel bad about it. It's only for certain people."

It wasn't too long after that talk when I discovered girls, and my brother's words rang truer than ever.

When it was time to choose a high school, I chose B.C. High. Academic excellence and family tradition were my incentives for wanting to attend. My father was a graduate, my brother was already enrolled, and I felt I would fit in comfortably. The school's slogan is "to form leaders of competence, conscience, and compassion who seek to do things for the greater glory of God." Implicit is the ideal of being a man or woman for others.

Under the close supervision of the Jesuits, we studied Latin, Greek, math, literature, history, and a language. I loved to read, so I enjoyed history, Latin, and literature, but I shied away from the sciences and religious classes with those frustrating formulas designed to prove the existence of God. Rather I developed my own spiritual life grounded in the Christian principles of faith, service to and love of my fellow man. More important than the formal curriculum were the principles of helping others that we learned from our priest-teachers.

B.C. High reinforced my parents' lessons that the world wasn't all about me and that the acquisition of things—money, status, objects—is not the sole reason we are put on Earth. Acquiring things is only satisfying for a while. Once the novelty wears off, you're where you started, looking for your next acquisition. Yes, it is important to excel academically and have a fulfilling career that allows you to support yourself and your family. But our *raison d'être* includes helping others, particularly those less fortunate—family, friends, coworkers, the public, the nation—and the satisfaction derived from service will last a lifetime, because it's built on love of mankind, and love never fails.[2]

---

2 St. Paul to the Corinthians, Chapter 13.

Our teachers insisted that spending too much time with girls could lead one into temptation, which didn't seem like a bad idea to me! Thus, we were encouraged to avoid those "occasions of sin." Ironically, the very same priests who were warning us about the evils of sex were sponsoring dances for us at parish halls where the lights were dim and the music slow, and where there weren't enough chaperones to ensure we "left room for the Holy Ghost."

I grew to admire most of my Jesuit teachers. These highly educated men had given up worldly pursuits, marriage, and children to serve God and pass on their knowledge to us.

Charlie McCoy, as a former marine with exotic World War II service in China, impressed me the most. When he enlisted in the Marine Corps after his first year at Boston College, and just after the Japanese surrender in 1945, they sent him to occupied northern China. He returned home, graduated from Boston College, and then went to B.C. High to teach and to coach football and baseball. Later, he entered the seminary and became a diocesan priest. He must have missed the adventure of the military, because he joined the navy and served as a chaplain, earning a Purple Heart in Vietnam for his combat injuries. Twenty five years later, he retired as a navy captain.

The story goes that Charlie, a marine private first class, left a pair of boots to be repaired at a local cobbler in Okinawa, Japan, in 1946, days before he was deployed to China on short notice. Many years later, now a priest and navy captain, he returned to Okinawa on official business for the Marine Corps and remembered the cobbler's shop. He told the cobbler his name and said that he was there to pick up his boots. After disappearing into the back of his shop, the old cobbler returned and announced: "Come by tomorrow. They'll be ready then."

Charlie was a good teacher, tough but fair. He took no guff from his pupils, and anyone who had the privilege of being one of his students or one of his athletes came away a better person, or at least with a thicker skin. My high school experience taught me lessons that led to my choice of career. There I acquired the principles that I have held on to all my life.

And my initial spark of desire for navy service was further fueled by a famous World War II Navy hero, John F. Kennedy.

I actually served Kennedy (then a U.S. senator) his breakfast as a room-service waiter at our Maine hotel. He was staying with us while recuperating from war-related back surgery. He was already married to Jackie, but she had not come with him. As a waiter, I got to know what he liked for breakfast. He would call down with his order for double eggs, double orange juice, double toast, bacon and, of course, two pots of coffee. Naturally eager to please, I would promptly deliver the order to his room.

Wow! The guy has an appetite!

He would greet me at his room door with his magnetic personality and put me at ease. Handsome, friendly, an Irishman, and, on top of that, a glamorous naval war hero who had operated patrol boats in the South Pacific—he was an icon, even then.

It didn't dawn on me until much later that there was usually a shower running in the background . . . and that someone else (certainly not Jackie!) was taking it when I wheeled in his . . . double orange juice.

Kennedy was a Catholic and since he didn't have a car with him, he'd asked my father to take him to Mass on Sundays. At collection time, he'd fish around in his pants pockets for some change and coming up empty, he'd turn to my father and ask him for a dollar. Apparently, he didn't carry cash around and depended on others for such acts of charity. I'm not sure he ever repaid my father. In any case, he was a hero of mine.

CHAPTER 4
Roots

_~_

THE 1950S AND EARLIER

ALTHOUGH THOSE MAINE SUMMERS WERE magical, I like to say that I consider myself lucky to have had a perfectly unremarkable and ordinary childhood. My parents were not demonstrably affectionate, but they truly loved and respected each other. I don't remember a serious argument between them. They were strict, yes, but they raised us with gentle patience and understanding. John and I certainly felt loved and looked after. My father was kind, hard-working, honest, and humble. He passed his love of books and the opera down to me. My mother stayed at home, as did most mothers and wives in those days. When John and I were older, she worked part-time in a book shop.

John and I were three years apart, but we were close. I looked up to him, and he watched out for me at school and at play. He patiently allowed little brother to tag along with him and his friends until little brother found friends of his own. Among his many great qualities, he was highly intelligent, intense, and outspoken; whereas I was more even-tempered and eager to please. I was crushed if I disappointed anyone, especially my parents.

I was about eight years old and making every effort to impress my brother and his friends when I fell off my bike in front of the house.

"Fuck!" I yelled.

Like a shot, both parents rose out of their chairs on the porch. "What did you just say?" asked my father.

"Fuck," I repeated, this time under my breath, head bowed.

My mother wanted to know where I had learned that word.

"From Tommy O'Keefe," I muttered. Tommy was the neighborhood tough guy who lived on the next street.

"Do you know what it means?" she asked.

"No," I whimpered, tears forming.

That answer made them happier than if I had never used the "F" word. I told them the truth, but if I had said "yes," they would have had simultaneous strokes on the porch. In those days, most Catholic families kept their kids in the dark for as long as possible about the facts of life. This made it far more interesting for inquisitive young minds.

The military is in my blood going back to the American Civil War. John Gunning, my great-grandfather on my mother's side, hailed from Limerick, Ireland, and emigrated with his family to the Roxbury area of Boston in 1842 when he was three.

There he spent his childhood and grew up to work as a laborer. He married but left his pregnant wife, Maria nee Downey, in 1862, a year after the Civil War had begun, and volunteered to join the Union Army.[1] Whether it was because the army offered a decent wage for an Irish immigrant who otherwise couldn't find work, or because he harbored strong Unionist or abolitionist views is something I'll never know.[2]

Unfortunately, he was not as lucky in his military career as I would be in mine. He didn't get a second chance. In August 1864, he was captured at the Battle of Weldon Railroad, Virginia, after a heavy engagement with Confederate forces. Union General Ulysses S. Grant had interdicted a key section of the enemy's railroad supply lines.

Young John Gunning was captured along with 200 other Union soldiers and imprisoned in Salisbury, North Carolina, where he died, at the age of twenty-five, probably of starvation or disease like so many others. A few years ago, I visited the football-field-sized mass grave where my great-grandfather was buried. The simple marker read:

---

1 My great-grandfather joined the 39th Massachusetts Regiment, Company B.

2 Joining the army then was a risky occupation as it is today. Many choose such an occupation for the same reasons as my great-grandfather: to pay bills, develop skills, or go to college.

IN THE TRENCHES JUST SOUTH OF THIS SPOT REST THE BODIES OF 11,700 SOLDIERS OF THE UNITED STATES ARMY, WHO PERISHED DURING THE YEARS 1864 AND 1865, WHILE HELD BY THE CONFEDERATE MILITARY AUTHORITIES AS PRISONERS OF WAR IN A STOCKADE NEAR THIS PLACE.

As I stared at the grass under which my great-grandfather was buried, a single question ran through my mind: *Was it worth it?*

The same question strikes me every time I visit the Vietnam War Memorial in Washington, D.C., that honors the 58,000 who died in one of the longest and most controversial wars in the history of this country. Although 620,000 lives were lost in the Civil War, it brought us the emancipation of slaves and the preservation of the Union. There is no similar weighty statement I can make for the Vietnam War.

While my ancestor John Gunning was at war, Maria gave birth to Thomas Gunning, their only child and my grandfather and namesake. Maria never remarried. I assume she was strong and resourceful to have raised her son on a military widow's pension—something I would eventually learn much about.

Perhaps because Thomas was a successful underwear salesman in Boston and could afford it, or maybe because he had been an only child, Thomas and his wife Mary had thirteen children of their own. My mother, Elizabeth, was born in 1900. She was the fifth born of five brothers and seven sisters. Thomas raised that big brood in a single-family house on one of the nicer streets in the Dorchester section of Boston. They identified themselves by their local parish, St. Mark's, whose famous parishioner, Rose Fitzgerald Kennedy, the mother of President John F. Kennedy, sponsored my mother, vouching for her character, when she received the sacrament of Confirmation. Thomas and I never met. He died before I was born.

My mother was slender, attractive, and well-dressed, and she remained that way all her life. She had a strong will and independent spirit that I inherited, along with her sense of humor. As a young woman, she spent summers waitressing in Ogunquit, Maine, at an inn where, as my luck would have it, she met my father—a tall, shy gentleman from Boston.

John Basil Kelley was two years her senior and considered a good catch. Not only had he graduated from Boston College High School, a school that still requires applicants to pass a rigorous exam, he had a steady profession. After graduating from Boston College, he taught junior high English and math and would later become principal of one of Boston's elementary schools.

My parents started their married life together in Dorchester and soon moved to Boston's West Roxbury. John was born first and I came into their lives on Mother's Day, May 13, 1939, exactly one-hundred years after John Gunning was born in Ireland. My mother never let me forget, on every birthday, that my arrival on Mother's Day was the best Mother's Day present, ever.

CHAPTER 5

Officer Candidate, First Ship, My Own Family

⎯⎯⎯ঔ⎯⎯⎯

NEWPORT, RHODE ISLAND AND CHARLESTON, SOUTH CAROLINA, 1960S

INEXPLICABLY, OCS HAD LOWER VISION standards than ROTC or the service academies. Go figure! It goes to show that if you apply to enough programs, one might have slightly different admissions requirements, and you're in!

And just like that, I had a real opportunity to become an officer in the U.S. Navy. My parents were thrilled and very happy for me, not to mention somewhat relieved that they wouldn't have to support me after college. They thought that I had shown maturity and good judgment in picking a career.

OCS and its summer-friendly Newport Rhode Island location became my after-college plan. While at that time the surest road to success in the navy began at the Naval Academy, many officers had risen to command and other senior positions after starting at ROTC and OCS.[1]

One month after my twenty-first birthday, I raised my right hand and joined the navy family as an E-2, seaman apprentice, my rank until I completed training. I was warned prior to taking the oath that if I failed to complete the sixteen-week training program, I would "wash out" and be required to serve two years in the fleet as an enlisted sailor. I wonder, does the army call this getting "run over?"

---

1 It is possible to rise to the very top of the navy leadership by starting in the enlisted ranks, just as the late Chief of Naval Operations, Admiral Mike Boorda, did.

I reported to OCS at the Newport navy base on June 30, or "30 June," as I quickly learned was the military style. Check-in, issuance of clothing and gear, various immunization shots, and finally "marching" to our barracks went fairly smoothly.

Marching was a bit of a joke. One of my new classmates was a first class petty officer (E-6) who had obviously done this before. He got us going, shouting out some gobbledygook, which I later learned was called "cadence," designed to keep us in step. I was too busy trying to translate what he was shouting, thinking it might be about when supper was going to be served. I and several others struggled to keep up, while the rest marched on.

We were assigned to a thirty-man company in an open-bay barracks on the second floor of a World War II vintage building. The proper naval term for floor is "deck." There was a "head," otherwise known as a bathroom, at one end with open showers and sinks. We each had a tiny footlocker into which we placed our gear after being instructed on how to "stow" it in precisely the correct order so that everything fit. We then marched, again, this time to the mess hall for supper, moving our feet a little more smartly.

Every morning my company and ten or so others would muster in formation when the flag was raised as the national anthem played. Then we'd receive orders and instructions for the day. My company's spot was at the rear of the formation, which meant that for almost four months I couldn't hear an intelligible word. After we received the "plan of the day," we would march to class and spend the next several hours learning subjects like steam and diesel engineering, navigation, seamanship, weapons, including ships' armament and small arms, as well as customs and traditions that had kept the navy afloat since 1776.

Evenings were spent studying for the next day's quizzes, shining shoes and belt buckles for the next morning's personnel inspection, and "titivating"—formerly known as cleaning—our barracks for daily inspection. "Chow" or what I used to call meals, was pretty good as I recall, and there was plenty of it. Every now and then we were marched to the Navy Exchange that was a mini department store where we could purchase "gee dunk"—snacks and soft drinks.

About two weeks into OCS, I was uneasy about whether I could pass the academic part of the course. Although I'd developed good study habits in college, I was never at the top of my class. One afternoon, I was called in to see the guy in charge, the company officer. After I gave him my best attempt at a smart salute, he told me to stand at parade rest.

He let me know that my navigation and engineering grades were not up to snuff and asked me what the problem was. *Oh no, I've overcome the hurdle of poor eyesight. Now I'm having trouble with the coursework?* I didn't want to join the enlisted ranks for two years.

"Well, Sir, I was an economics major in college, so I didn't take any science or math courses."

"That may be true, but you can't skate out of here with these grades," he raised his eyebrows to emphasize the point. The hair on the back of my neck stood up. Not only would I disgrace myself if I flunked out, but I knew I'd disappoint my parents.

"You know," he said, "we only graduate people from this course who we feel are reliable enough to entrust with millions of dollars of government property and hundreds of lives. When we accepted you into this class, we assumed you had the potential to live up to that responsibility."

"I know that, Sir."

"I can see that you have a good work ethic, and I know you're trying hard. Here's what I'm going to do," he said, laying out a plan whereby I would be tutored on Saturday afternoons in "stupid study."

"You'll find that by working through the really tough problems with others, you'll be better able to do it on your own."

That bit of advice reminded me of how important teamwork can be. It saved me academically.

My study group consisted of a handful of guys, about half of whom pulled the underachievers up to their level. And everyone was rooting for the team. After a while my grades improved. While I was never at the top of my class, I happily placed somewhere in the middle and could eventually help others who were struggling.

After the first four weeks, we were allowed off-base liberty from noon on Saturday till "1800" (6:00 p.m.) on Sunday. That is, if we didn't have a "uniform discrepancy": tarnished belt buckle, un-spit-shined shoes, or an "Irish Pennant," an ethnic slur for having a loose thread on one's clothing, in which case you would spend Saturday afternoons marching around in circles on the "grinder," the parade ground. Being one of the least squared away of my classmates in military bearing, I usually didn't go ashore until suppertime. I say least squared away because uniform perfection and close order drills were not high priorities for me, even then. The larger goal of mission success was foremost in my mind. You could be the most squared away sailor in the navy, but if you lost sight of your mission, you betrayed your service.

Liberty was pretty routine. It meant meeting up with my pals, especially my two Holy Cross classmates, Domenic and Don, and downing a few beers and burgers. Having just turned twenty-one, I was able to drink legally for the first time, which didn't have quite the thrill as using my old fake ID card. Usually we would return to the base at night, but on a couple of occasions I trekked to Boston in uniform to let my folks know I was still in the navy. I am very happy that I did go home and spend time with my father who, as it turned out, wouldn't live to see me commissioned as an officer.

One of the coolest benefits of being an officer candidate was free laundry and dry cleaning service—or so I thought. Every morning before breakfast, a laundry truck would pull up outside the barracks and every few days I would give the driver my dirty "skivvies," underwear, and "dungarees," pants. The next day they would be back. Good deal! When I graduated in October, the truck driver was in attendance, not to congratulate me, but to give me a bill covering four months of "free" laundry service. I paid another bill for membership in a locker club in downtown Newport and all the "free" booze Wolfie, the owner, had so generously provided. Thus ended another lesson in real-world financial management for this economics major from Holy Cross!

My favorite area of training was damage control, which is nothing like what the White House does when a messy story is leaked. Damage control, the way I learned it, was how to save a sinking ship and put out a shipboard fire. We bonded as a team in the firefighting simulator battling real flames and smoke, and real world disaster training didn't stop there. In the USS Buttercup, we practiced working in flooded parts of the ship—pumping out compartments and shoring up "bulkheads," walls with heavy timbers. For the next thirty years I held on very closely to what I learned in those two training buildings. Fortunately, I didn't have to use this type of training to save lives.

I would venture to say that teamwork is more important in the navy than in the other services because of how dependent one is on the ship's smooth functioning, which is maintained by each person lifting his own load in concert with the others. If your tank or transport vehicle gets damaged or catches fire, you can rescue the injured and abandon the vehicle. Pilots can eject and parachute to safety; hopefully they land on terra firma. But on a ship in the navy, you are always operating with a certain level of vulnerability because you're on the water, hundreds or even thousands of miles from land with so many lives at stake—a few hundred on a typical ship and five thousand on an aircraft carrier. You can't just abandon the ship. Also, a ship costs a heck of a lot more than a single aircraft or tank.

While it was important that we learned how to take care of and maintain the ship, it was absolutely crucial that we knew how to limit damage and run the auxiliary systems. This training enabled one to act quickly without confusion in real life navy combat situations and emergencies.

My euphoria over finishing OCS and moving to the fleet was shattered by a phone call two days before graduation. It was my mother.

"Tommy," she paused, trying not to cry.

"Your father went to work this morning and—" A chill ran through me as I strained to hear her tear-choked voice.

"He's had a massive heart attack— The ambulance took him to the hospital— Can you please come?"

My father, who had just turned sixty-two, had never missed a day in the classroom. He had been a rock of strength for the whole family, and now my dream to have my proud parents see me commissioned in the navy was replaced with my fervent hope that he would simply survive, at least until I got to his bedside in Boston.

He knew I was there along with my mother and brother. I believe that if he could have spoken, he would have told me how proud he was of my choice to enter the navy.

He was a true gentleman. My first and best role model. I never heard him curse or say unkind words about anyone. It's true that in both areas I may not have measured up to his legacy, but I have always tried to be like him and adopt the values he taught me of integrity, kindness, humility, moral courage, and service to others. He taught me to tolerate different views and treat with sensitivity those who are less tolerant or less respectful of others.

My father's wake was held in our home over two days. It was a typical Irish wake. Mostly men and a few women, gathered in the kitchen to share stories of my dad while throwing back many drinks, and I mean many. Inevitably, a few loud arguments broke out as folks who hadn't seen each other for years renewed old grudges, but acting as peacemaker took my mind off the utter devastation of my dear dad's passing.

When I returned to Newport after my bereavement leave, my class had already graduated. My mom came to attend my private commissioning ceremony and spend some time with me. It was a very therapeutic time for both of us, but I hated the thought of her going back to an empty house while I set off on my new career. Fortunately, her sister, Rose, came down from Maine and helped her settle into her new life.

I attended communications school in Newport for six weeks and visited Boston on weekends. In mid-December, Mom and I headed for Charleston, South Carolina, my first duty station, so we could spend the holidays together. It was a leisurely drive down south in my first car, a 1954 Buick. Yet, my most vivid recollection of the trip is not so pleasant.

We were crossing into South Carolina, and I heard someone speaking a very strange language on the car radio. I could make out only a few of the words but one, repeated over and over, was "nigra." The voice turned out to be that of then Governor Strom Thurmond. And that marked the first of things I would come to learn about in the South.

My mostly southern shipmates introduced me to NASCAR, not a popular sport in Boston. It was my privilege to sample a Dr. Pepper long before New Englanders even heard of it. And I got my first mouthful of hominy grits (dried, ground, and boiled corn kernels) which still tastes like paste to me.

In any event, I was on my way to adventure on my first ship, or so I thought. When I joined the navy, I envisioned this moment and saw myself stepping onboard a dashing destroyer with a bone in her teeth—slang for cavalier—or onboard a mighty aircraft carrier striking fear into the heart of an enemy. Instead, I was assigned to a plodding, unglamorous repair ship—the USS Pandemus (ARL-18)[2] homeported in Charleston.

I don't remember having this aspiration before attending OCS, but my training in naval subjects, including command structure, and who does what job onboard a ship, quickly led me to want command at sea. I desired the top job on the ship—that of "captain" or "skipper," "the old man," and the team leader. For me, and mostly everyone else in my class, being captain was the pinnacle of every shipboard officer's dream.

My first assignment was out of my hands, but I was determined to make the most of it. I reported just before Christmas 1960.

As the operations officer I oversaw a department of thirty men whose job it was to operate radio gear and navigation equipment. It was my first morning. I was at work at my desk when a large man with a walrus mustache appeared.

"So I noticed you graduated from communications school. What did they teach you there?" he asked in a very deep voice that matched his commanding presence.

"Well, Sir, all about how to operate and maintain radios, radars, and such."

"We have talented enlisted men to do that stuff! I'm going to give you two simple chores: make sure the ship arrives at the right place at the right time and make sure we can communicate with the outside world. You'll be embarrassing both me and Holy Cross if you screw up. Got it?"

"You bet, Sir."

So went my first conversation with my new commanding officer (CO), Bob Kubizewski, who I was happy to learn, was also a Holy Cross graduate. Admittedly, I was a bit intimidated by him. As the captain he had absolute control. He could make you or break you, and on deployment the captain and

---

2 Pandemus had been a landing ship in World War II, like the ones that carried troops to Normandy, Iwo Jima, and Guam. The navy kept a few in commission as repair ships for mine sweepers at this time.

his crew would be together 24/7. So, it made sense to take steps to be on his good side, and fortunately he treated me well.

One day while operating at sea, we lost a major piece of navigation equipment, causing us to flail about in proximity to the ships we were supposed to repair. A collision was imminent. One of the chiefs went into a panic and started yelling at his men to fix the problem on the double. Without missing a beat, our captain calmly ordered the deckhands to drop the anchor. He intended to stabilize the ship first. The ability not to lose your head, when all around you people are losing theirs, is common to all effective leaders. Calmness is contagious. When demonstrated by the captain, it gives all hands a sense of trust and confidence that the situation is under control. Even when panic gnaws at the edge of your gut, it's easier to push aside when you have a strong leader.

A Bostonian named Bill Somerville was our executive officer (XO), or second-in-command. With more than twenty years as an enlisted sailor (such officers were known as "mustangs") he knew a thing or two. From Bill I learned to love my sailors almost as a father loves his children. Like a good father, being a good officer means letting your team know when they don't measure up and praising them when they do.

Our ship spent most of the time in Charleston repairing the minesweepers based there. A couple of times a year we'd get underway and travel to Norfolk, Virginia, or Panama City, Florida, where a smaller number of minesweepers were based.

Leaving port for an underway period was always a rare, big deal for most of this crew. Since they were on a repair ship, they viewed their assignment as "shore duty," never expecting to actually get underway. When the orders came to deploy, the running joke was that the area under the ship's bottom would be dredged to get rid of our weeks of accumulated coffee grounds before we could shove off.

Being a Northerner, I immediately pulled the charts for Central America when the captain told me to get the maps for Panama City. Everyone else seemed to know that Panama City, *Florida*, was just below Georgia.

"Watch standers" were in short supply so the skipper decided that the warrant officers would be trained as officers of the deck, in charge of the ship while underway.[3] The warrants' normal job was repairing ships' parts and while they were good at that, they knew very little about ship driving. In fact, none of them had ever set foot on the bridge of a ship, and it was my job to qualify them.

"Okay, gentlemen," I said. "Do I have a deal for you! In six months, I'll teach you everything I've learned about driving a ship. In return, you teach me about machinery repair, electrical systems, and the finer points of damage control."

"Aw c'mon, kid," one of the warrants said. "We don't belong up here on the bridge any more than you belong down in the repair shops."

I explained that to stay in the navy, I would need to learn from the experts how to keep the ship and its gear running. Then I said, "Let's give it a try, okay?"

Initially they resisted, but I knew my way around the bridge and was able to help them become acclimated in navigation, ship-handling, and communications. They actually seemed to enjoy standing duty on the bridge with me. In turn, they became terrific mentors in my navy education. Maybe in their new role they saw themselves with greater responsibility, performing tasks they never dreamed they were capable of? Empowering those junior to me in rank and learning from those senior to me in service was the bedrock of my leadership style.

Those brief and infrequent times at sea gave me an opportunity to practice and improve the seamanship and navigation skills I'd learned in OCS. Our top speed was about eleven knots, which was hardly cool. I continued to wish I were assigned to a destroyer—a greyhound—that would dash around at speeds of nearly thirty knots. Instead, our ship was like an overweight basset hound slowly making its way. To take command of my own ship, I had to advance in the ranks, meaning I had to get a department head assignment next. To get that, I'd have to apply for destroyer school and complete the department head course.

---

3 All services have warrant officers who are senior to the enlisted ranks but junior to the officer ranks. In the navy, warrants are former enlisted sailors, highly skilled in a specialty such as carpentry, electricity and machinery.

The upside to serving on a ship that rarely left the pier was that for the first time in six months, I actually had time for a social life. We used to hang around a bar in Charleston on East Bay Street called Big John's. Supposedly the owner, John Canaday, had played professional football for the New York Giants. The place was scruffy, dimly lit with shuffleboard and air hockey games, sawdust on the floor, and cheap beer.

We got to know the local girls. One was a schoolteacher named Gwen Qualey who caught my eye. She was smart, pretty, and fun. Gwen's mother had died when she was eight, and her father had moved the family from New Jersey to Charleston where he became the operations manager of the port. He married a South Carolina woman. So Gwen grew up with a mixture of Southern gentility and Northern street smarts.

There were three other junior officers aboard the Pandemus. Two were married and one was a bachelor like I was. The bachelor, Frank Bollinger, and I became good friends. After a few months, we decided to rent a house on the beach, along with two officers from other ships. A stucco ranch out on the Isle of Palms, about a thirty-minute ride from the naval base, it was affectionately known as a "snake ranch," meaning a house rented by bachelors. We were off duty about three nights out of four and very seldom got underway on the ship, so there was plenty of time to party. And party we did!

One of my college friends, Vince Promuto, came to town in 1961 as a member of the Washington Redskins to play an exhibition football game. With promises of beer and girls, I invited him to bring a few of his teammates to a party at our snake ranch after the game. They arrived about midnight, and the wild partying began. Since the guys had been in training camp for about a month and hadn't had a drink, after about two beers some got a bit boisterous.

Fortunately we were the last house on a dead end street, because between us and the rock and roll blasting from the stereo, the noise level was several decibels too high. Noticing we were short of Ripple wine, I was on my way through the smoke-filled room into the kitchen for more when my jaw dropped. Bob Toner, a former Notre Dame tackle, was holding this petite girl over his head and twirling her around like she was a human baton. It was my friend, Gwen. And the look on her face was terror. She was begging him to stop.

"Hey," I yelled at him. "What are you doing?"

Apparently he hadn't heard me above the din. I grabbed the muscled arm of his six-foot, six-inch frame and held on.

"Knock it off, guy. Can't you see she's scared?"

"Huh, what the—?" The hulk finally noticed my one-hundred-and- fifty-pound presence.

"Look, you're scaring this girl. Will you please stop and let her down?"

Amazingly, he did. The expression on Gwen's face was pure gratitude and I was proud to have been her rescuer. Later I wondered what would have happened to me if Bob hadn't been so acquiescent. That moment was probably the spark that led to Gwen and me marrying a year later.

Gwen left in September to teach in upstate New York, but she had introduced me to her family, and they treated me very well, inviting me to Sunday dinner and such. Gwen and I were a good match. We were Northerners; we liked to have fun with our friends and didn't take ourselves too seriously. When Gwen came home for Christmas, we decided that we'd be married the following summer. I did the formal thing, asking Gwen's father for her hand. His face lit up and he welcomed me with a hug. It was nice being accepted into the family, but the navy would eventually pull me away from my new bride.

When the Cuban Missile crisis broke out in the fall of 1962, after the failed U.S.-led invasion of the Bay of Pigs, the Soviets assumed the U.S. was weak.[4] They thought President Kennedy would acquiesce to their ballistic missiles stationed in Cuba and positioned to take out the continental U.S. Tensions increased until both sides seemed to be on the brink of a nuclear strike.

---

4 In the early 1960s the U.S. led an invasion into Cuba of those exiles opposed to the new revolutionary leader Fidel Castro. It occurred in the Bay of Pigs, Cuba. But the failed invasion caused Castro to increase his ties with the USSR. We watched TV in horror as missile launch facilities were being built in Cuba, only ninety miles from U.S. shores. For thirteen days the U.S. was in a standoff against Cuba and the USSR. The U.S. established a military blockade to prevent further missiles from coming into Cuba and demanded that the weapons already there be returned to the USSR.

This was my first exposure to wartime danger. Although it was exciting, it was more filled with trepidation. The entire U.S., not just a few Southern states, faced annihilation if the Soviets launched a missile strike on us.

Pandemus and just about every ship in the Atlantic Fleet got underway and headed toward Cuba. We were part of the military blockade ensuring that no further USSR missiles made their way into Cuba.

Action, finally!

There were dramatic moments in which a U.S. Navy destroyer, coincidentally named the USS Joseph P. Kennedy (DD 850) after the president's brother, stopped a Lebanese cargo ship, but let it through after it was cleared. If the Soviets hadn't backed down and removed their nuclear weapons, we would have invaded Cuba in a moment's notice. Thankfully, the Soviets did back down and removed their missiles.[5] We were told to stand down from general quarters.[6]

Curiously, the people at home knew more about what was going on in the big picture than I did. We had no TV at sea and no instant news, and fortunately most of the action was diplomatic and, therefore, took place in Washington, Moscow, and the United Nations.

As it turned out, our role on Pandemus had been to go alongside every ship of the dozen in our destroyer group each day and transfer their trash and garbage to us. What a letdown! Here I thought I had an opportunity to influence the balance of world power. I had visions of a grand sea battle (in which no one was mortally hurt) and in which our little ship was part of the U.S. defensive coalition. Maybe this one episode would have resulted in the Berlin wall coming down, and I could claim credit for my tiny role?

I chortle to myself when I think I spent a very significant time in history milling about in a glorified garbage scow with only forty millimeter

---

5 The president was playing brinksmanship close to the line. Just two days before the crisis ended, Kennedy was convinced we'd have to invade Cuba and launch a nuclear strike on the Soviet Union at the same time to preempt their retaliation. The president's advisers persuaded him to give diplomacy more time. Pope John XXIII begged both sides for a peaceful resolution, and it worked.

6 General quarters is a signal aboard a naval vessel for all hands to man their battle stations and remain there until ordered to stand down.

anti-aircraft guns. But I'm sobered by what could have happened and grateful for the success diplomacy played in saving the day.

Up to this point I hadn't questioned my decision to join the navy, but this garbage detail made me wonder what kind of future I'd have without the proper qualifications to advance. After completing my obligatory two-year tour on Pandemus, I applied for destroyer school, only to suffer a serious blow to my ego when I was turned down for reasons that were not shared with me.

But this turn of events was fortuitous, as it meant Gwen and I could start our family. The next year she delivered our first child, Elisabeth (Liza), named for my mother. In the summer of 1963, I received orders to a destroyer home-ported in Newport: the USS Davis (DD-937). Finally I had an assignment to a real fighting ship! We headed off to Brunswick, Georgia, where I would attend navy school for four months and learn how to control friendly aircraft with radars and radios on the ship.

Looking back, I realize how many changes Gwen and other navy wives weathered in a short period of time. Here we were newly married—new parents—and I uproot Gwen from her family and friends in Charleston and move her to a place where she knew no one. She adapted and didn't complain.

We were still in Brunswick on November 23rd when an instructor came into our classroom and informed us that President John F. Kennedy, the hero to whom I'd served a double order of eggs, had been shot. The next morning, while giving baby Elisabeth a bottle, my tears fell on her face as I explained to her what had happened. She couldn't understand what I was saying, but I'm sure my tears conveyed my grief. I had my own personal memories of him, but I, like so many other Americans, revered him as our president and we were all devastated by his death.

CHAPTER 6

Onboard and Underway

~~∽~~

Action from Afar, 1966

After my navy school ended, we headed north to Newport where my newly assigned ship was homeported. Although I was eagerly seeking a challenge, I'm not sure Gwen felt the same. Now, in addition to the move and being a single parent when my eventual overseas deployment kicked in, she was pregnant with our second child. My leaving gave us an additional challenge we hadn't expected: I needed to teach Gwen how to drive. I don't think she had ever sat behind a steering wheel, and she could barely reach the tall gearshift of our VW camper, standing or sitting![1]

My June deployment was clearly on the top of my mind while we trained in port and underway. And since I had been led to believe that I would be promoted to head the operations department before deployment, I attempted to learn all I could about the divisions that I would be overseeing. Then in April, bad news. It was very hard to take.

The personnel folks in Washington stuck to their policy: no one could be a department head on a destroyer without first graduating from destroyer school. As I had already been turned down for destroyer school, I would be reporting to a new lieutenant who had been ordered to the ship to become the operations officer. I was stuck.

---

1 In my opinion, being a spouse in the navy was harder than in the other services. Separation was more complete because of lack of communication. The single parent was left behind with a host of responsibilities and sometimes resented being left by the partner. While at sea, the deployed parent often felt helpless, worried, and guilty. Marriages had to endure multiple stressors.

Constantly on alert for advancement opportunities, like a ship's rotating radar, I took advantage of a situation right across the pier: another ship in our squadron, USS Stickell (DD-888), also a sleek destroyer, had an immediate opening for a department head. The XO had unexpectedly been transferred to take command of another ship, and the operations officer had fleeted up to become XO. That left an empty slot for me and I called my detailer in D.C.[2] I told him three things: (one) the ship across the pier was due to deploy in a week, (two) there was not time to find a new operations officer, and (three) I was ready, willing, and able to fill in. A call from Washington followed and I was transferred to Stickell, where I assumed duties as the operations officer the very next day.

Stickell opened up a new world for me in many respects. For example, I learned to see things differently at the end of my very first day, a Friday, when I approached the XO to request his permission to go ashore. I bid him a nice weekend and said that I'd see him Monday. But as I turned to leave he told me to sit down. He then recited for me a list of ways that destroyers were different from the "laid-back navy" I was used to. At the top of his list was a half day of work on Saturday. Within minutes, I learned that there was enough work to justify at least a six-day workweek, especially since we were to deploy soon. This XO had, until the day before, occupied my new position, so he knew exactly what needed to be done in the operations department and could easily look over my shoulder to see how I was doing. It was a rude awakening.

The makeup of the crew was opposite that of Pandemus. I now found myself with very inexperienced junior officers and enlisted men right out of boot camp or initial skill training. I had to get familiarized with this ship and then turn the crew into professionals who could operate the ship and its gear.

Our first deployment was like a pleasure cruise. We sailed from Newport to Annapolis to embark sixty midshipmen from the Naval Academy for their summer cruise. We were then off to Portland, England; Cherbourg, France; Copenhagen and Aalborg, Denmark.[3] While deployed, we had to integrate

---

2 A detailer is a person who makes your future assignments.

3 We would spend three or four days in each of these ports, then get underway for a few days to reach our next stop. It was a busy time for me: scheduling the port visits, arranging logistics, and coordinating *rendezvous* at sea with other U.S. and foreign navy ships.

these "middies" into our team by assigning them meaningful work so they could pull their weight and further their education at the academy.

The ship returned to Newport in early August 1964, just in time for the birth of our second child, Catherine (Kate). Gwen had risen to the occasion and was exercising her new found independence with her VW camper skills. She had made close friends with new neighbors in our apartment complex, a classmate from Holy Cross, Kevin Healy, and his wife, Sally. They remained among our closest friends and would support Gwen again and again when my career took me away.

For the next six months, we deployed to the Mediterranean where we operated primarily with an aircraft carrier battle group. It was the height of the Cold War and we were on alert for hostile activity. The Soviet Navy was everywhere in that region in submarines, ships, and long-range aircraft. Both navies were playing a game of cat and mouse.

The Stickell returned to Newport and sailed up and down the East Coast on short deployments for a year, prior to training with our aircraft carrier task group in the Caribbean. Despite frequent deployments, the ship's schedule actually gave me a fair amount of time to spend with my now growing family. It wasn't unlimited time, so I tried to make every moment count by taking them to playgrounds and the beach and making them special pancake breakfasts on weekends.

The Kennedy family entered my life again during the summer of 1965. My good friend Jack Walsh was a Secret Service agent assigned to protect Jackie Kennedy and her children. They were in Newport for the summer, so Jack asked if they could come by the ship. Their visit was the highlight of the year. The children had ice cream on the mess decks with the sailors, while Mrs. Kennedy graciously met the crew. But what I remember most was eight-year-old Caroline asking if she could wear my very expensive navy hat. I handed it to her and watched, horrified, as she promptly pitched it over the side into Narragansett Bay. I'm sure she forgot the incident a lot sooner than my wallet and I did!

In early 1966, Stickell was deployed to the waters off Vietnam as part of a carrier task group. Our mission was to provide gunfire support to troops on the ground, and to assist in the rescue of downed pilots in the waters off the coast. While this duty off Vietnam was exciting, I felt detached and distanced from what was happening in-country. Radio transmissions of the pilots going in to conduct strikes were my only sense of the war. My pulse thumped when I heard, "over target," from the pilots and the sound of enemy anti-aircraft fire. Several times I heard various aircraft getting hit and going down. My gut wrenched as the pilots' chances of survival hung in the balance.

Unfortunately, this was all passive involvement. We were technically part of the war effort, but it didn't feel that way. My country was at war, and while others were putting themselves in harm's way, I was just a bystander enjoying the good life: safe comfort at sea and in liberty ports. When I wasn't on deployment, I was home at night with the family. I had joined the navy to see the world and for personal enrichment, but I wanted to do more.

I returned to Newport in July 1966 to Gwen, Liza, Kate, and our two-month-old daughter, Jane, born in April while I was away.

My next two-year assignment was to Destroyer Development Group 2, also in Newport. The group created and tested new tactics and innovative equipment primarily for anti-submarine warfare. As operations officer, I scheduled at-sea tests for the squadron's ships in the Caribbean and other locations.[4] One of my shipmates had just returned from an in-country Vietnam tour operating logistics boats to resupply the marines near Danang with food, ammunition, and equipment. Of course, the big question when I had a minute alone with him was:

"How was it?"

"It was exciting," he said. "They give you a lot of responsibility as a junior officer. And since you're in a war zone, there are no higher-ups to give you a hard time. They tell you just get the job done and leave you alone. You're kind of a free agent."

"Were you afraid of being shot?"

---

4 While the Caribbean may evoke thoughts of fun in the sun, the days and nights were so busy with ship's operations that we never went ashore. It was hardly a vacation. The navy chose Caribbean waters for its exercises because they had good characteristics for testing anti-submarine warfare.

"Only a couple of times. The marines took pretty good care of us. I got to work with other services, too."

His adventure stories fueled my longing to get into the action. A *Time* magazine article highlighted the navy's new Mobile Riverine Force (MRF) operations in the Mekong Delta. I thought this might be a good fit for me since I was skilled in ship-handling in tight spaces. Naturally, I had second thoughts when I got to the part about the very high casualty rates in the MRF. I considered the very real possibility that I would leave my family and never return, but naval warfare was the reason I'd become a naval officer. Here was an opportunity to serve, to lead, and even to make a difference.

I didn't let Gwen know that I had volunteered because I didn't want her to worry while I waited for orders, but I told her I might be called to serve in Vietnam. When my orders to the MRF came through, Gwen and I discussed whether she'd stay in Newport with the three girls or move.[5] At that time, the navy was very generous with its policy of relocating families when the service member was deployed to Vietnam. We could select any location and the navy would move us. Gwen's fascination with Hawaii led to our decision to move to Oahu.

I was itching to get closer to a "hot" war. Soon I'd be right in the middle of one.

Before I deployed to Vietnam, I underwent two months of intensive small-boat and riverine training in the narrow rivers and canals of Mare Island off Vallejo, California. This involved traveling in close formation with other boats, learning how to fire the various weapons onboard, and how to communicate in the heat of action in mock battles. The navy had established a training facility there a couple years earlier to prepare us for river warfare.[6]

"Good morning" and "How are you?" were the two phrases in the Vietnamese language that we were taught in the unlikely case we were invited for tea. But the more unnerving possibility was that we'd be taken prisoner

---

5 In 1968, the military gave one-year orders to Vietnam. Individuals who wanted to serve longer had to request additional tours. Obviously, if you were seriously wounded during your twelve-month assignment, you weren't required to serve out the rest of the tour in Vietnam.

6 The school was called the Naval Inshore Operations Training Center.

and held. Becoming a POW grew all the more real—and terrifying—during the five days of Survival, Evasion, Resistance, and Escape training (SERE).

The program involved a scenario in which we were captured, and the enemy employed its strategy of psychologically breaking the senior officer first, thereby diminishing morale and making it easier to break the lower-ranking crewmembers. Our role playing was rough and terrifyingly real.

The instructors were all navy men, some of whom had actually endured enemy imprisonment and torture in the Korean War. In their role as our captors, they forced our senior officer into a dog collar and made this man crawl on all fours and bark.[7] Repulsed and angered, I stepped forward to protect him by confronting them and drawing their attention to myself.

"I'm in charge," I yelled. "Go fuck yourselves."

I knew I had succeeded remarkably well when the first punch landed. It did not stop and it got worse—something we were taught to anticipate. I was subjected to the "black box"—a windowless, pitch-black container about the size of a dog kennel, in which a man will not fit unless forced into a tight fetal position. Inside the box you sweat profusely, your eyes sting, your head throbs, every muscle in your body aches, and time ceases to exist. I would have sworn on a Bible that I was in there for twelve hours. After thirty minutes they pulled me out, but it wasn't over. I was greeted with a rotten egg shoved into my mouth. I had pissed off my captors and they were making me pay. I vomited all over them which earned me a few more punches, and then they left me to staunch the bleeding myself.

Horrific as that was, nothing compared to waterboarding, a term unfamiliar to me at that time. When they covered my face with a cloth, and poured water over my mouth, terror shot through my entire body. My brain could not hold any rational thought that might comfort me. This was not "training," and it certainly wasn't an "enhanced interrogation technique".

---

7 In 2004, the Defense Department revealed that in the War on Terror in Iraq, the U.S. Army and other agencies had committed abuses on prisoners there, including torture and reported rape and homicide. Some of these actions are eerily similar to what I experienced in my SERE training.

This was drowning. This was torture. How could I believe otherwise as I lay there sputtering, gagging, choking, and gasping for air?[8]

But my instructors saw things differently. For them this was routine training, and, as quickly as they pinned me down, they sat me up again—ears ringing, head throbbing—and sent me back in formation with the troops. The troops had been instructed to form up in order to watch me being disciplined—just in case they got any ideas.

As I struggled to stand up straight, I felt like I was nearing the end of my rope and began to dwell on disturbing thoughts like: *What if some of my instructors went a little too far? Would I become a "training accident"? Could I die, here, at the school?* I owed it to Gwen and my girls to come back in one piece and even in this early step of my journey into combat, I began to feel like I might be letting them down. This punishment all had a chilling effect on my behavior. I was no longer eager to rock the boat. I could be seriously injured. But I was proud of what I had done. By diverting the captors from the man they were trying to break, I had supported my team.

At midnight on the fifth day of SERE training, we were ordered to gather in formation outdoors on the parade grounds for what we expected to be additional punishments. Instead of the anticipated brutality and darkness, the lights came on illuminating the flagpole with an American flag fluttering and the "Star Spangled Banner" playing on loudspeakers. We were inspired in this moment. We were relieved that we had endured, not to mention survived, the hardships of training that were meant to prepare us in the event of the real thing. Our captors, who by some trick of the light had turned back into our instructors, embraced us and wished us the best with the sincerest intent. We couldn't wait to hightail it out of SERE training.

In August 1968, the family and I flew to Hawaii. We spent a day together before I had to leave them in temporary quarters at Fort DeRussey on Waikiki. Gwen found a home for us in the town of Kaneohe.

---

8 The U.S. has used waterboarding purportedly to gain information from terrorist prisoners during the War on Terror. Based on my experience I believe it should be classified as torture. Further, I'm not convinced of its effectiveness since I would have said anything—and not necessarily based in fact—to stop the waterboarding. I don't believe it to be a reliable means of obtaining useful information.

It was hard saying goodbye to the girls who were ages two, four, and five, and even more difficult leaving Gwen at Hickam Air Force Base. We both knew the danger I faced in my new assignment and that it would be next to impossible to communicate during my year-long tour in-country except by very slow mail delivery. The unspoken question between us declared itself in our eyes. If I could have promised her that we would see each other again, I would have made that promise on the spot, but I couldn't. So I kissed her goodbye and boarded a chartered Boeing 707 with a few hundred other service members for destination: Vietnam.

My sea bag was packed with underwear, socks, sunscreen and, because I was going into a war zone, not much else. How much more did I really need? My excitement and anticipation of what lay ahead kept me awake during the ten-hour flight from Hawaii. But then a sobering sense of clarity came over me on our final approach over lush green jungles to the Tan Son Nhut airport in Saigon. Smoke rising from hundreds of cooking fires in the villages surrounding the city had an oddly peaceful look. I could have been arriving at some exotic vacation destination.

This will be no vacation.

Down there the army guys would soon be humping it over rough terrain into enemy lines, and we sailors in the MRF would be getting shot at from the cover of thick palm trees and foliage lining the waterways.

CHAPTER 7

Hot War

⎯⟋๑⟍⎯

SAIGON AND DONG TAM, 1969

NO SOONER DID MY FEET hit the ground in Saigon than an oppressively hot blast of air hit my face. The steamy August heat was more intense than anything I'd ever experienced on previous deployments, even in the Red Sea. Our uniforms were soaked, and to add to our discomfort, we lost no time in getting painful shots for more tropical diseases than I care to remember, and taking malaria pills that had side effects. Welcome to Vietnam!

Vietnam was divided into separate countries after World War II: communist North Vietnam and democratic South Vietnam.[1] South Vietnam had been a French colony, but, after the war, communist insurgents initiated hostile activity there. After suffering defeat by the local communist forces, the French withdrew. The U.S. saw an opportunity to contain the communist threat in that part of the world and sent military advisors into South Vietnam.

The Eisenhower and subsequent Kennedy and Johnson administrations believed in the "domino theory"—if South Vietnam came under the influence of communists, then the surrounding countries of Laos, Cambodia, Thailand, and Indonesia would follow suit, toppling like a row of dominos. The U.S. wanted to prop up the South Vietnamese government that was struggling against takeover by the local communist forces, the Vietcong, who were supported by North Vietnam. They, in turn, were supported by the Soviets. The number of U.S. advisors in South Vietnam rose eight-fold between 1961 and 1964.

---

1 The Geneva Convention of 1954 had formally divided Vietnam into two separate nations.

Starting in 1964, the U.S. conducted a bombing campaign against North Vietnam that resulted in U.S. pilots being killed or captured as POWs. But the bombing had little effect in overcoming the enemy and only strengthened its resolve. In 1965 the initial deployment of combat troops on the ground occurred with the landing of 3,500 marines in Danang.[2] That same year, the Tonkin Gulf incident occurred in which the navy maintained it was attacked by North Vietnamese small boats. With this "event," President Johnson justified the beginning of the build-up to 500,000 troops.[3]

The North Vietnamese had been smuggling weapons, ammunition, and supplies by sea and river into South Vietnam. And when the navy began an operation in 1965 to intercept the flow of these supplies at the seacoast and on the major rivers, the enemy countered by moving inland into the maze of waterways called the Mekong Delta, covering 24,000 square miles of rivers, canals, and rice paddies. Most of its eight million inhabitants were farmers or fishermen, many living hand-to-mouth near the riverbanks.

The Vietcong were also in the Delta in force, confiscating crops and gathering recruits. There were dozens of pockets of enemy resistance. Most were inaccessible by road and the enemy operated there with near complete impunity.[4] It made sense that to stem the flow of arms, the U.S. had to control the small waterways that fed into the main rivers. In these small spaces, the navy needed a different kind of force that could withstand enemy ambush and unload troops off the boats, thereby taking the fight along the shallow rivers and canals of the Delta and into the swamps, jungles, and rice paddies where the enemy hid.[5]

---

2 Danang was a strategically large coastal city in the north of South Vietnam.

3 In August 1964, the USS Maddox (DD-731), operating in international waters off the coast of North Vietnam, was attacked by three North Vietnamese patrol boats. Although the boats launched torpedoes, the Maddox suffered no damage. The next night, the Maddox and crew of another destroyer observed numerous radar and sonar contacts they assumed were enemy patrol boats. Both U.S. ships fired torpedoes and guns at the contacts but never actually sighted the boats. The U.S. military on scene concluded that the contacts were false images. However, officials called the "attack" real, and the U.S. responded accordingly.

4 Jack P. Smith, "From the River to the Sea," from *Vietnam: The Soldier's Story*, a television documentary series on the History Channel, 2000.

5 Ibid.

The fact that my great-grandfather's unit had engaged in the same type of military operations—cutting enemy supply lines at the Weldon railroad in Virginia—that I was engaged in on the other side of the world in Vietnam, some 105 years later, is not lost on me. My job and his was to deny the enemy the essential food, water, and ammunition they needed to fight. The elements of warfare don't change much over time.

That different kind of force was called the Mobile Riverine Force, a combined army-navy force used for both small and large unit search-and-destroy missions. The MRF operated in groups composed of converted World War II landing craft. Each was manned by a navy crew and carried thirty to forty army soldiers. When the boats reached their mission location, the troops would disembark on ramps lowered while beached on the canal's edge. The entire operation was controlled by a navy officer onboard a boat called a Monitor.[6] Once the soldiers began their operations ashore, the commanding officer would order the rest of the team to a safe location until the soldiers reported their mission completed. Then the boats would pick up troops and take them to the next mission or return them to base. We fought a cat and mouse game with the enemy hidden in the thick tropical cover of the inland waterways. There were no tactical books on this type of engagement, so improvisation and innovation were key in developing strategy and tactics. And it was the ultimate in teamwork.

As part of our indoctrination we spent a couple of days learning the local customs. We had been taught everything from the obscure— "Never point a finger or show the bottom of your foot to a local. It is a sign of disrespect."—to the self-evident—"Stay away from the women. Do not befriend them or use them as prostitutes."

Our instructors added "never drink a local beer" because the Vietcong had been known to sprinkle tiny pieces of broken glass into the bottle. I was

---

6 The Monitor was designed after the original Civil War ship, the USS Monitor, which had armor cladding and a rotating gun turret. The U.S. Navy hadn't been involved in riverine warfare since the Civil War, when the Union Navy used small boats in the Mississippi delta to disrupt Confederate military actions by blocking harbors in the south and then pushing up the river in small armored boats.

never sure if this was an admonition to keep the troops sober or if there was any truth in it, but I decided not to tempt fate.

Several days after landing, we newly arrived soldiers and MRF sailors climbed into a small transport plane for a short flight to our new home south of Saigon, a U.S. Army base at Dong Tam.[7] It had been built on a dredged portion of the river that was located near the city of My Tho and consisted of airfields, ammunition depots, offices, and barracks housing thousands of troops. In contrast, the navy had a mobile base that was made up of repair and supply ships along with barracks barges that housed our communications and support staff. Each ship contained berthing facilities for the riverine sailors and army troops who lived with us during operations. When we arrived at the Dong Tam base, the soldiers went to their land barracks and administrative office buildings, and we MRF sailors embarked in small boats and headed to a barracks barge anchored in the river, where I expected to live for the next twelve months.

The Tet Offensive was recent history and the enemy was everywhere. It had started seven months earlier on January 31, 1968, when Vietcong and North Vietnam forces broke the traditional truce over the Tet (lunar) New Year holiday and launched a surprise attack in South Vietnam on one-hundred cities, plus the U.S. military headquarters and U.S. Embassy in Saigon. The enemy was everywhere.

Every evening to avoid becoming a target while sleeping, the entire MRF would get underway and relocate several kilometers up or down the river. Some of the ships had significant hospital facilities and could land helicopters that provided urgently needed air resupply and medical air evacuation (medevac) capability.

My new boss, Commander Jim Froid, was a really decent guy.[8] But like other COs in my past, he lost no time in pushing aside the polite formalities and getting down to the job.

---

7 The base, home of the U.S. Army's 9th Infantry Division, was located in Kien Hoa province. It was also the headquarters of the navy's MRF from where we were assigned to transport the Army's 2nd Brigade of the 9th Infantry Division as it conducted its missions throughout the waterways of the Delta, the southern part of Vietnam that flowed into the South China Sea.

8 Jim Froid was Commander of River Assault Squadron 9.

"You're going to be my chief staff officer," he said. I didn't need an interpreter to know that meant I would remain behind at headquarters while he went out on the squadron's operations. I caught my breath and immediately put up some restrained resistance while I still had a fighting chance. This sort of pushback was almost expected from any young sailor who had just been told he wasn't going into the fight. Ultimately, though, if you didn't want to be deemed insubordinate, you did whatever your boss told you.

"Sir, I was hoping to go into operational command right away and see some action."

"Nope, I need you here on my staff, Tom. We need to plan operations and logistics and make sure that everyone's accounted for after the operations."

"Aye, Skipper."

When all was said and done, this non-combat assignment would help save my life.

I got busy and soon recovered from the disappointment of not being assigned a command. By September 1968, I was deeply involved in the planning and execution of MRF combat operations.[9] Sometimes there were several operations in a day, and I got to go along and actually command a unit.[10] Getting out was not only a great opportunity for me to get to know the troops and to experience what was actually going on in the field, but it was also excellent training. This sort of navy training prepared its people for tough situations, so that life and death would not hang on some untried seat-of-the-pants approach. On one such outing, I saw very clearly why my boss had not placed me in charge of an operation right away.

It was early morning and I was an observer on an Assault Troop Carrier. The sun rose over the canal stoking up the oppressive heat that beat against us. Even at sunrise we were drenched in sweat. Fermented fish smoking on wood fires permeated the air. The only sounds were our engines humming along, the gurgle of the slight wake we left, and the occasional radio command to the boat crews by the officers-in-charge.

---

9 My assignment had been to River Assault Squadron 9, consisting of two divisions, 91 and 92. Each had a couple dozen boats and two hundred sailors.

10 Depending on the size of the operation I might have commanded three to five boats with forty soldiers on each.

We were slowly passing a village. Children were playing on the canal bank. This was a good sign. When the Vietcong were around, the kids hid with their families. These children stopped their play to wave, smile, and call out to us. I might have been watching my own little girls at play and a pang of homesickness shot through me. It was easy to see that some of our crew members, including the gunner seated next to me, were missing their own kids, too. We all waved back silently as we moved by, no doubt lost in thoughts of home. The presence of children at play in the village allowed us to relax a little. I was enjoying this bucolic moment on the canal when the popping sound of small arms fire from the village changed everything. The waving gunner next to me was hit in the face. I caught him in my arms, instantly sickened by the rusty metallic smell of his bloodied body and the sight of his partly decapitated head. I yelled at the boat captain to request a corpsman (medical specialist) from another boat. By the time he arrived, five minutes later, the gunner was already dead. At least he didn't suffer long.

In the blink of an eye I was stunned and angry, but I'd transitioned to this bloody hellhole. This was war. I had forgotten why I had thought it would be gallant and noble at every minute. It was full of darkness, destruction, death, fear, and suffering. *Kill the enemy before he kills you.* I was already expressing doubts to myself about what I was doing here. *Shouldn't I be at home with my own little girls? Why am I putting them and myself through this?*

This, my first experience with death in combat, reminded me—about as closely as one can be reminded—of life's vulnerability. The lesson that was imprinted on my brain that morning was to never, ever, let your guard down. You have to assume there is danger even in the most benign and tranquil setting and be on guard every single second. As some wise person said, "Being in war is ninety-nine percent total boredom and one percent total chaos." You need to be totally alert one hundred percent of the time in order to be ready for the one percent. I was fortunate to have learned this lesson early in my tour, when I was not in charge of the operation or responsible for others' lives.

Ironically, that Christmas in 1968, we learned that Bob Hope and his USO troupe were coming to Dong Tam. The need for diversion in an unceasing life-or-death situation is wholeheartedly welcomed during the holidays.

But my unit drew the short straw, and we were ordered to provide waterborne security for the base while the soldiers and sailors enjoyed the show, which was to include fireworks. The enemy decided this was an excellent opportunity to attack our security perimeter. Soon, we had our own fireworks in the form of mortars, launched by the Vietcong on us from an island in the river. We fired back quickly and quelled the attack. No harm was done, and the show went on. After a few somber thoughts about how fast the night could have turned fatal, my team and I rejoiced in knowing we'd protected our men during this most special time.

By February 1969, the Vietcong had shifted their supply lines several kilometers north of the Mekong Delta, much closer to the western approaches to Saigon where there was a dearth of U.S. boats and troops. This raised the threat of another Tet offensive that would possibly lead to the fall of Saigon. That's when Admiral Elmo Zumwalt ordered the MRF to counter the threat.[11]

Nowhere is the old saw about history repeating itself truer than in war. Weapons, equipment, and tactics may change, but the mission is always the same—take the offensive and all the ground you can. Deny the enemy his supplies, troops, and armament. Kill or be killed. Fortunately I never had to kill anyone. But as I watch events unfold today in the Middle East, I'm stunned by how we're repeating the same mistakes we made in Vietnam. The goal of our involvement is fuzzy. Send in the advisors. When that doesn't work, start an air campaign, and then when that doesn't work, send in the troops, but not enough troops to be successful. When Americans tire of the death tolls of our troops, the enemy, and innocent civilians, pull the American troops back. The new government doesn't work and the soldiers we trained can't manage on their own (or their government isn't paying them), so they stop fighting. An even worse enemy slips into the power vacuum and takes the weapons we left behind. Why don't we learn?

To counter another major offensive, I was placed in command of six boats and directed to operate in this new high-threat area. Our mission was to

---

11 Admiral Elmo Zumwalt was commander of naval forces at the time. Subsequently, he became chief of naval operations. So respected was he for his service that the navy named a line of guided missile destroyers after him, beginning with USS Zumwalt (DDG-1000).

deploy on the rivers for a month and interdict the enemy's boats. We had to be ready at a moment's notice to aid our own boats when they needed us on their night operations, or when they radioed for help in tight situations. And because we were a relatively new fighting force, and no one had written the text book, we were in charge of our own mission: able to innovate and improvise as we saw fit. I decided that in our off-duty hours (daytime) we'd live alongside the local Vietnamese population to see if they were collaborating with the Vietcong. This would inform our strategies and better allow us to avoid causing civilian casualties. We bonded with the children by beaching our boats at a village or hamlet and allowing the children to come by and meet us. If we had extra food or candy, we shared it with them.

While visiting the hamlet of Hiep Hoa, we befriended a six-year-old boy and his four-year-old sister who'd shyly approached us. Their twig-like arms and legs spoke of hunger and malnourishment, and that's all we needed to know. We gave them food, and they quickly became regulars visiting us each day. As far as we could tell, they had no family. On one such visit my heart sank when I noticed significant cuts and bruises on the little girl's legs and face. Once again, my thoughts ran to my own little girls at home.

I asked a local interpreter to find out what had happened to her and after a quick exchange with the child, he looked up at me and said solemnly, "land mine." She'd been hit by shrapnel from one. Our corpsman kneeled to look closely at her, but quickly rose to his feet saying that she needed a doctor and nothing short of what a hospital could offer her. I grabbed the radio, requested a medevac and, within an hour, a U.S. military helicopter appeared. Barely touching down on the riverbank, it whisked the little girl away to the nearest U.S. medical facility.[12]

Within the next hour, a second helicopter appeared over the trees and landed. Out jumped a red-faced U.S. Army general officer.

"I'm looking for the idiot who ordered the medevac for a gook girl," he bellowed.[13]

---

12 The nearest U.S. hospital was at the 25th Infantry Division Headquarters in Tan An, about forty kilometers away.

13 "Gook" was a derogatory term meaning Vietnamese person and similar to terms used in other wars, such as "Kraut" referring to a German soldier in World War II.

I identified myself as the officer in charge and stepped a bit closer to him. "I don't know what you're talking about, Sir. I requested a medevac for a Vietnamese girl who urgently needed attention."

"I'm going to remove you from command for wasting valuable assets!" the general spat back.

"Sir, I'm not in your chain of command," I replied, trying to contain any sign of disrespect, although I was feeling self-satisfied.

Furious, he huffed and puffed his way back to the helicopter. And that was the first time I saw a helicopter full of hot air rise like a balloon! That was a very good day! It felt good to get in trouble for a humanitarian purpose, and I would do it again for the right reasons.

In the weeks that followed, we had relatively little contact with the Vietcong. We were on normal maneuvers in the canal. The moon was nearly full; the sky was cloudless and we could see a good distance. Although a few of us complained about not getting enough sleep during the heat of the day in preparation for night operations, the coolness of the evening and the anticipation of enemy fire at any second kept us sharp and on edge.

We were visited frequently by senior officers, politicians, athletes, and entertainers—Secretary of Defense Melvin Laird, Ann Margaret, and, as mentioned, Bob Hope to name a few. Most of them appreciated what we did and were easy to be around, with the exception of the comedian, Jocy Bishop, who came to entertain the troops at Dong Tam.

I didn't know Joey Bishop from Adam. I had never watched him on TV, or in the movies. All I knew was that after touring one of our boats he insulted my boat captain.

This boat had just returned from a three-day combat mission. It was littered with spent ammo shells, odd pieces of uniforms, and empty food containers, because the crew had been too exhausted to clean it up.

"This looks like a pig sty!" said the star.

My boat captain was not amused. He told me about it. And I approached the man on a matter of manners.

"Sir, I'm the officer in charge. Could you possibly be a little more diplomatic in dealing with my sailors?"

He snarled at me. "Who the fuck are *you* to be talking to *me* like that!"

"Until this morning, Sir, I had never heard of you. And, right now, you are a guest on my boat. Act like one!"

He was even more irritated that I didn't know who he was and gave me a little shove. So, given that he was only about five feet, four inches and a lightweight, I figured I could take him, and shoved him back. Fortunately, someone yelled at us to break it up, and I backed off so that the comedian could get off my boat and continue his "good will" tour elsewhere. I had grown very protective of my men and their well-being. No degree of abuse would be tolerated, not even from a big star like what's-his-name.

The Tet offensive in early 1968 was a turning point in the war. It revealed an intelligence failure on the part of the U.S. and resulted in increased loss of domestic support throughout America. This meant that our air war in the north was reduced. It also precipitated the beginning of limited troop drawdowns and a greater push to turn the war effort over to the South Vietnamese in a strategy known as "Vietnamization." In this process two of the four MRF squadrons, including my own, were decommissioned and the boats were turned over to the South Vietnamese Navy. We would spend a couple of months preparing for the boat turnover and training our Vietnamese counterparts who would replace us. With most of that training behind us, I was essentially out of a job.

Except that I still had about four months left on my in-country tour. My options, however, presented themselves as a no-brainer. I could transfer to navy headquarters in Saigon for a staff job, or I could stay with my men on the boats and take command of one of the remaining divisions.[14] I chose the latter. I really enjoyed doing what I was trained to do and I was in my element when leading operations. So, Vietnamization did not change the MRF's day-to-day operations. We continued to transport army troops to points along the canals and rivers, provide fire support to them, pick them up and move on. We were still getting shot at and taking casualties. I can't help but imagine how different my life would have been if I had taken the first option and relocated to Saigon. I've never regretted my decision. Things happen for a reason.

---

14 I would command Division 152 in River Assault Squadron 15.

Part Two: Joan

CHAPTER 8

A Totalitarian State

_6

BERLIN, 1970

THE HALF EMPTY TRAIN SCREECHES *slowly out of the station in West Germany, as though reluctant to leave. Denise and I observe, while looking for a vacant compartment, that the train is almost empty. We munch on our cheese sandwiches as the late fall landscape and small country houses slip away silently under the remnants of daylight. After dark, Denise curls up on the bench while I choose to stretch out on the threadbare carpet. The gentle rocking of the slow moving train lulls us to sleep.*

At 9:00 p.m. we awake to the sound of grinding metal as the hulking train slows to a complete stop at a station. There are no passengers on the platform, only East German guards with machine guns.

"What's going on?" I ask Denise, rising from the floor and joining her on the seat.

"Border crossing," she whispers. We're mesmerized watching. Suddenly, the shuddering metallic sound of all the train's car doors locking in unison echoes through the car. We are trapped. As Americans, we aren't used to being confined in our travels. Still, I think, Why lock all the doors? Who would be crazy enough to attempt escape with all the armed guards around?

Our heavy compartment door slides open efficiently as an East German guard enters and demands our passports. We hand them over wordlessly. After a perfunctory check, he hands them back. Once again, the night train is underway and we settle back into our sleeping positions, but are now too restless to sleep.

A couple of hours pass. The door slides open again. I hear it just in time to move away as a leather boot is about to land on my head. Another passport check in silence. We avoid eye contact and he leaves. Why are they continuing to check passports when clearly no one can enter or leave the train because the doors are locked and, if anyone did try, they'd probably be shot on sight? Then the coin dropped. They're doing this because they can. *We get the message. This is intimidation. We give up on sleeping. After dawn we arrive in West Berlin.*

From West Berlin we take a day trip into East Berlin through Checkpoint Charlie on the American side. The guidebooks recommend that we "register" with the U.S. Marines there. When we ask a marine sentry about this—he's very helpful—but says if we fail to return, even after registering, that, "Anything could happen to you, and we can't come after you." This is hard to believe, given the marines' reputation for rescuing U.S. citizens abroad. We enter East Berlin anyway.

Partially collapsed buildings riddled with bullet holes welcome us to the city. How can this be? The war ended a generation ago. *The streets are deserted yet it's mid-morning. Most buildings look uninhabited. There's little in the way of cars or shops. Occasionally a person disappears into a building, but no ordinary people are bustling about their daily routines chatting with one another. There are no birds singing, no sounds of children playing. Even though it's November and you wouldn't expect to see trees and plants in bloom, there aren't even leafless trees here. No shrubs, no evidence that any grass or even weeds grow here. Hardly a sign of life exists. I take no photos as we were warned to leave cameras behind.*

As we cross a river, I peer over the side of the bridge into the dirty water below. I wonder what the suicide rate is. The cold, damp, gray weather accentuates the bleakness of the place. It seems to permeate my soul.

We visit a museum where ancient Greek sculpture and other artifacts are on display in a cold, cavernous room whose floor is covered with soot and debris. Under the dim lights, we struggle to see these priceless treasures with years of grime in their crevices. What's more remarkable is that they aren't identified as to where they come from and how old they are. They're simply left where they were placed as if to say, "it doesn't matter." We take this as a Soviet affront to our Western culture. Here, in this museum, we are seeing life through a totalitarian lens—the creative individualism we value doesn't matter. Independent spirits are crushed in favor of the state. The state is everything, and will dog your every step if necessary.

In a newer, slightly brighter part of the museum, with a carpeted floor, hangs a wall-sized map of the world clearly marking the countries already under communist rule. The hair on my neck rises as we view the countries expected to be under communist rule at future dates. Among the states marked to fall to totalitarianism are South Vietnam, Cambodia, Laos, Thailand, and Indonesia. Here, in front of us, on the wall, as if to challenge the assumptions we college students had made in the antiwar movement is a snapshot of "the domino theory," a threat that justified for many Americans our presence in Vietnam. What we had called a conveniently made-up myth by the U.S. military-industrial complex is real!

Although I'm aghast, I keep my thoughts to myself, as does Denise, lest we're overheard and whisked off for interrogation by the secret Stasi police, who might be lurking in the shadows. This is a place where people disappear for no reason.

We do not feel welcome here, nor do we have any inkling to stick around after a cafeteria lunch consisting of gray unidentifiable substances that we push around on our plates. The metal cutlery is so flimsy that the fork tines bend as you try to pick up a piece of food. After a quick trip to the restroom where we are watched by a burly, stern matron, we decide to abandon the rest of the East Berlin itinerary, and leave rather than spend the night.

When we return through Checkpoint Charlie, Denise goes first, and then it's my turn. The East German border guard looks at my passport and vanishes into a back room. When he reappears, he looks concerned in a ministerial type of way. He's not threatening, so I'm not fearful, but his every move has my full attention. If anything, he seems anxious to sort something out. He asks me in English,

"Do you speak German?"

"No," I reply, thinking this somewhat of a stupid question. After all, I'm an American! Everyone is supposed to speak our language.

"Come with me," he says signaling me to follow him into the same back room. It is Spartan, with a tiny table and a couple of chairs. He sits and offers me the other seat so we're facing each other across the table.

He begins to question me in surprisingly good English—about my passport. Where did I get it? When? Who took the photo? Had I lost it? Had it been kept by anyone else?

By the time he excuses himself and leaves the room—still holding my passport to freedom—I'm hoping Denise, now on the American side, has notified the marines to report that I'm being detained. Although the marine's warning echoes in my head, I'm pretty certain that this passport problem—whatever it is—will be resolved. Just the same, I whisper a prayer.

The guard returns and hastily points out what was wrong with my passport. He explains that the U.S. State Department stamp made a single impression on the front side but a double impression on the back side. Fortunately, this is not enough of a printing error to give cause for alarm and he lets me go, anxious, I assume, to get on with his duties.

Denise hadn't spoken to the marines yet, but was about to. Although my interrogation had only been twenty minutes, it seemed a lot longer. When I saw the U.S. flag as I crossed over, I almost broke down sobbing. The next morning we lost no time in returning to West Germany.

Impending graduation and unsure futures sparked this trip. Denise, my college roommate, and I were in our dorm room, and graduation was not far away. While she had a substitute teaching job lined up, it could be postponed. I had no job plans at all and was eager to find any excuse to avoid my career search. We figured we could travel on the cheap staying with her relatives in Ireland and mine in Italy for a while. We'd skimp on hotel rooms by sleeping on overnight trains when possible and dine on cheese, chocolate, bread, and fruit picnics.

We worked all summer, saving our money, then took off shortly after Labor Day. Our tour began in London and continued on to Ireland and her family. Berlin and East Berlin, both situated inside East Germany, were also on our itinerary. In 1970, West Germany was a sovereign state, and East

Germany was part of the Soviet bloc. To go to Berlin we had to cross from one country into the other.

My experience at the border, which could easily have spiraled beyond my control, had a deep and lasting effect on me. It strengthened the unmistakable gratitude I feel to this day for being an American, blessed with the freedoms we enjoy. I found a new respect for our military that only a few months back I'd painted with the same broad brush as the evil military-industrial complex. I became less cynical about America's military involvement in other countries and more aware of our role in the world. And I will always remember that marine with the utmost respect for the way he conducted himself.

Ultimately, my Berlin experience would change my life. It would lead me to re-examine earlier thoughts and feelings about the military, setting me up for a future I never could have imagined inside that dorm room.

CHAPTER 9

Earlier Thoughts

⤡

CAMBRIDGE, MA, 1950S

THE BITING NOVEMBER WIND BLEW through Veterans' Stadium, and as the afternoon sun faded, we drew our coats tighter and stamped our feet. The crowd roared and my father jumped up out of loyalty every time Navy did something with the ball. "First down! Come on Navy, you can do it!" I caught my dad's enthusiasm at these games.

I was ten. My father, Thomas Joseph Chiara, and I were at the annual Army-Navy game where the U.S. Military Academy and U.S. Naval Academy, archrivals, were battling it out. The game was in Philadelphia, the half-way point between West Point, New York, and Annapolis, Maryland, where the academies were located, respectively. Throughout the big stadium crowd, military custom and tradition prevailed. The gold braid and buttons on the midshipmen's navy blue bridge coats dazzled me. Even on a bleak November day, the gold was brilliant to me.

My Dad had served as a U.S. Army medic during the invasion of Sicily in World War II, and then became an interpreter for the Allies after they discovered he was fluent in the Sicilian dialect.[1] But he always pulled for the navy at these games. His younger brother, Matt, had graduated from the Naval Academy in 1948. Matt had studied navigation and French, the language of

---

1 In World War II it was common for second generation Italian, German, and Japanese citizens to fight for the U.S. against their ancestral homelands.

diplomats then. He was in the Korean War as a supply officer aboard ship and left the service in 1953 with the rank of Lieutenant Commander.[2]

It was clear to me, especially at these Army-Navy games, that my dad was very proud of his younger brother. My father held his head a little higher and his voice deepened whenever he told anyone that Matt had graduated from Annapolis. It was as if our family had earned the right to tie our name to that great academy. After all, Annapolis was a long way from Sicily, literally and figuratively. And, on that side of my family, going to the Naval Academy was a bigger accomplishment than going to Harvard. Not only would you receive an excellent education, but you'd also serve as a leader in the finest navy in the whole world.

My paternal grandparents, Gaetano and Giuseppina Chiara, emigrated from Sicily in the early 1900s to escape poverty. They arrived in Lawrence, Massachusetts, with only a few possessions and the desire to work hard in the woolen mills as unskilled laborers. Gradually they saved enough to buy a small store with an upstairs apartment, where they lived. They sold specialty foods to other Italian immigrants hoping to achieve the same dream of American prosperity themselves.

Carmine Antonio Russo and Elisa Clementina D'Onofrio, on my mother's side, emigrated separately from Italy in about 1910 and settled in Cambridge, Massachusetts. Friends introduced them, and they married and had two children. Carmine, the youngest of nine, had come from a family that could barely scratch out a living on a farm in a tiny hillside village east of Naples. At eighteen he immigrated to the U.S. with his two older sisters. He worked as a stone mason, managed to acquire carpentry skills, and eventually became a residential contractor. Long hours paid off and he prospered enough to become a small-time landlord.

My mother, Gemma Raffaela Russo, was born in 1921. Her only sibling, Rudolph Romeo Russo (really!) was born six years later, and may have been named after the then-popular matinee idol, Rudolph Valentino. In 1947,

---

2 Korea had been ruled by Japan from 1910 through August of 1945, when Japan was defeated in World War II. In 1948, the Soviets occupied North Korea and the Americans, South Korea. In 1950 the North Koreans invaded the South, and war ensued. But in 1953 an armistice was signed permanently dividing both nations. The U.S. lost 35,000 casualties.

she married my father, and two years later I was born. My brother Thomas Carmine Chiara followed in 1954.

We lived downstairs in a two-family house in Cambridge owned by my mother's parents, who lived upstairs. Every school morning after I washed and dressed, I would go upstairs and my grandmother would vigorously brush my brunette hair until it gleamed, her hard-working hands coaxing my thick hair into two braids, which she tied with elastics and ribbons. After school I'd sit at her enameled kitchen table drawing on the white cardboard she saved from her hosiery packages, while she went about her routines. Usually the radio was turned to "Queen for a Day," where down-on-their-luck contestants would make their best case as to why they should be queen and win a cash prize or a washing machine.

When I was old enough I took piano lessons and very willingly practiced upstairs on my grandparents' piano, acquired from a tenant during the Great Depression in lieu of rent. Practicing my music after school became a cathartic exercise for me and still is today.

My grandmother was a shy woman and had modest ways. She partnered with my grandfather in taking care of the rental properties—cleaning, gardening, collecting the rents, and banking. She seemed continuously busy with one domestic task after another. I was fascinated by the numerous housekeeping duties she undertook every day, usually following a schedule.[3]

I was amazed at how the seasons governed certain routines. Spring started in February or March when I helped her plant the tomato, marigold, and petunia seeds she'd dried from the previous fall. Later, my grandfather planted the seedlings in the ground and placed a glass panel over them until it was warm enough to let them flourish on their own. All summer she weeded and watered. In the fall, my grandfather and uncle would harvest the grapes, pears, and figs. My grandmother picked the herbs, then dried and stored them. Fall days involved making and canning grape jelly, our home-grown

---

3 Monday was laundry; Tuesday, ironing; Wednesday, grocery shopping; Thursday banking; and Friday cooking for the weekend. I can still see the homemade fettuccini pasta laid out on her spare bed overnight to dry.

pears and store-bought peaches. The goods were stored in the cellar, and there was plenty for both households.

The holidays brought special cooking and baking. My grandmother would start preparations for Christmas and Easter dinners a couple of weeks before. Since both were also religious holidays, we had to save time for church, especially at Easter when we seemed to go every day for a week. Our holiday dinner involved antipasto, soup or pasta, turkey with all the trimmings, nuts and fruit and desserts. Our Easter dishes included seasonal cheeses from Italian markets, creams, and ham. I can see my grandmother sitting in front of the TV at night, her fingers flying over crochet work even while she "relaxed."

My uncle, Rudy, also my godfather, became a surrogate dad for me because my father was always working. A World War II army veteran, Rudy helped my grandfather run his contracting business and lived next door with his wife, Betty, and their two daughters, Elise and Amy. When his sister-in-law's house burned down and her disabled daughter died in the fire, her husband took off. My uncle was on the front page of the paper the next day helping her sort through the debris. He took her sons to buy suits for the funeral and stood with them in place of their missing dad. Birthdays, graduations, and the day my son was born, Rudy's face was there; his dashing appearance was a constant in my life. He was my first hero.

Unfortunately, even though I was young, I knew my mother wasn't happy. My father's work in the family business was all-consuming, and we wouldn't see him much of the week. On the weekends, if he wasn't working, he would catch up on his sleep. There were fights, mostly about my father not being home enough and not bringing enough money home. My mother's troubles were deepened by my brother's small size as a child. He was born prematurely and had trouble in school. We later learned there was a ticking time bomb in his brain that hadn't fired yet.

I found the warmth, nurturing, and security missing from my own house in my grandparents' apartment. In the quiet pastimes and routines that characterized my life with Nana, I knew what to do, and I knew what to expect. There were no surprises.

Despite the tension I felt at home, there were many happy times in my childhood, and most of those I associate with the beach. The sea has never been very far away in my life. I can go back a long time to sizzling hot summer afternoons with my mother, brother, and grandmother at a beach, surrounded by other families on their blankets. Gleeful children's voices competed with those of shrieking seagulls. When the east wind blew in, it made the sea smell stronger and the water warmer.

When I was seven, I learned to swim at a local summer camp, and I was making progress, but couldn't synchronize the kick and arm movements. My brother and I were playing in the shallows, splashing and trying to do the dog paddle. Without thinking about it, I let go of the bottom and suddenly all my movements were working together. Much to my amazement, I was swimming!

"Hey, I can swim!"

I ran to my mother and grandmother sitting on their blanket warmed by the sun. I could see my excitement reflected in their smiling faces. They cheered and applauded me, while I did my victory dance by the sea elated by the notion that—

"I can swim!"

And, of course, ever since that glorious moment in the shallows, swimming has been my main form of exercise.

—⟋⟍—

Sebastian (Sebby) Ranieri was a family friend who worked with my grandfather. My mother always seemed happy to chat with him. One day Sebby appeared at our kitchen door, with his dazzling smile and rugged good looks, wearing army green fatigues. His dark brown eyes sparkled against his Mediterranean skin. My mother turned away from the sink and smiled back as she greeted him. I looked up from the kitchen table where I was playing with a doll.

"Gemma, I came to say goodbye," he said, looking proud while casually lounging against the door jamb, hands in his pockets. It was 1953.

"Where are you off to?" My mother asked.

"The army and eventually Korea."

"When will you be back?"

"I don't know, but I'll keep in touch with my parents. You can get news from them," he said.

"Look, Sebby, Korea is a pretty dangerous place," she said moving closer to him. "I'd try not to stay too long. Take care of yourself and good luck."

As he turned to leave, my mother patted him on the back and resumed her dish washing. I went back to my doll without any sense of danger ahead. Maybe they downplayed their concerns because I was listening.

Several months later, perhaps during the summer, I overheard a conversation between my mother and grandmother that something terrible had happened to Sebby. Time passed, and that handsome face never graced our doorway again. From his disappearance, I learned that people who went to war sometimes never came back.

One of my sharpest early memories is of the air raid drills in primary school thanks to the war from which Sebby never returned. I don't remember any explanation as to why they happened, but the sternness in our teacher's voice told us that these drills were to be taken seriously. A school alarm would sound, and we'd line up in single file and walk, without rushing, to the cloakroom. Spreading out carefully along the walls, we'd kneel in place, cover our heads with our clasped hands, close our eyes, and wait for what came next—an all-clear from the teacher.

From a child's perspective, it wasn't any scarier than a fire drill, and we didn't have to kneel in the cloakroom for very long. From an adult's point of view it seems laughable that we would move to the cloakroom in a thermal nuclear attack. But it was the most we could do to protect ourselves, and I credit our teachers for conveying a sense of calm to us, despite whatever personal beliefs they may have had about the effectiveness of those drills and the implications of doing them. Inasmuch as I depended on my teacher for a sense that someone was in charge, this was an early exposure to good leadership.

These vivid early remembrances about the sea, military, and war would marry up with my later experiences at the Army-Navy games and help form my future self.

CHAPTER 10

Ballet and Baking

⁀᧢

CAMBRIDGE, MA, 1960S

MY CHILDHOOD UNIVERSE WAS NEATLY contained within a few city blocks where my home, the Morse Elementary School, the Blessed Sacrament Church, and my best friend Linda's home could all be found.

Linda and I were third-generation friends. Our grandparents, who'd arrived to the same Cambridge area from Italy stood up at each other's weddings as best man and maid of honor. Our mothers pushed our baby carriages together as they swapped childcare tips and shared their concerns and dreams. Linda and I went to each other's birthday parties. When we were three or four, we took ballet lessons and later art classes together.

After school Linda and I would attend religious instruction known as "released time," which I thought sounded like prisoners out on parole, but were actually lessons preparing us to receive the sacrament of Holy Communion. Most Saturdays, Linda and I went to confession to be forgiven by the priest for our sins, and on Sundays we went to Mass with our families. Before confession, we'd check the movie listing by the National Legion of Decency to be sure we hadn't seen any "condemned" films that we'd have to add to our list of sins.[1] Films like—heaven forbid!—*The Apartment* with Jack Lemmon and Shirley MacLaine were on the list. The Church was guided by its reluctance to

---

1 Before the movie industry itself rated films suitable for adult and general audiences, the Catholic Church operated the National Legion of Decency to grade films on the basis of morally objectionable content.

acknowledge sexuality outside a marriage, even though the film is about the redemption of the two main characters.

Linda and I still share a love of art and frequent Boston's great Museum of Fine Arts. Long-standing friendships are like antique embroidery, where multicolored silk threads carefully weave together over time to form beautiful patterns.

Later when I switched schools, Frances became a good friend. She was born in Italy, and she had a younger brother, too. We both loved clothes, fashion, and movie stars, and bonded over long phone conversations about Sophia Loren, Gregory Peck, and Paul Newman.

Another Italian-American friend who lived in a nearby town invited me for sleepovers with her daughter, Janet, after she'd cleared it with my mother.

Janet and I chatted on her bed as we flipped through her array of Mickey Mouse Club magazines and caught up on the latest involving our favorite stars on the *Mickey Mouse Show* on TV. We liked the child actors, dancers, and singers who won their way into our hearts—as only Disney can do. We would have given our entire piggy banks to become Mouseketeers, especially like the pretty Annette Funicello, our favorite because she was Italian-American and became a teen idol in beach party movies with Frankie Avalon.

Despite these good friendships, I seemed to be dogged by insecurity, mostly due to average grades and being overweight. My poor self-image came into sharper focus when I watched Annette, and I felt a little neglected at home because my mother was so focused on my brother.

Tommy needed a lot of her attention. Today he'd probably be diagnosed with attention deficit disorder, because he had trouble focusing in the classroom. His dyslexia, not diagnosed until much later, slowed his reading and spelling. Amazingly, almost every toy in his hands ended up broken, and not by intention. But somehow he figured out how to solve a Rubik's cube puzzle at a young age.

We moved to a new school in the fourth grade that had a cafeteria. We no longer had to tote our lunches, and since the meals were subsidized, they cost very little. They were delicious, too. My favorite was the tuna salad sandwich served on a hot dog roll with chips, salad and dessert. I didn't worry about fat, sugar, or empty calories then.

In the fifth grade, the city began a new program for the gifted. To be selected you had to perform high enough on the IQ test. My mother asked if I wanted to transfer to the school that had these gifted classes. Though I missed the first cut by a few points, I was offered a seat anyway. Apparently, complaints from another parent whose kid didn't get in led to the bar for entry being lowered.[2] My mother wanted me to understand how my acceptance came about in case, once in the new school, I was unable to compete with the others. I was glad she shared this information with me, because I did transfer to the gifted class and it helped me understand why my grades were near the bottom in anything math- or chemistry-related.

Despite average grades, I felt I had joined an exclusive club. We hung out together after school. We learned conversational French starting in the sixth grade, which was a mark of culture in my home where the southern Italian dialect, rarely spoken, lacked a certain *je ne sais quoi*. And because I took two public buses by myself to get to my new school, I felt very grown up.

With my mother focused on my brother, regular library trips kept me supplied with young adult mysteries like *The Dana Sisters* and *The Hardy Boys*, and teen romance novels. When my mother complained to one of my teachers that I was reading too much junk, he said to let it go; the fact that I enjoyed reading was enough, and eventually I'd pick up literature. This is only true lately!

I kept myself busy outdoors with bike riding, roller-skating, and playing with my cousins and the neighborhood kids. I would lord it over my younger brother and cousins as we played cowboys and Indians. Being the oldest, I decided who played what role and who got the guns.

My piano and art lessons gave me an early sense of accomplishment, and I enjoy both diversions today.

I spent a fair amount of time in Aunt Betty's kitchen watching her supreme baking skills and imitating them at home with the child's cookbook

---

2 Later I'd have another experience with just missing the bar by a few points.

and cake pans she gave me. Unfortunately a lot of what I baked ended up in my mouth, and I was becoming plump.

After three years of ballet, I hoped to earn the beautiful pink satin toe slippers of an advanced dancer. I begged my mother to ask the instructor if I could take toe dancing classes. I think my attraction had less to do with dancing *en pointe* and more to do with the shoes that tied with satin ribbons. Also, the directions were mostly in French.

But the instructor told my mother I was too heavy. No wonder I had an inferiority complex. The teacher might have been less critical and more constructive, but such are the emotional travails of childhood.

When it came time to choose a high school, my parents said I could stay with my gifted classmates and go to the public school, or attend a private Catholic girls' academy. Making new friends would be disruptive and awkward. From the visits I had at those girls' schools I thought I might not fit into the earlier established cliques. Besides, I wasn't sure I'd enjoy school without boys. They were witty in the classroom and, well, nice to look at. So I stayed with my friends—and made new ones at the large Cambridge High and Latin School.

CHAPTER 11
Family Issues

~⁀~

HOMEFRONT, 1960S

I THINK I MUST HAVE been anorexic then because I spent the summer of 1962, before my freshman year, dieting like crazy. I feared that eating would make me fat and unappealing, but no one really talked much about the causes of food disorders then. Food depravation caused me to take long afternoon naps during which I'd dream about food.

Soon, though, my mirror and I became close friends as I admired my new, narrow shape from every angle, smiling. When I wore a fitted skirt or slacks, my pelvis bones showed and I looked like Audrey Hepburn. But when I stopped having periods, I thought maybe I'd gone far enough and tried to resume normal eating, while maintaining my figure.

Showing off my new figure was motivation for a carefully shopped cranberry shirtwaist dress to wear during those first days of high school. It had a black patent leather belt that skimmed my slender waist. Matching flats made me feel like I'd stepped out of the pages of a teen fashion magazine, and I eagerly sought approval from others to bolster my self-image.

After all, wasn't high school where I'd meet my dream boyfriend? That's what all my teen romance novels told me and I had to be ready. I'd also stocked up on three-ring binders, notebooks, and pens preparing to shine academically as well.

I learned that the books didn't tell you everything. On the first day of school, the administration let us go early in the afternoon. I left right after my last class and as I was making my way toward the bus stop, some boy appeared out of nowhere and shoved me in the back, knocking my books to the ground.

He ran off laughing. My cheeks burned with anger and tears were streaming down my face as I bent over to pick up the books.

A woman who'd witnessed the scene from her yard came over. She helped me gather up my books, gave me a hug, and walked me to the bus. She assured me that hazing was an anomaly I'd never have to endure again. "You've survived your first day of high school!" she said with a smile. And so I had. But I'd also learned that a small act of helping someone goes a long way.

Speaking of which, a polite boy I knew from grade school asked me to my first high school dance. His father drove him to my house, then dropped us at the school gym. The anticipation of something big happening was intense, something on the scale of being swept away by a Middle Eastern prince (a peace-loving one) or jumping into a James Bond movie. The reality was that he danced with me, and then he went to get a Coke. I can't remember whether he asked me if I wanted one.

While he was gone a tall well-built blond boy asked me to dance.

"No thank you," I replied.

"Oh, okay," he shrugged and disappeared into the crowd.

When my friend returned I told him that I had turned the blond boy down, beaming with self-assurance that I had done the right thing,

"Why didn't you dance with him?"

"I thought I wasn't supposed to. I came here with you."

"He's my friend for heaven's sake! Would it have killed you to dance with him?"

"I guess not," I said uneasily, disappointed that he didn't consider this a date. I was beginning to appreciate just how difficult living the life I read about in my romance books could be.

As we early teens were feeling our way socially, serious world affairs were looming over us. We didn't understand the politics behind it, but we watched TV news and saw Soviet missiles being off-loaded near Florida in Cuba. And from the grown-ups' vibes, we knew things weren't good.

Distracted from homework, all I could wonder was how we'd survive a nuclear attack. One day after school, I asked my mother, as she was sorting laundry,

"What are we going to do if the Soviet Union hits us with an atom bomb? Shouldn't we have a bomb shelter?

"Why, we can always go to the basement. Nana has all those vegetables and fruits she preserved stored there."

"What about protein?"

"We have canned tuna. We'll pack up all our canned foods—peas, coffee, evaporated milk—and bring them too."

I knew the cellar would make a lousy bomb shelter. It had windows, except for one tiny interior space; it was drafty, so those atomic particles would have no trouble coming in; it had no stored water, and lastly there was no heat unless we kept our incinerator going.[1] I didn't want to argue with her. I didn't want to know what our real chance of survival was. In any event, what she said gave me enough comfort to turn back to my homework as she finished sorting. The arms race and the Cold War continued to weigh on us like a sodden coat.[2]

One day there was a giant roar in the sky while I was at home. Moments later, the whole house shook causing the windows to rattle in their frames. In fact, one or two of our large porch windows may have shattered. *Is this an earthquake or have the Soviets launched an attack on us?*

These disturbances turned out to be nothing more than sonic booms caused by aircraft exceeding the speed of sound. Westover Air Force Base, some hundred miles away, was testing supersonic jets, trying to keep pace with the Soviets in the arms race.[3]

I was a sophomore in 1963 and remember the Civil Rights movement because my high school ran an essay contest on the importance of desegregation in the Southern schools, and in public places as a whole.[4] I remember upper

---

1 Houses of that era, built in the 1930s, sometimes had incinerators in which to burn paper trash before the days of recycling.

2 On Saturday mornings we had tests of the emergency broadcast system. This is when TV and radio transmission would be interrupted by a reassuring voice, "This is only a *test* of the emergency broadcast system. If this had been a real emergency, instructions would follow . . ."

3 The U.S. Strategic Air Command was located at Westover Air Force Base, Massachusetts, at the time.

4 The protest marches resulted in the Civil Rights Act of 1964 that guaranteed equality of all individuals, regardless of race.

classmates talking about the marches down South and watching Dr. Martin Luther King on TV. Since my parents weren't getting along, and my brother had problems, I felt detached from the movement then.

But another national tragedy led me to try my creative skills, which made me feel better about myself. Like most Americans, I remember exactly where I was that November when I learned that President John F. Kennedy had been shot. It was a crowded school corridor, and I was moving between classes when the headmaster came on the public address system with an announcement that would momentarily disorient and stop a lot of kids in their tracks. The president had been shot in Dallas.

We were dismissed early, and Frances and I walked home in silence. The headmaster had said his condition was unknown, and in this, for a very brief time, there was hope that he would live. But when we heard the mournful bells tolling in Harvard Yard, we knew that Kennedy had died. President Kennedy was beloved by the nation because of his idealism and youthfulness. He was especially loved by Bostonians because he was a native son and the first Catholic president.

To capture the moment and my feelings, I wrote a short piece and submitted it to the high school newspaper. There was some debate among senior editors on whether my article merited publication. At issue was originality versus a commonly held perspective. Is there a time and place in the news for the latter? In the end my "everyman's" perspective was published and this would soon help me along a somewhat bumpy road, because it gave me confidence that my opinion mattered and was expressed well enough for someone to print it, and for others to read it.

When you're in high school and your family has a domestic crisis, whether it's health or money issues, you keep it to yourself under the false assumption that no one else's family could possibly be as dysfunctional as yours. Later, you discover others had it as bad or worse.

My parents divorced around the same time the elementary school was sending home reports that my brother was socially behind and having trouble reading. I couldn't share any of this with my friends because I was deeply embarrassed that my family wasn't "normal." My shoulders slumped in deeper humiliation when I had to drop to a lower level of algebra and geometry courses, because I couldn't keep up with my peers, despite tutoring. I felt my classmates knew why I was absent from math classes, like I'd been a pregnant teen, or similarly disgraced.

Both of the above situations could very well have happened to me because of distractions in high school, including unchaperoned house parties involving rock and roll and hard liquor. I got pretty good at finding my way home, drunk and stumbling down the spinning hallway into my bedroom, without waking my mother.

But I also found healthful distractions when Frances and I joined the drama club. We reveled in our roles in *Camelot* and *A Midsummer Night's Dream. Maybe this would open the way to Hollywood or Broadway? How many movie and TV stars had started out as child actors?*

We occupied ourselves with making sure our costumes fit perfectly and that we got the makeup right. It didn't matter that we had non-speaking parts as town people; we were part of the acting *team.* Our club had a good reputation among high schools under the exacting direction of Mr. Robert Guest. We made the state competition one year and those of us who played extras took as much pride in the award as the leading characters. Years later, the club would help launch two famous local actors, Matt Damon and Ben Affleck, to Hollywood, after their early movie, *Good Will Hunting.*

Of course, there was the ultimate distraction: boyfriends. I met my first boyfriend in *Camelot.* He was cute, smart, and nice, and he played the part of a town person, too. After several months of dating, he realized he was gay. Since he was too embarrassed to tell me, a mutual friend delivered the news. For years after I assumed my boyfriend didn't think I was pretty enough and used sexual orientation as an excuse (meaning he really wasn't gay) to save me heartbreak. Dating continued to be a tricky proposition for me and for comfort I turned to boxes of sweets, resulting in extra pounds.

It's a miracle I didn't become the size of a house, but my love of dancing saved me. I listened to a lot of Beatles and became an English Mod girl, which involved wearing black tights and as much black clothing as possible without being stopped by my mother.[5]

"You're wearing too much black," my mother would shout as I escaped the house for another school day.

"It's the British style," I would shout back over my shoulder.

Fortunately, she also liked listening to the Beatles, especially "Money Can't Buy Me Love," which resonated personally with her, so she let me wear what I wanted.

In my group of friends folk music was popular because of its messages about racial equality and anti-materialism. Joan Baez was a special favorite, because she got her start locally. We'd listen closely to Baez and artists like Peter, Paul and Mary and pay attention to their lyrics, but I found their music tiresome and lacking a beat. In the privacy of my own home, I'd play the Beach Boys and daydream about losing enough weight to wear a bikini and become a surfer girl. I could only dream about it, because I lacked the will and self-discipline to diet and exercise more. Sweets were a kind of soothing drug, especially chocolate. When the sugar high hit, I'd whip out my Chubby Checker records and dance the twist in front of the mirror. And I'll still boogie to the music with a good beat in the aisles at the drugstore, if no one is looking.

And dancing was a good diversion when my mother injured her back in an auto accident shortly after her divorce, and was confined to bed for months. I became the cook, but my suppers didn't always turn out well because I was too busy watching myself dance to "Twist and Shout" in the mirror.

My insecurities followed me into the work place. The summer I was sixteen, I had my first full-time job doing administrative work for the accounting firm that my father used for his business. No one there was my age, and I'd cry at the slightest criticism from my supervisor.

That summer, my mother rented a house far from my friends and near the beach. On weekends, I strolled along the sand, hoping to find a new friend,

---

5 "Mod" was an urban style that started in London in the late 1950s and was named for style-conscious youth who liked modern jazz. It made its way to the U.S. in the 1960s along with popular British rock music.

but most girls my age were in tight groups. I'd pass a group of blondes, chatting and animated about what I supposed were their boyfriends.

Only once did a girl look up and smile. But a smile wasn't enough encouragement for me to interact with them. I suspected they'd known each other since they were kids. How would I even approach them? I'm afraid I wore my loneliness and isolation on my sleeve. Who would even want to approach such a sad girl? I allowed my extra weight and the emotional turmoil at home to gnaw at my self-esteem.

As graduation approached I applied mostly to women's colleges. The few coed colleges in Boston were large universities where I didn't think I'd be comfortable. The one exception was Tufts University, my first choice, because my father had gone there, and it was a good school.

My mediocre grades and minimal extracurricular activities didn't add up to much and I was accepted to exactly one school—Emmanuel—a Catholic women's college in Boston. Nana was the only one home when I received my acceptance. I was in a rare, ebullient mood, feeling good about myself, and I hugged her. She told me she was proud.

I had one woeful reservation about going to Emmanuel. I was grateful that I had been accepted *somewhere* and I looked forward to earning my B.A. degree, but there weren't any boys there. Fat, without a boyfriend, and not expecting much from myself, I trudged off to Emmanuel in the fall of 1966.

CHAPTER 12
College Protests

◦━◦

BOSTON, 1970S

ON FRIDAY NIGHTS, HERDS OF us girls from Catholic women's colleges put on our best dresses, high heels, and makeup to ride buses to Holy Cross. There we were discharged into the field house for dances. Because there was safety in numbers, the boys hung together shooting the breeze while the girls clustered in twos and threes. I was unsure of myself and what to expect.

But the music was exceptional and the kind I danced to at home in front of the mirror. The already famous soul man Wilson Pickett was there—live— on the campus stage belting out "In the Midnight Hour." A boy whisked my roommate, Denise, away to the dance floor. With any luck my turn would be next.

"Wanna dance?" asked a guy appearing from nowhere as if I had imagined him.

"Sure."

A couple of fast numbers including "Mustang Sally" got our blood pumping. I liked the fast numbers; we could dance at a safe distance. I grew uncomfortable when the tempo dropped and he pulled me closer. It didn't occur to me that I could just thank him and wait for another fast dance—or a new partner.

Pickett left the stage for the intermission.

"Want to go outside and see the stars?" the boy asked. I fell for it because I liked looking at stars, too.

"Sure."

Once outside and on the hilltop, he was upon me with a very wet kiss reeking of beer.

"Um, I have to go now," I said, freeing myself from his gangly embrace, but it was he who disappeared like a shot back into the cavernous field house. I followed at a safe distance, relieved. After a couple of similar experiences, I ended my trips to Holy Cross.

Sometimes Emmanuel would import a busload of boys for our on-campus mixers. I was never clear on what schools they were from and feared they might have been from the local technical institute and not have B.A. degrees. So I rarely went.

As a freshman, I commuted from home to college with my friends, but by sophomore year my father had encouraged me to move into the dorm on campus. He thought living with other students and making new friends would be good for me and eliminate the daily battles I was having with my mother for control of my life.

That's when I met Denise. Bright, easy going and of Irish descent, she made my transition from home to the dorm easy. Since I grew up in a neighborhood with many Irish families, we related well from day one. Another new friend, Judy, lived down the hall. I admired her intelligence and poise, along with her disciplined scholarship. We too remain close friends.

One warm Sunday afternoon in September, my father drove me back to campus to begin my junior year of college. I had just finished a summer job as a playground instructor and had a crush on a senior colleague, whom I was sure was going to ask me out for a date when the summer ended. But he chose to date someone else, and the inscrutable elements of social interaction eluded me once again.

I was hurt and returning unhappily to a mediocre academic career. Being at Emmanuel and not Tufts was a disappointment, but it didn't move me enough to improve my grades and apply for a transfer. I wasn't pleased with myself. I was an underachiever who would never find a good job. I was an overweight young woman whom no one would want to marry. *Poor me!*

But this was the year that things would begin to turn around. It was beginning to dawn on me that if you don't take the opportunities that life offers you for happiness, it's usually your own fault. Also, that giving up on goals is easy. No effort required there, consequently, no risk of failure. Persevering in goals is harder, requiring sacrifice and stamina. But when you see your efforts pay off, it's the ultimate reward.

One experience that helped put my life on a new course was becoming the associate editor of the college paper. While many of my friends had steady guys, and others spent their weekends getting dolled up and dating, I decided to put my unspectacular dating life on hold. I wanted to learn about writing news and editorial pieces, layout, and the creative and technical aspects of photography.

I began putting in more time at the newspaper, including Sunday mornings. I scrutinized mainstream periodicals and other college newspapers trying to stay on top of current events so that I could write about them. Being an English major and art minor provided a solid foundation for editing, and since Emmanuel had a curriculum-sharing program with Simmons College next door, I took courses in news writing, copyediting, and proofreading.

To be a paid journalist would solve all my problems, or so I thought. I'd have a job, my self-worth restored and—I'd be too busy writing about current events to even *think* about dating! Then tragedy struck. Judy found a serious boyfriend. At twenty, I felt doomed to become a spinster.

An opportunity presented itself when a navy recruiter came to campus. She was stunning and shapely in her navy blue skirt-suit with all the gold braid and stars. This was my first time since childhood seeing a naval officer, and my first time ever seeing a female naval officer. She had a beautiful face and a bedazzling smile. She was intelligent and eloquent, and I wanted to be just like her. I took a brochure home that weekend.

"Hey, Ma, guess what? I went to see the navy recruiter when she came to school this week."

"What! Did you sign anything?"

I assured my mother that I hadn't and that I was interested in learning about the officer candidate program. Her tone implied disapproval, and she said that I should talk to my father. Apparently she talked to him first because, in no time, he was on the phone.

"Your mother told me she wasn't happy that you saw a recruiter."

"Yes, but I remember how proud you were of Uncle Matt's navy career. I thought this might be a good career for me too."

"Look, what about being a teacher or a librarian?" he asked. "You'd have summers off and—"

"Sounds boring."

Then he blew the wind out of my sails with a few words I will never forget.

"Well," he paused. "Your mother and I feel the navy is no place for a woman. That's all there is to it. I'm sorry."

I've never been sure whether the objection came solely from my mother and she wanted backup or whether they both objected. I'd been sure my father would see things my way. I was definitely hearing mixed messages from my Dad: the navy was the greatest thing in the world—but only for men? In any event, if my father had supported me, I might have risked my mother's disapproval, but I wasn't about to take on both parents.

When my parents said no about the navy, a part of me was relieved. The decision was out of my hands. At that time, I didn't have the confidence or discipline to get into the navy, let alone stay in the service. Better not to risk failure. But I wasn't going to be a teacher either, darn it!

In time, I would deal with the twin images of the beautiful women, by which I mean—the Siren and the poster-perfect recruiter. They would call on me again.

If I didn't have much belief in myself then, at least one man found me attractive. My father would sometimes take me clothes shopping or out for nice dinners where he'd tell me I was getting "prettier and prettier" every day and turning into a "real glamour girl." I still didn't feel pretty, but hearing it from him lightened my spirits. Even better were our political discussions. Dad, the Republican, would listen carefully to my Democratic views. He agreed with my antiwar position on Vietnam and made me feel like an adult, with a worthy point of view.

I was deeply immersed in the antiwar movement like most college students of the time. We were losing too many young men to unclear and unobtainable objectives. We wanted them back home where they would be safe.[1]

Perhaps America's involvement in the Vietnam War may have been justified in its early days, but by 1969–1970, it couldn't be sustained. No matter how you looked at it—on moral, economic, or humanitarian grounds—it made no sense. The North Vietnamese communists weren't a direct threat to the U.S. from what we could see. They weren't going to invade, and if there were vital American interests in Vietnam, we couldn't see them.

The heart-wrenching sight on the evening news of Americans returning home for burial was a growing source of resentment. Investigative proof of the torturous conditions in which our downed pilots were held for captivity for years deeply disturbed us.[2] We were outraged by the My Lai Massacre in 1968 in which 350–400 South Vietnamese civilians were killed indiscriminately by our ground troops.

That famous photo of a naked young girl running with her body on fire near Trang Bang after America started bombing South Vietnam turned our stomachs. Sentiment was so strong against the war that even John Kerry, newly decorated for his brave service on the Swift Boats in Vietnam, testified before Congress on the wastefulness and immorality of the war. Yet there seemed to be no stopping the slaughter.

Many of us in the antiwar movement had friends who died in Vietnam or who walked off the plane physically intact, but not mentally. Our rallying protests called for the U.S. to declare victory and bring home the troops, now!

---

1 Although some Vietnam veterans talk of their unwelcome return home from the war, I never saw any evidence of it. No one I knew felt hostile to these veterans. We separated the war from the warrior, much as Americans do in today's wars. Then, we blamed our leaders in Washington and the military-industrial complex for continuing an unjust war.

2 Not many Americans were aware of the long and inhumane captivity these POWs suffered until their wives brought it to public attention after many months of lobbying the White House. Sybil Stockdale, the wife of navy pilot Jim Stockdale, later admiral, led the wives in their successful effort to get President Nixon to negotiate with North Vietnam for the captives' release.

"Hell no, we won't go!" was the refrain of thousands of massed student voices gathered at marches and rallies from colleges across the region, the state, and the country. As we marched we sang, "And it's one, two, three, what are we fighting for? Don't know; I don't give a damn. Next stop is Vi-et-nam." The most popular of the antiwar lyrics was John Lennon's "All we are say-ing, is give peace a chance." Did we think we could just sing peace into being?

Why don't we have antiwar protests like that anymore? Because then, half of us had a personal stake in stopping our involvement halfway around the world: able-bodied young men who were not in school or college. There was something called the draft. Being drafted meant going straight into the army, unless you had a deferment. Being drafted wasn't a cheery prospect, since the army served primarily on the ground engaging the Vietcong (guerilla warriors) and the North Vietnamese Army in the jungles, rice paddies, and mountains.

By volunteering for one of the other services, young men could avoid the draft, but not the war. There were many who avoided both. Some would beat the draft by deliberately raising their blood pressure or blood sugar just before the physical.

Besides the college exemption, there was one for conscientious objectors. However, evidence was required supporting a personal belief that it was morally wrong to kill another human being. If you were the fortunate son of someone with influential family connections, you might avoid service altogether. Not so fortunate? Well then, you could drive north to Canada where there was little possibility of extradition for draft evasion. Some became Canadian citizens. These groups who avoided military service ran the risk of being known as "draft dodgers" by those who disagreed with their actions.

For obvious reasons, the draft couldn't touch us women at Emmanuel, but we protested with the same gusto as the others on campuses across the country. When we weren't attending the big all-school marches and rallies on weekends in the heart of Boston, we held small discussion groups about the war and protest tactics. Our newspaper staff worked with the editorial staffs of other college newspapers. We strove to combine editorial ideas and share news stories. Many staffers were cute, shaggy-haired boys who expressed themselves intelligently. *But wait! Ending the war is serious business. No time for frivolous thoughts about men!*

The massive antiwar protest marches and rallies were growing even larger. President Nixon didn't appear to be moving fast enough to conclude our involvement in Vietnam. It was empowering to partner with thousands of other college students marching in Boston, home to more colleges than most other cities. We were united in our common cause to bring our troops home. I was starting to feel better about myself.

But things took a quick turn. In my junior year, I signed up for a course in constitutional law at Emmanuel. My father was hugely supportive. If he hadn't had to work in the family business, he would have gone into law himself. He saw the way I argued with my mother and thought I'd be good in a courtroom. I didn't work hard enough, and when I told the professor about my thoughts of applying to law school, he told me I was dreaming. The self-doubt was there like the returning tide.

But if I didn't always believe in myself, at least I felt better engaging in worthwhile group activities. By senior year, we had burned our bras and traded our matching cardigans and wool skirts for work shirts and jeans. Our freshman teas, requiring dresses and high heels were just memories. Woodstock had happened the summer before, and we were now listening to Janis Joplin and Jimi Hendrix—the upbeat Beach Boys lyrics about cars and surfers left behind.

Feminism was on the rise and female college students demanded equality in everything from sports to leadership roles in student government, and no men could tell us what to do. We were our own bosses. The sexual revolution was happening, but not to me personally. I still wasn't dating in my senior year. I wasn't ready. I didn't even know what I was going to do after graduation.

Alas, another setback occurred in my final year, but one that would provide a guiding lesson. Most of my free time went into our class yearbook as its editor-in-chief. I learned about composition, sizing, and cropping of photos. By selling ads, I learned about some of the business aspects too. *Maybe I could get a paying job after college?*

One day, we decided to play a prank on a nun who was our yearbook advisor. A dour woman, she was not our favorite. We resented her authority (that of censorship) and kept her out of the loop as much as possible. The prank may also have been partly fueled by the anti-authoritarian movement sweeping campuses. Students, frustrated that they couldn't change U.S. policy on the Vietnam War, used campus authority as a surrogate.

We suspected that Sister Anne was poking around our yearbook office after hours and checking on our work. To test our suspicions, we mocked up layouts of full-page photos with captions such as "Nude Man and Partially Clothed Woman Embracing" and "Mary and Jane Try Marijuana." We laughed ourselves silly as we strategically laid the boards around the office. What could possibly go wrong? A couple of days passed.

A secretary from the president's office phoned inviting me to a meeting. No subject was given.

In the president's office, with its Persian-carpeted floor and leaded glass windows framed by solemn draperies, I felt out of place in my jeans and work-shirt. President Sister Marie looked up at me from behind her desk when I said good afternoon. Her mouth was drawn in a tight line as she gestured for me to sit. I had a pretty good idea of what she wanted to discuss. I thought that in the context of campus protests, students cutting classes and smoking pot in their rooms, the yearbook prank would be a minor hiccup in her day. Maybe she'd even see the humor in it? It wasn't like at some other schools. We didn't take over a building, for heaven's sake, as they did across the river at Harvard, ending in the state police being called in.

"Joan, I called you here because—" she paused trying to check her emotions. "I want to know—" her face was red, her jaw tightening. "I want to know if *you* know anything about these?" Without taking her steely blue eyes off mine she pushed the offending layouts at me.

Our suspicions had proven true, I smiled ruefully. This was exactly one second before the panic started welling up. Suddenly, in her look, I saw that the prank had turned into a serious indiscretion and I was entirely to blame because I was the editor. *Why hadn't I thought of that sooner?* "Yes, Sister, I do. We put these mock layouts around to see if we were being monitored. Obviously we were." I tried not to sound snippy.

That's when the panic really set in.

She told me that Sister Anne's oversight was necessary because of the public exposure the yearbook gets. And that we didn't want to embarrass the trustees and scare away donors or cause a lawsuit. "Oh, I hadn't considered that part—" I mumbled, remembering that I'd briefly considered going to law school.

A lecture followed on seeking a compromise as the mature alternative to what I had done—if only I could have talked with Sister Anne and shown respect to the college and myself. It seemed to me that Sister Anne was the one sneaking around. It was that sort of conflicting message that kids were pushing back against all over the world.

I was told never to expect a recommendation from the school upon graduation, and then she dismissed me with a flick of the wrist.

"Okay, then. Fine."

I stood up. And in an attempt to recover my dignity, I walked out of the office with my head high. Lesson learned: I was the editor—the captain of the ship—and the captain takes the blame when the ship goes down. (Also, don't burn any bridges when you leave a place.)

Like so many other schools, Emmanuel suspended final exams that year. They wanted us off the campuses. I had spent so much time protesting the war, who knows what my final grades would have been?[3] Yet, we were all awarded our degrees.

By senior year, I accepted the fact that Emmanuel had been better for me than a coed college. In a larger, male-dominated institution, I wouldn't have had as many leadership opportunities. And maybe—I would have been distracted by the boys.

---

3 Maybe that's why I still have the classic nightmare in which I'm about to take a final college exam, but can't find the classroom because I've cut too many classes.

Part Three: Tom

CHAPTER 13

The Ultimate
Second Chance

～

DONG TAM, JUNE 15, 1969

I AM CERTAIN WE'LL BE attacked today. My 3:00 a.m. wakeup call and the relentless afternoon heat have sapped every ounce of energy. Exhausted, I wipe my forehead with the back of my hand and stare at the sky. Gray, again. The humidity has swallowed the blue. It's three in the afternoon; perspiration stains have turned my green uniform white. The hair on the back of my neck stands up. My hearing is extra sharp, as though I could speed up the firefight that I feel is coming just by listening hard enough.

Into the soporific air my radio crackles. "Hey Skipper, this is Tango 2."

"Go ahead, Tango 2."

"The troops are all onboard, but my bow ramp is stuck in the down position. I'm going to have to winch it up by hand!" Mike Harris, boat captain of one of the armored troop carriers, is excited. His boat will sink if it moves from the shore with the ramp down. But his greatest concern, and I can feel it in his voice, is that he is exposed to the enemy and extremely vulnerable.

"Winch it up, Harris," I say, climbing onto the perch of my boat to better assess the situation.

We are on our last operation of the day in an area where we'd been ambushed and suffered heavy casualties (including fatalities) only three days before. The Vietcong considered this area, dubbed "Rocket Alley," their own backyard, and it's bad territory for us. Not dumb by any means, when the enemy sees a group of

U.S. Navy boats go up the river, they simply wait for the return trip. Then they attack. The only unknowns in all of this are when and where and how quickly we can return fire. The enemy is nearby. And we are sitting ducks.

I'm commanding a group of eight navy river assault boats. All day we've been dropping our boatloads of army troops at their pre-determined locations for routing the enemy and disrupting its supply lines. We do our part, and then steam around the canal waiting for a radio call to pick them up and take them to their next assignment. It is mindless, boring, and exhausting work, but to succumb to the monotony can be fatal.

As usual my role is to provide fire support from my heavily armed Monitor.[1] I'm in the middle of a column of eight boats. This way I can cover both the head and rear of the column. Army artillery and navy helicopter gunships have been covering us all afternoon, but now they've been diverted to another mission. I am not alone among my crew in sensing that something is up. Everyone is more alert than usual and on edge. The air is ominous. We are grimly silent as we proceed down the canal; our eyes scan the dense foliage lining both sides of the canal.

Seeing the vulnerability of Mike's boat, I order the rest of the boats to break formation and encircle Tango 2. As if reading our playbook, it is precisely at that moment—when we are not quite in place—that the Vietcong open fire from the shore with the popping of small arms and the rata-tat-tat of automatic weapons.

"Return fire with all you've got!" I shout into the radio over the racket. At the same time, I order my Monitor to a position directly between enemy fire and the crippled boat, so we can unleash our superior firepower. Without hesitation, I act instinctively. My unit is in deep trouble and as their commander, it's my job to protect them. Fear is not on my mind.

Ear-splitting gunfire shatters the air. Acrid smoke swirls as bullets and rockets explode around us. The humidity seems to accentuate the smell of hot metal and the heat of fire. My men on the Monitor—now in constant motion—yell directions to one another, working as a team to repel the enemy.

A puff of gray smoke billows from the canal bank. The enemy has launched a rocket-propelled grenade. The grenade arcs towards the Monitor in slow motion.

---

1 The Monitor's firepower includes a 105-millimeter Howitzer, 20-millimeter cannons, grenade launchers, and 50-caliber machine guns.

I am already in a trance; my mind is preparing to take the blow. Oddly, I don't think to duck as the rocket screams toward me. I cover my ears and lower my head, my heart thudding. The deafening blast of the RPG on a pipe stanchion nearby hurls me like a rag doll up into the air and down ten feet into a narrow passageway in the boat. My ears are ringing, and I am wedged in tight and can't maneuver myself because of my injuries.

Hey, this can't be! It's not supposed to happen to me. It's supposed to happen to the other guy!

I gag on the blood flooding into my mouth. My stomach wrenches again with the sickening realization that I am blind and badly wounded. It feels like a portion of my skull has been crushed and that I've taken shrapnel in my head, upper body, hands, and arms. No one can get to me in the middle of a firefight. Mercifully, the pain hasn't arrived, but it's coming.

"He's dead!" I hear someone shout over the roar of the firefight.

"No, I'm not!" I yell back. I am angry and indignant that the enemy chose our most vulnerable moment to open fire on us. And I am in mortal fear of letting my men down. I have been charged with getting them home safely and I am going to finish my mission. I need to get back into the fight and take control.

"Continue firing," I shout. Somehow the blast has not knocked away my radio handsets, and they're still working. Adrenaline courses through my broken body trying to stave off the pain. If it takes my last breath, I'm going to quell this attack and get my men to safety. I know Tango 2 is still on the beach with a disabled ramp and unable to get underway. The harder I push, the more the pain kicks up. The more I fade, the tighter my grip on my radio handsets.

The firefight continues to erupt around me. Still wedged, I'm receiving reports from my crew on the radio. My men are loading and reloading rounds and letting loose with all our firepower, furiously pounding the enemy.

"Skipper, Tango 2 has raised its ramp and is proceeding to rejoin the other boats," says Harris.

"Roger that. Keep firing," is my order to the other boats. I want to ensure the attack is over before the medical boat comes for me. I don't want to interfere with

our return fire, and I don't want the troops on the medical boat exposed. No more casualties today, I say to myself.²

I hear someone shout through the chaos and noise "re-load those guns ASAP!" Even though my ears are ringing, I can hear bits of conversation. As if to make up for my loss of sight and inability to move, my ears seem extra sharp, and I'm aware of our unit's medical boat, which I'd not wanted exposed, coming alongside my Monitor. I hear navy corpsman, Richard "Doc" Nelson, jump aboard. He begins attending to me even as the battle continues. I'm unaware of the total extent of my injuries and have adrenaline to thank for getting me this far. Doc puts a sterile compress on my head wounds to staunch the bleeding and then stabilizes my condition with an injection to prevent shock.

Is the gunfire becoming more sporadic and distant, or I am slipping in and out of consciousness?

At last, a crackled voice on the radio telling me what I am waiting to hear.

"Fire suppressed, Skipper,"

"Roger that," I reply through bloodied and parched lips, "Move the boats to safety and request medevac for me."

I suddenly feel at peace and greatly relieved that my men are safe. A medevac army helicopter takes me away. When it lands I'm aware of being carried into an army field hospital and a voice saying, "He's not going to make it."

Oh, yes, I am. Yes, I am.

---

2 As it turned out, I was the only casualty that day. Although I have not seen it, several years later Michael Harris visited the spot where the ambush took place. He sent me a photo of a monument the Vietnamese had erected to the June 15, 1969, battle with River Assault Division 152, commemorating their victory over the "imperialistic" America, whom they viewed as trying to replace the French in their efforts to colonize the country.

CHAPTER 14

Fighting for Another Second Chance

⎯↶⎯

HAWAII, THE WHITE HOUSE, CALIFORNIA, 1970S

I WAS IN A COMA for fifteen days. The casualty assistance team had visited Gwen right away, yet all she or anybody knew from early reports was that my prognosis was poor, and I wasn't expected to live. Then the military's personnel accounting system lost track of me. Seriously, they didn't know where I was and, I guess it's fair to say neither did I. No news was forthcoming, and Gwen was scared and frustrated. But one of her pals in Hawaii was a friend of Carol McCain, wife of Lieutenant Commander John McCain who was then imprisoned in North Vietnam.[1] McCain's father was Admiral John McCain, commander-in-chief of the U.S. Pacific Command. That's all it took. As soon as the admiral heard about this missing wounded sailor I was found in the system, and Gwen got the good news that I was improving. According to my medical records, I'd been transferred to a military hospital in Vietnam, then one in Japan, then one in the Philippines. That time was hardest on loved ones.

Getting home to Hawaii and being reunited with my family was a gift beyond belief. I was lucky, and I thanked God, as we all did. Before our operation I'd remembered it was Father's Day, and I had gone to Mass, praying that I would return to my three girls. Survival renewed my faith in a higher power

---

1 John McCain has been a U.S. Senator for Arizona since 1987, and was the Republican presidential nominee in 2008.

and gave me a new lease on life, the ultimate second chance. I was determined to make every day special for the rest of my life.

In spite of having been on death's doorstep with very serious injuries, I was in remarkably good shape. My skull had been broken by the shrapnel from the RPG exploding on the stanchion twelve inches from me, and my right eye was gone. So I had to spend a few more weeks at Tripler Army Hospital in Hawaii for reconstructive surgery to fill the dent on my forehead and create a socket for my prosthetic eye. These successful procedures eventually left me feeling as normal as before my injuries. I was blessed to have survived with my brain, nervous system, and all my faculties intact. Gwen and the girls, having prayed so hard, were joyous and grateful for my safe return.

An officer came by and told me I was to be presented with a Purple Heart by a three-star admiral and that the awards ceremony would take place in the patient lounge at Tripler. This was a big deal! A three-star admiral dressed in his summer white uniform, with abundant gold braid and a chest full of ribbons! Not to mention the Purple Heart.

The next morning three of us were waiting in the lounge when an older gentleman, dressed like us, in his pajamas and bathrobe, shuffled into the room, accompanied by a navy administrative sailor.

"Now, which of you is Kelley?" Admiral E.R. Aurand mumbled. He motioned me over to his side, reached into his bathrobe pocket, pulled out a medal and pinned the Purple Heart on my robe. I'm humbled and pleased.

"Well done, son," he said, switching his attention to the two other sailors before shuffling off to have his gall bladder removed.

At least I was fine physically. Stoicism was guiding me. The truth is, I returned as a different person. My temper was shorter. Although I tried to be patient at home, I could explode quickly elsewhere. Sure, I'd seen death, including my father's, but that's not the same as seeing lives brutally cut down in their flower, especially those you knew. I'd seen poverty in the U.S., but not the abject bare survival like that of the peasants in Vietnam. The orphans we tried to help were a gnawing reminder of my little girls half a world away. I had lost my innocence. Whatever emotional trauma I'd encountered, I bottled up and buried inside for the time being. I had to continuously put one foot in front of the other.

Once healed, I was able to go home in July. Gwen was ecstatic and relieved to have me back in Kaneohe. Single parenting was difficult, but she hadn't been made one permanently. The girls were a little shy at first but we soon returned to our playtime routines and I was reading to them every night as was my custom before leaving. But there was a hiccup in my recovery. The blood transfusions I'd received resulted in infection, and I had to return to Tripler for a few days. This meant that recovering my strength and weight would take a few more weeks. Family and friends, I later learned, were concerned about my head wounds and my skin-and-bones look courtesy of all the time I spent in various hospitals.

After being released from Tripler—again—in August I was anxious to get back to work. The navy wouldn't put me back in a full-duty capacity because of my injuries, so they placed me in limited-duty status, an opportunity to prove myself. This was standard procedure. The navy had to decide if I was worth keeping.

My orders were to the Fourteenth Naval District, a shore station headed by an admiral responsible for personnel administration and logistic support for the ships homeported in and visiting Pearl Harbor. I was assigned as the recreation officer for the gym, playing fields, and swimming pools on the base. Yes, this fully qualified surface warfare officer had to make sure that at the end of each day we had the same number of basket and racket balls we had started out with. Two months earlier, I was protecting our soldiers from the Vietcong. Now I was protecting basketballs from thieving sailors and marines? I was not happy.

Fortunately, one of my pals from Newport was assigned to the staff of the Pacific Fleet commander and I shared my frustration with him. He talked to his bosses and I was reassigned with new duties and responsibilities. When there was a need for an extra person I rotated through the plans division's four branches: political and diplomatic, nuclear plans, war plans, and foreign military assistance. I learned a lot about high-level staff duty, too. We handled major operational issues such as preparing for the reversion of Okinawa from the United States to the Japanese government.[2] We developed plans to mine North Vietnam harbors, and we provided military aid to friendly nations in the Pacific area. My Vietnam experience served me well when, after a couple of months, a new branch was established to implement Vietnamization and I became the number two person in the Vietnamization branch. By 1969 America had started the process of turning the war over to the South Vietnamese forces, a measure hastened by the unpopularity of the war at home. As aircraft, boats, and equipment were transferred to South Vietnam, the number of U.S. troops was being reduced.[3]

On two occasions, I was sent back to Vietnam to monitor the progress. I spent some time in my old stomping ground, Dong Tam, where I shook my head in disappointment to see half sunken boats that we had labored so hard to put into mint condition for the Vietnamese Navy. They had been neglected by our allies. Their engines were inoperable and their weaponry had been eaten away by rust. If I hadn't realized the war was lost before, this certainly convinced me that the future of South Vietnam, at least from a navy perspective, was doomed.

My navy career was also at serious risk. While duties at the fleet were intellectually stimulating and broadened my perspective on our position in the geo-political world, I was anxious to get back on a ship and go to sea with my sailors. This turned out to be a challenge. I had assumed that my navy career would resume as soon as the medical people found me fit for duty.[4] Not so. A Medical Board and a Physical Evaluation Board (PEB) each had to review my case and recommend me to a higher authority for final deci-

---

2 Okinawa, Japan, which had been under U.S. control since the end of World War II, was returned to the Japanese government in 1971 in accordance with a post-war agreement.

3 Vietnamization was a dynamic and politically sensitive area. The Nixon administration was anxious to get the U.S. out of South Vietnam without appearing to abandon its ally. The chain of command, including my bosses, wanted to finish the job they had set out to do—defeat the Vietcong and preserve South Vietnam. Guidance was constantly changing, depending on the whims of the administration and/or Congress.

4 I had lost an eye, but adjusting was easy. I had to be a little careful with depth perception and peripheral vision, but otherwise I was fine. That's not to say it didn't take some getting used to. I feared falling while going down stairs, so I exercised more care. The first few times I tried to catch a baseball or hit a tennis ball directly in front of my face, I got smacked before I learned to move the glove or racket a bit to the right. These were minor and temporary setbacks.

sion. Consisting primarily of medical folks, the Med Board would determine whether I was healthy enough to continue serving with or without continuous access to medical facilities. After a two-hour meeting where they asked me a few questions and reviewed my medical records, they pronounced me medically cleared to continue serving.

The PEB proved to be the greater hurdle. Made up mainly of line officers, its role was to determine if my injuries would keep me from serving on a career track leading to command at sea. From the tone of their questions, I could sense that they were uneasy in their role and would have preferred the Med Board to have ruled differently. We were clearly on a collision course, because I was not ready to take a disability pension and leave the navy. When the PEB finally made its decision, I was called into the admiral's office.

He looked up from the files on his desk and said,

"Son, I'm sorry, but I have bad news. Due to the loss of your eye, the PEB has found you found unfit for duty. Their recommendation is that I muster you out of the navy."

I felt like I'd been hit in the head again. I was stunned and devastated that the navy was rejecting me. The fact that I had been part of the greatest team on earth for a decade made no difference to the admiral, who was duty bound to follow the recommendations of the PEB.[5] The irony is that I did the "right thing" in saving four dozen men, and now I was being punished for it.

"But, Sir, I've only lost one eye. I can do everything as well as I normally did."

I appealed the PEB's recommendation. Another interview session followed where, this time without panic, I confidently made the case that I was a damn good naval officer who had served his country for ten years and that the only thing that had changed was that "now I can see only half as well with one eye." Whoops! I wished I had phrased it more like—"Now I can now almost as well as I could with two eyes"—but that's the way it came out. It didn't

---

5 At that time sailors missing a body part were considered unfit for duty. Fortunately, this policy has changed so that today's Global War on Terror warriors, even those missing limbs, can continue to serve in their old units or at other commands in certain capacities. This humane policy helps them recover faster because they are wanted and needed by the very organization for which they gave so much.

matter because good fortune smiled on me that day and the board upheld my appeal. I would continue to serve in the navy!

But here was the hitch: I couldn't serve as a sea-going line officer. They recommended that I transfer to one of the staff corps such as supply, intelligence, or public affairs, of all things. To my mind these positions were second-string jobs. Supporting the active fleet would keep me in the navy but not on a path to command at sea. Still, the glass was half-full and I was determined to make the most of it. I would be able to serve my country. Perhaps there would be more I could do in the pursuit of my ultimate goal?

Good fortune smiled again in the form of Admiral Zumwalt, my former boss in Vietnam, who had just been selected to the top job in the navy.[6] Although I didn't know him well, and I was sure he wouldn't remember me, I wrote a note congratulating him on his promotion and subtly whining that although I was able to stay in the navy, I really wanted to remain as a line officer. Lo and behold, a few days later a message came back from Washington overruling the PEB recommendation. I would remain a line officer and the glass was full again. I was overjoyed in knowing that my original career goal—sea command—was still in sight, no pun intended.

In May 1970, the navy ordered me to Washington, D.C., where I'd be presented with the Medal of Honor by President Richard Nixon. Yes, I was astonished at the news. I'd been awarded the Purple Heart, but I hadn't been told anything about the Medal of Honor and frankly hadn't given it any thought. A shiver ran down my spine as I remembered the other men I had served with in Vietnam carrying out their duties, every day, in extraordinary ways. We were only doing our job. Only a few months ago the navy was trying to retire me, now I was receiving its highest award.

The next few days were a blur. The navy arranged for Gwen and the girls to be flown from Hawaii to D.C., and I went to Boston to gather up my mother and brother, John.

In the East Room of the White House we were joined by eleven other nervous and awestruck soldiers, sailors, marines, and airmen, also there to receive

---

6 Admiral Zumwalt had become chief of naval operations.

the Medal of Honor, with their families in tow.[7] That day, I failed to appreciate the grandeur of the place—the portraits of past presidents, antiques, and the rich furnishings—that I noticed on subsequent visits. Instead, I was concerned about what I would say to the president if he started a conversation?

President Nixon entered the room and, one by one, he presented each of us with the Medal of Honor. When he came to me, he shook my hand, and we both listened as someone read my citation for the award.[8] He placed the medal around my neck, shook my hand again, and then asked me where I was from.

"Boston, Sir," I said. *So far so good.*

"Oh," the president said, "do you eat baked beans every night?"

"No, Sir, only on Saturdays," came my eloquent reply to which he gave a sharp harrumph and moved on to the next person in line.

---

7 At the White House ceremony I was joined by my brothers-in-arms, soldiers Paul Bucha, Frank Herda, Allan Lynch, Ron Ray, and the late Charles Rogers. Also with me were marines James Livingston and Jay Vargas, airmen James Fleming and the late John Levitow, and sailors Don Ballard and Bob Kerrey.

8 My Medal of Honor Citation reads: "For conspicuous gallantry and intrepidity at the risk of his life above and beyond the call of duty in the afternoon of June 15, 1969 while serving as commander of River Assault Division 152 during combat operations against enemy aggressor forces. Lt. Comdr. (then Lt.) Kelley was in charge of a column of 8 river assault craft, which were extracting 1 company of U.S. Army infantry troops on the east bank of the Ong Muong Canal in Kien Hoa province, when 1 of the armored troop carriers reported a mechanical failure of a loading ramp. At approximately the same time, Viet Cong forces opened fire from the opposite bank of the canal. After issuing orders for the crippled troop carrier to raise its ramp manually, and for the remaining boats to form a protective cordon around the disabled craft, Lt. Comdr. Kelley realizing the extreme danger to his column and its inability to clear the ambush site until the crippled unit was repaired, boldly maneuvered the monitor in which he was embarked to the exposed side of the protective cordon in direct line with the enemy's fire, and ordered the monitor to commence firing. Suddenly an enemy rocket scored a direct hit on the coxswain's flat, the shell penetrating the thick armor plate, and the explosion spraying shrapnel in all directions. Sustaining serious head wounds from the blast, which hurled him to the deck of the monitor; Lt. Comdr. Kelley disregarded his severe injuries and attempted to continue directing the other boats. Although unable to move from the deck or to speak clearly into the radio, he succeeded in relaying his commands though 1 of his men until the enemy attack was silenced and the boats were able to move to an area of safety. Lt. Comdr. Kelley's brilliant leadership, bold initiative, and resolute determination served to inspire his men and provide the impetus needed to carry out the mission after he was medically evacuated by helicopter. His extraordinary courage under fire and his selfless devotion to duty sustain and enhance the finest traditions of the U.S. Naval Service."

After the ceremony, the staff graciously took my mother, whose health required a wheelchair, on a tour of the White House. Two weeks later she passed away from a heart condition. Our relationship had always been strong, including the time leading to her death, even though I had the dual task of healing and fighting for my career. She died as she wished: a proud mother. Over the next few years she would have been even prouder of my fight to take command.

The White House ceremony in 1970 was the turning of a chapter, and our lives fell into a comfortable pattern. My navy career was on track and I was well on the way to regaining all my strength and adapting for the loss of my depth perception and peripheral vision. I was working long hours at the fleet, but I could get home every night and had most weekends off. This gave me ample time to spend with the girls who were then four, six, and seven, and we whiled away precious hours exploring the pristine beaches of Oahu and neighboring islands. I tried to make up for the worry I caused them when I was recovering from my injuries. I succeeded in turning all three daughters into Boston sports fans, although one defected to the Yankees later. (We Bostonians take our sports passionately.)

As a Medal of Honor recipient I was asked to make appearances and give talks at various civic and military gatherings, like the Memorial Day celebration in Kapiolani Park in downtown Honolulu. One of my fellow honorees was an old Filipino veteran who had survived the Bataan Death March.[9] Another was the singer Don Ho, Hawaii's favorite son. Ho was a no-show when the program started at the outdoor venue.

I had already spoken, and the Filipino man was weaving a spellbinding story about his wartime experiences when a limo pulled up to the stage area. Out hopped Ho with a scantily clad female companion. He moved quickly to center stage and started to wrest the microphone out of the old man's hands, insisting that it was his turn to speak.

---

9 The Bataan Death March occurred in 1942 when U.S. and Philippine soldiers surrendered to the Japanese Army. The surviving prisoners were marched sixty miles to a POW camp where they were interred for the duration. During the march that included U.S. Army female nurses, the Japanese brutally beat and killed those prisoners unable to keep up.

I could not believe his rudeness and jumped to my feet from my seat on the stage. Not only did I give Ho the old heave ho, I told him to shove off! He aimed a few choice profanities at me as he retreated into the crowd, leaving me and the old Filipino warrior who thanked me with tears in his eyes. A local photographer captured the moment in a photo that ran the next day on the newspaper's front page showing me in that unmistakable navy dress white uniform with the baby blue ribbon around my neck attached to the medal. It was a pose not befitting a Medal of Honor recipient.

This taught me a lesson that all recipients need to keep in mind every day: that the privilege of wearing the medal and the celebrity status associated with it changes our lives forever. We also wear the medal for those who didn't survive. Any action we take in public is public, whether it appears in the media or not, and we have to uphold the dignity of the medal. It's not just all about us.

My orders were to attend the Naval Postgraduate School in Monterey, California and take a one-year master's degree in management. The curriculum looked challenging enough to keep it interesting for me, but we had to leave our idyllic family life in Hawaii. Gwen and the girls were good sports about the move. On the pro side, I had a regular schedule and family time on nights and weekends. This was a ticket I had to punch if I wanted to move my career plan forward. I completed the program and waited for my next assignment, one more step towards heeding the Siren's call and taking command at sea, and, sure enough, it came through. Not only were we going back to Hawaii, I was returning to sea, ordered as XO of the USS Sample (DE-1048), homeported in Pearl Harbor.

Gwen and I eagerly relished the thought of returning with the girls to that tropical climate with its laid-back way of life and of resuming friendships. But before assuming my XO duties, I had to attend a four-week course for prospective XOs in Newport. This gave us a chance to see old friends while enjoying Newport at its best (in the summer, of course!) and drive down the East Coast to visit Gwen's family in Charleston. Life was good in the navy for the time being.

Although there were many officers who, like me, were becoming XOs, the student body included officers who were further along in their careers—those about to become COs—and we benefited from working with one another. We shared many classes as well as numerous bull sessions where the senior guys related many of their XO experiences to us fledglings. Another advantage of hanging around with prospective COs and listening to their stories was that we could study and evaluate a variety of command styles. These included the detail-oriented micromanager at one end of the spectrum, the big picture guy at the other, and everything in between.

The big picture guy sought to empower individuals by bringing out the best in them. This was a leadership style that I admired and aspired to learn. It was exemplified by one individual I met, Captain Frank Donovan, who became a major influence in my career because of his kind and gentle way in always putting the sailor or marine first.[10] A Boston native and former enlisted sailor, Frank Donovan was en route to assuming command of a large amphibious ship, USS Tarawa (LHA-1). We later served together when he achieved flag rank. Frank reinforced the importance of taking care of people, entrusting them with responsibility, and by so doing, empowering them. His inclusive nature enabled team building, team cohesiveness, and ultimately team success. He saw the intrinsic value of each team member from the lowest enlisted rank to the highest officer rank. Needless to say, he treated minorities and women no differently from anyone else. When you worked for Frank, you admired his even-handed fairness. He made you want to do your best for him, and more importantly, for the good of the team. Why? Because he taught us the team is more important than any one person.

At the end of that summer in Newport we were Hawaii bound. This time the navy really showered us with gifts, as if to make up for what it would later demand from all of us. Instead of being crammed in a chartered 707 we were "forced" to take a passenger ship from San Francisco to Honolulu. The SS President Wilson was an elegant ocean liner chartered by the navy to carry cargo, military personnel, and their families across the Pacific between mainland U.S. and Hawaii. For six days we lived in the lap of luxury with all the

---

10 The late Vice Admiral Frank Donovan later commanded the Navy's Military Sealift Command and would be a keynote speaker at my navy retirement.

food we could eat, movies for the girls, swimming pools—you name it, old Woodrow provided it.[11]

I had a few days before reporting to the USS Sample, enough time to find a nice home in Kailua, just outside the Marine Corps Air Station at Kaneohe, and a couple of miles from where we lived during our previous tour in Hawaii.

Gwen settled the girls into their school routines, and I reported aboard the Sample, confident that my career was on course and the navy viewed me as one of its future leaders.[12] But I had to successfully complete this assignment in order to earn my command at sea qualifications. I knew at this point that I had a fifty percent chance of being selected for ship command. Those were the odds for everyone. If you failed selection, you could continue to serve in other capacities, but your sea-going career would be essentially over. I was grateful for this opportunity. The reason I chose the navy was to serve by leading my crew at sea. That's where all the action was as far as I was concerned.

As the XO, I was tested in ways far more challenging than what I'd encountered while heading up a department. The captain and I were the senior leaders of the ship. No longer could I complain about command policies or commiserate with my fellow officers. I had to be on the same page as the CO. But this proved to be a near impossible task since the CO and I were very different people with extremely different leadership styles.

The CO was a driven, demanding and an unforgiving taskmaster, far less inclined towards the inclusive "big picture" style of leadership that I naturally favored. He gave the impression that nothing good could happen unless he was personally responsible for it. It was his way or the highway. This dictatorial form of leadership struck fear into the hearts of the sailors and created resentment. Fear will only get a leader so far. You may get people to perform, but you'll never earn their full measure of respect, enabling them to exceed expectation.

---

11 Coincidently this was an historic trip, the final voyage for this ship and the end of an era that gave way to air travel.

12 The Sample was a Garcia-class destroyer escort comparable to the Stickell in size, but with a newer type of propulsion plant of poor design that we struggled to maintain. Fortunately I was surrounded once again by some very talented sailors, and we managed to stay on top of our commitments.

The captain's attitude resulted in somewhat of a role reversal between him and me. Traditionally, the CO is supposed to project the "good cop" while the XO is the take-no-prisoners "bad cop." In the eyes of the men of Sample, I was generally considered the good guy. My tour on Sample would become extremely valuable where future tours and civilian employment were concerned. I was able to develop a leadership style and achieve success by empowering and encouraging the crew to perform above their expectations.

We'd been at sea for several weeks when we pulled into Guam to celebrate Thanksgiving. Due to the need to conserve fresh water, the ship's laundry had been unable to clean dress uniforms. The CO announced that only those with clean dress uniforms could participate in the sumptuous Thanksgiving dinner prepared by our own food service team. In spite of my heated protestations, this edict meant that the majority of the crew had to find food on the base, if anything was open. In a display of solidarity, most of the officers who did have clean uniforms, myself included, chose not to enjoy the Thanksgiving dinner on the ship.

Another more striking example of his leadership occurred when he left me in charge during a port visit to Penang, Malaysia. He handed me a phone number where he could be contacted in an emergency and said, "I'll see you in five days." This was unusual. Commanding officers didn't leave their ships in foreign ports for that length of time, except in emergencies.

As fate would have it, while the CO was away all hell broke loose. The ship received a "flash" message—the highest category of importance—directing the Sample to get under way within twelve hours and proceed to a rendezvous point off the Cambodian coast. The Cambodian government was about to collapse to the communists and we were to stand by to assist in evacuating American citizens living there. Getting a ship ready to sail normally takes days. We had overnight.

The first order of business was to send the shore patrol out to round up all the sailors. Since they were on leave, it was reasonable to look for them in bars, hotels, and restaurants, and not in libraries and churches. Next, we had to expedite the delivery of food and other supplies that had been scheduled to arrive two days later. Once the supplies were delivered, they had to be loaded aboard and stored. All ongoing maintenance and repair had to stop, and all machinery had to be made ready for full use. Finally, I had to contact the CO and tell him to get back to the ship. When I reached him, in spite of the antiquated Malaysian phone system, he was 150 miles away from Penang and had no means of transportation to get back in time. I contacted the Malaysian Navy, explained the situation and begged them to send a car for him, secretly hoping that he would not get back in time. He was derelict in his duty, and I looked forward to leading the men in a way that they deserved, and in a style I had always admired going back to my dad.

We continued to make the ship ready for departure. At the appointed time, I was on the bridge, binoculars around my neck when I gave the salty order to "take in all lines." We were under way, minus the CO! I stood straighter and took a deep breath, hands on my hips. My dream of being in charge had come true. I was in command of 250 men and 2,600 tons of fighting metal!

But no sooner were we under way and proceeding out of the harbor than I spotted a small speedboat astern of us. As it made headway, the song playing in my head about the wonderful day growled to a halt as if someone had pulled the plug on the record player. It was the fighting mad CO. He'd caught up with us and was coming aboard. My short stay in command made me realize how badly I wanted it.

"Kelley, how *dare* you get under way without me!"

"Sir, we received a flash message to help rescue Americans in Cambodia. The communists are about to take over, and lives are at stake! Besides, I didn't want you to get in trouble." I put an extra emphasis on the last word to let him know that I knew he could be in a world of hurt if I'd let the powers that be learn the real story.

Here I thought was an opportunity to earn his respect, by either demonstrating my competence and loyalty or by instilling fear that I could blow the whistle on him. But he was still unable to show me any respect.

When my twenty-four-month XO tour was up, I detached from the ship in Pearl Harbor. In his final evaluation report of my performance, the CO made the comment that I should not be given command of a ship at sea. He stated that my lack of sight in one eye made me a risk in ship-handling. In fact, I had trained the officers and senior enlisted men in ship-handling with outstanding results. I tried to let it roll off my back, but his comments roiled around in my head, and I seriously worried about whether his report would keep me from command at sea.

I had another one of those ticket-punching assignments in 1975 you run into along the way: a six-month program at the Armed Forces Staff College in Norfolk, Virginia. This is where mid-career officers studied high level subjects such as diplomacy, world affairs, military history and strategy, and inter-service collaboration.

My preference would have been to return to Newport, where we still had lots of navy and civilian friends, and spend nine months at the Naval War College studying similar topics. There, I could keep in touch with my beloved Boston Red Sox, Bruins, and Celtics, but this was not to be.

The student body in Virginia was divided evenly among all the service branches with a few foreign officers thrown in as well. Together we shared a wide range of backgrounds and experience in our careers. This was my first chance to meet officers from other services and see how they operated, which was essential for the joint and allied responsibilities we were to assume down the road. The president of the college, Admiral Jerry Denton, was an inspirational figure, because of his leadership role as a POW after being shot down and imprisoned by the North Vietnamese in Hanoi.[13]

One of the best parts of that program was meeting with visiting dignitaries in small groups to exchange ideas. I felt like a big shot—meeting all the service chiefs, secretaries of defense and state, and the CIA director. After this I had fully expected to be ordered to a joint staff, or at least a navy staff involved in worldly affairs. Instead, I faced the type of two-year assignment that most of us in the military dreaded and went out of our way to avoid: duty in Washington, D.C., at the home office.

I had eluded this tour for fifteen years but now my time was up. "Driving a desk" in Washington meant you were away from operational ships and sailors and working in the highly politicized environment of the company's

---

13 Admiral Jerry Denton kept his team of POWs together by maintaining morale under arduous circumstances.

headquarters, commonly known as the Pentagon—or stress city. And if that wasn't enough, I had the negative evaluation from the skipper of the USS Sample, which I tried not to think about. If I had any chance of being selected for command, I needed a good evaluation from this tour.

I arrived at the Office of the Chief of Naval Operations to work in manpower planning and programming.[14] I was surrounded by people who really knew their jobs, including senior civilians who had been doing this work for years. Our primary task was to plan for the number and occupational mix of sailors needed to man the fleet in the years ahead, and to ensure that we properly justified and requested adequate funding from Congress to meet those needs. We were forecasting the navy's future and what it would cost. Finally my economics degree was of use! It was a pleasure to go to my new assignment every morning.[15]

Added benefits were that our office wasn't in the Pentagon pressure-cooker building itself, and that we worked across the hall from the detailers who assigned sailors to their duty stations. Whenever we devised a theory, like adding two dozen mid-grade sailors to the Pacific fleet in the next fiscal year, our colleagues could tell us how feasible it was.

I had thought that compared to driving a ship on an operational mission, anything to do with personnel was boring. But it wasn't. Among the issues we worked on was studying the manpower requirements for a navy that would expand to six hundred ships, a very controversial issue that lingered into the 1980s.[16]

---

14 The chief of naval operations is the person in charge of the entire navy, similar to the commandant of the Marine Corps or the chief of staff of the army or the air force.

15 Besides crunching numbers we crafted position papers in which we made best-case arguments as to why the funding was necessary and how it would meet the navy's future needs. We recommended the number and type of ships and aircraft to carry out missions in support of the country's military and diplomatic commitments.

16 When the Vietnam War ended in 1975, the military reversed its rapid expansion into the war effort and funding was greatly reduced. As the Cold War continued to be a concern, navy leaders determined the U.S. had a slim margin over the Soviets, who had begun staging vessels in former U.S. ports in South Vietnam. This gave the Soviets potential presence in all seven seas. The six-hundred-ship navy concept bit the dust during the Reagan years due to Congressional budgetary restrictions beginning in 1986. The Soviet Union dissolved in 1991, making the need for a six-hundred-ship navy overtaken by events.

It was a quantity versus quality issue. Many in decision-making roles felt we needed fewer ships because the newer ones were technologically superior, and we could be effective with less.[17] Ultimately, my newly acquired knowledge would make me a better commanding officer because I understood the process involved in properly manning my ship.

One Friday afternoon in 1976, we were told to actually prepare the manpower requirements needed for a six-hundred-ship navy of the future, or about one hundred more ships than were currently in the fleet. We worked through the weekend, sleeping little and did a hasty, but accurate analysis of the manpower requirements needed to run a fleet that could match the Soviet might. We delivered the finished product to our bosses first thing on Monday. It was tedious work, but we had a lot of laughs about becoming the famous architects of the six-hundred-ship navy. It was a great example of teamwork in that no one cared who got the credit, and we all took pleasure in being part of the team that delivered a first class product on short notice.

Finally, while still on my Washington tour, I received the news I had been hoping for ever since I joined the navy, sixteen years earlier. The board of senior officers charged with selecting the next generation of commanding officers had screened me for command at sea! This was a big deal, the fulfillment of my childhood dreams and an immense challenge. I didn't know it at the time, but my case may have been helped by two of the board members who were old shipmates and friends: Captain Joe Nolan, a Boston guy, and Commander Mike Boorda, who was the recorder of the board proceedings. Apparently they were able to convince the other board members, based on the evidence in my record, that my former CO's comments about my inability to handle a ship were nonsense.

This was a personal achievement to be sure, but its true significance was the realization that the navy trusted me with this immense responsibility. I would have life and death power over the lives of my crew. I would be responsible 24/7 for the welfare of the men I had the privilege of leading.[18] It was at

---

17 Some thought we had to keep our numbers up to compete with the Soviets. The other services were advocating for the same dollars. In the end, all plans were meaningless unless Congress appropriated the dollars.

18 It was not until the 1980s that the navy began integrating women on combatant ships.

once a most humbling and challenging moment, and I couldn't wait for orders to the actual assignment and to get started.

My orders came through in the spring of 1977. I would command USS Lang (FF-1060), a Knox-class frigate homeported in San Diego. Once again, I was forced into another "hardship" tour in Newport. I would enroll in a four week program for prospective captains and my family would be able to accompany me for another great summer in Newport. All of a sudden, my duties in Washington became far less interesting compared to the perceived excitement that lay ahead.

CHAPTER 15

Command

⟿

PORTLAND, OREGON, 1978

"SABOTAGE!"

"What are you talking about?" I couldn't believe what my XO was saying when he came rushing up to me on the main deck where I was standing gazing out the porthole and having a quick cup of coffee.

Choking, I set the cup on the table, wiped my mouth with my hand, and bolted for the door. Words were still spewing out of his mouth as our feet thudded down the metal ladders on our way to the engine spaces. I could barely understand what he was saying, and didn't want to. The day of our final engineering inspection was upon us, and he was talking about someone setting us up to fail.

The Lang was in a civilian shipyard in Portland, undergoing a complete nine-month overhaul.[1] As the new skipper, I was responsible for the entire project. Assuming command of a ship and the responsibility for three hundred sailors assigned to the ship's company is a daunting experience, at least it was for me. I was replacing a man who had led his crew through two years of challenges, including extensive deployments, who had fostered deep loyalties and who, in most cases, was beloved by the crew because he treated them as family. He was obviously more qualified for command than I was, because he'd been doing it for the past couple of years, and I was the new guy. While

---

1 Ship overhauls involved repairing and replacing equipment with newer versions, cleaning the hull while the ship was in dry dock, painting, and overall sprucing up. The work was done in navy shipyards or contracted out to civilian shipyards and could take nine months.

I'd been driving a desk in Washington, he and his crew were steaming around the world keeping the sea lanes of commerce open.

To make my earliest days of command even more challenging, during the "hail and farewell" parties, where people greeted me and said goodbye to my predecessor, all the speeches and toasts highlighted how much the old CO would be missed. I had to prove myself to the crew by coming out of the gate running, and here I was running through the ship with my XO about to face a situation no captain wants to deal with. Be careful what you wish for.

We had already endured several months of the harsh shipyard environment working closely with our civilian counterparts to make sure the work was done properly. Wearing hardhats and goggles and protective equipment all day came as naturally as putting on your pants every morning. Shipyards and the deck of a ship in dry dock are dirty, loud, and crowded places. Flying paint chips, metal, and soot are everywhere. The smell of paint, oil, and hot metal hangs in the air, and there's always a taste of dirt and grit in your mouth. Also, you have to attend to overhead work and the possibility of heavy objects falling.

Besides staying alert and being physically dexterous, patience is required. Sharing our workspaces in this close environment with dozens of technicians, who sometimes left messes of trash at the end of the day, became annoying, and cleaning up grew tiresome.[2]

Other challenges involved the lines of authority every time a change had to be made. The superintendent of shipbuilding's office was assigned to ensure contract compliance and oversee the work. But my bosses in San Diego would jump in as well, not to mention the fleet headquarters in Pearl Harbor. It could get very frustrating.

The hardest part for me and the crew was seeing Lang in overhaul with no heart and soul, totally dependent on shore connections for electrical power, water and steam. It was like watching the unconscious body of a favorite uncle

---

2 However unpleasant these working conditions were, there was a daily respite in the fact that we only had to come onboard during the day to perform our duties. The extensive ripping out and installation of equipment made our ship uninhabitable. This meant that the crew lived on a barracks barge nearby or outside the yard in civilian housing. I lived in housing with my family, as did many others.

in the hospital on life support, with tubes running every which way. For me and the other new guys who had not yet seen Lang under sail, it was especially hard to get a feel of the sleek, fast frigate she would become.

Gradually, she transformed into a fighting ship of the line. Machinery was repaired or installed, openings in the ship's hull were closed up, welding lines withdrawn, and the compartments and passageways were cleared and cleaned. We intensified our training programs, particularly in engineering—the actual mechanics of making the ship run—in anticipation of a tough outside inspection, without which we would not be permitted to operate the ship's propulsion and electrical systems.[3]

All our efforts had been focused on that inspection, scheduled within days, when my XO approached me as I drank that cup of coffee with his awful news that the chief engineer could not activate one of the main generators that had been rendered inoperable.

"When was it last turned on?" I asked swinging my way down the last ladder rails to the hot engineering spaces below with the XO trailing behind.

"Yesterday, Sir, but it was functioning fine then."

When I reached the engineering spaces I found the chief soaked in sweat. His men were spreading the parts of the disassembled generator across the deck.

"What seems to be the problem, chief?"

"Sir, it appears someone deliberately poured a hardening compound into the guts of the generator. Look, see for yourself."

He backed away and directed my attention to a whitish cement-like substance covering the turbine. I was incredulous. *Who would do such a thing?* We'd been working months and months towards getting this ship back on the line and now, within hours of our final inspection, someone sabotages it? Who? And why? Questions, but no answers.

---

3 During inspection a team of outside experts would come aboard to make sure that all equipment was fully operational and that engineering watch teams were fully qualified to operate the systems and to be able to respond to all emergencies. The engineering spaces had to be spotlessly clean. All administrative records such as training and testing of water, oil, and fuel had to be perfect.

"All I know is it's going to be weeks before we can replace the damaged parts and get it operational again," said the chief wiping his brow with his forearm.

This was terrible. Being delayed in the shipyard due to scheduling issues was one thing, but a deliberate act of sabotage, quite another. Now navy investigators would have to come aboard to interview me and the crew to determine who was responsible.[4] Who knew how long it would take? And, of course, as the commanding officer, responsible for all parts of the ship and all members of the crew, I fervently hoped this would not spell the premature end of my command tour before we could even get the ship to sea. Notifying the crew was one of the toughest tasks I had in my two years aboard Lang. Our team was used to high morale: we operated not just as a military unit, but also like a family. I felt like a parent having to explain to a child that his or her sibling had deliberately crashed our car. *How could he do such a thing? What was he thinking?*

The investigation team came aboard and two days later it had a suspect. He was in the family, alright. Even worse, the likely perpetrator was a senior petty officer who was one of the most competent, trusted, and well-liked men onboard. But before we could confront him, he went missing. Later that night, I received a call from the state police that sucked the air out of me.

Apparently he had fallen in love with a local woman and could not stand the thought of leaving her when the ship sailed back to our home port of San Diego. He destroyed the generator to delay our departure, but this series of events and other unfortunate factors in his short life seemed to hasten the end of his. The sailor had deliberately driven his car into a bridge abutment and was killed instantly. We had lost a dear shipmate. None of us had been given the opportunity to help him through his tough personal situation. We were helpless and frustrated after the fact.

While my combat experience and the devastating impact of bullets, grenades, and mortars had taught me the fragility of life, this was my first

---

4 Naval investigations were handled by the Naval Investigative Service then. Now that agency is called Naval Criminal Investigative Service, or NCIS, the inspiration for a TV show of the same name. Since shipyards have high security, sabotage had to be by a crew member or, but unlikely, by a civilian contractor.

experience with the equally devastating results of untreated psychological problems, a major issue facing returning veterans today. However, for my crew, if anything, this incident brought us closer together as a family. As the CO, I was more resolved than ever to get to know my men better on a personal level and head off any potential crisis before it became life-threatening. This was a tough undertaking. A leader can get only so close to his or her subordinates and, naturally, they will try to hide their personal feelings to cover up something. In spite of this challenge, I was beginning to take great pleasure in my new role of service through leadership.

Predictably, our stay in the shipyard was extended for a few weeks until we could pass the final inspection. During that time, the spotlight of general scrutiny by navy higher-ups shone brightly on the ship and me. What could have become a firestorm ending in my being removed from command, resulted instead in me and my crew receiving solid support and backing from our chain of command.

Once we were fully operational, we spent six more months training for a western Pacific deployment by practicing with other ships. Training involved operating off the coast of southern California with the carrier task force, followed by two weeks in port in San Diego where we trained on simulators ashore. We were always training.[5]

Unfortunately, like on any team, there were a few sailors who didn't want to play by the rules. This was at a time in the navy when drug use, although not nearly as prevalent as it had been a few years earlier at the end of the Vietnam War, still posed a challenge to good order, discipline, and unit cohesiveness.

An administrative discharge procedure allowed commanding officers to get rid of bad apples by discharging them "for the good of the service."[6] I applied this procedure where sailors had used, sold, or encouraged others to use

---

5 A naval task force is like an athletic team: a group of ships of various dimensions and capabilities being molded into a single unit in support of the mission assigned to it. And like a sports team, every member (ship) has to be focused on the task at hand and be ready to jump in and support each other.

6 As a result of these administrative discharge procedures, we were able to clean house and get rid of the bad guys, which provided great moral support to the rest of the team.

drugs, or had run loan-sharking operations. It was easier and quicker than apprehending and prosecuting them.

In one such case, while still training in San Diego, I was escorting an admiral around when we stopped in a passageway to chat with a couple of crew members. I placed my hand on top of a vent just above my head and unexpectedly felt something resting there. Curious, I grabbed it and took it down. There in my hand, in full sight of the admiral, was a nickel baggie of weed, obviously some crew member's stash. I was crimson with embarrassment, but fortunately the admiral had been around enough ships to know that this was not unprecedented.

With the overhaul successfully behind us and our personnel problems put to rest, we were ready to deploy—and to have some fun! But I couldn't have anticipated the adventures lying in wait for us.

—6—

I awoke one warm, sunny day in June 1978 and thought, *This is it! Finally, I'm at the pinnacle of every surface warrior's dream—in command of a fighting ship. I'm now the captain of a freshly overhauled, fast frigate steaming out of Portland.*

We picked up speed as our sleek bow sliced through the dark blue waters of the open ocean, and we churned up a powerful white wake. Portland had disappeared astern. I'm on the bridge watching my men working around me, but my spirits are soaring in the white cumulus clouds overhead.

Away from the safety of the U.S., and into potentially hostile environments, I was ready to put my leadership skills to the real test of command at sea. Most sailors will tell you that while leaving loved ones behind is tough, the very act of getting under way is a bittersweet relief. It means that the long hours of preparation are over. No longer is anyone looking over your shoulder, micromanaging every deed. Finally, you can do what sailors are supposed to do, go to sea!

As the CO, I now had the freedom of individual thought and action to carry out the ship's assigned mission. But it was an awesome responsibility. Nowhere is teamwork more important than at sea, because you are isolated from the outside and totally dependent on one another to get from point A to point B. You need to find the way together.

The hours at sea can be long. Days are divided into four-hour watches in which you're assigned duty on the bridge, in gun mounts in the communications centers, in engine rooms, or in lookout positions. Additionally, you must find time for your "normal" job, which might be in repair, maintenance, training, or administration. Oh, and somehow you are supposed to be well rested before coming onto your next watch. Since there's not much else to do besides working and sleeping, keeping busy passes the time. In some ways, the skipper has it easier. There is no assigned watch, but he or she is on duty 24/7 and ultimately responsible for everything. That's the reason why during the two years I was in command, I never had a full night's rest while at sea.

My leadership style meant that I trusted and had total confidence in those responsible for driving the ship and in operating propulsion and weapons systems. We'd spent months practicing for every conceivable scenario, and the crew had increasingly earned my confidence.

One of the trickiest ship-handing evolutions in the open sea is called "underway replenishment," or maneuvering alongside another ship to receive fuel or supplies. This requires coming alongside the other ship, usually an oiler, or an aircraft carrier, from astern, ten knots faster. You then slow your ship directly across from the other ship, about eighty feet away, so that fuel hoses can be run across. At best, even in calm seas, it's a white-knuckled event because you have to control two huge, fully manned machines in close proximity to one another while sailors manhandle heavy rigs and hoses from one ship to the other, often in rough seas. With little margin for error, it's one of the ultimate tests of expert ship-handling, and it always distinguishes the leaders in the pack. Failure can end one's career. Every aspiring young sailor wants to experience being in charge of the operation, but usually the CO is either performing the act himself or hovering over the person to whom he's delegated the task. On the Lang we did it a little differently.[7]

---

7 This is what I call service by leading. One of Lang's greatest achievements was to become the top ship in the Pacific destroyer force in the number of enlisted sailors who qualified to be officer-of-the-deck. This led to high morale that translated into high re-enlistment rates of those who would serve in the navy as long as they could continue to be on the Lang.

Once a sailor had proven himself in other evolutions, I would allow him to drive the ship alongside the refueler-ship. And while he did that, I would stand slightly out of his sight, but close enough to monitor his performance. On a few notable occasions, the admiral on the aircraft carrier would radio over,

"Who's driving the ship?"

With a great deal of satisfaction and pride, I would radio back, "Petty Officer Second Class Gomez, Sir, and fully qualified officer-of-the-deck."

One day, while steaming with another frigate in the South China Sea, we received a radio message from the aircraft carrier in our group.

"Our planes have spotted a small boat possibly in distress fifty miles from your location. Stand by to proceed to assist."

I got on the horn with the engine room, "Main control, this is the bridge. Bring second boiler on line ASAP."

Both Lang and the other frigate had been operating with only half-boiler power, limiting our speed to about twenty knots. I wanted us prepared to move fast in case the call came in.

Sure enough, about a half hour later, we received another radio message from the more senior CO on the other frigate. "The boat is in distress. Proceed to its location at best speed."

"Take position astern of me while we both proceed to the small boat's location."

"Negative," I responded. "We have two boilers on line and can make twenty-seven knots. I will take the lead and meet you there." The Lang crew loved this. It was like challenging a big kid to a footrace and beating him!

Lang steamed to the location where we found a derelict sailboat packed with fifty Vietnamese civilian men, women, and children, from the very young to the very old, on the edge of peril. They had fled their now-communist country about ten days earlier in an attempt to reach the Philippines or Indonesia, where they could find a new life. They were out of food, nearly out of water, and in desperate need of help. The sight of these Vietnamese taking enormous risks was heart-wrenching. In fact, it was very much like the heart-breaking scenes of today's refugees from Syria and the Middle East trekking to Europe, who would have been killed for their political and religious views if they remained.

Under the diplomatic rules at that time, U.S. Navy ships were allowed to give such boat people food, water, and medical supplies, but were not allowed to "rescue" them by taking them onboard, unless their boat were sinking. So, I made a quick decision. We brought everyone safely aboard Lang, then shot a few rounds into their small boat and watched it sink. Indeed, "their boat was sinking." I called it removing a "hazard to navigation," while performing an act of mercy.

The Vietnamese were weak from starvation, not very clean, and their clothing was in tatters. We fed them some good American chow—burgers, hot dogs, soda, and milk—and gave them use of our bathrooms and showers to clean up. We eagerly came up with spare dungarees, shirts, and civilian clothes for our new guests, and soon they were clean, comfortable, and well dressed—sort of well dressed. We found mattresses and bedding, and because our "bird" was off the ship, we were able to bunk them down in our helicopter hanger. Once settled, we showed them a few Hollywood movies, mostly cartoons for the children, but every single one of our guests sat transfixed for hours at a time.

The other frigate showed up about an hour after we did, and although slightly miffed that we had beaten them to the punch, their CO graciously transferred more bedding and food for our guests. None of us will ever forget the initial desperation in those Vietnamese faces compared to the relief we saw when they realized their sea-crossing was over and that they were in the hands of a nation who cared about them.[8]

These people had taken unfathomable risks to get this far. Their boat was too small and fragile to make such a crossing and pirates were known to prey on such defenseless souls, taking the few possessions they had and frequently killing them. For a few days, looked after and much respected by our crew, our guests were safe in America until our arrival at Subic Bay in

---

8 This contrasted with the feeling many Vietnamese had four years earlier when the U.S. abandoned them to their communist conquerors.

the Philippines, where we dropped them off.[9] Most of them eventually made their way to the U.S., after spending months in refugee camps, and, no doubt, didn't forget that their first sign of hope and freedom had been the good ship USS Lang. Many of the crew made new friends for life and still keep in touch.

About midway through the deployment, the Lang was ordered to Australia to take part in an annual celebration. This event commemorates a vital battle in the Coral Sea during World War II, when two U.S. carrier task forces blocked an attempt by the Japanese Navy to strengthen Japan's foothold in the South Pacific.[10] As a result, and at a high cost, the allies were able to start their slow but steady push toward the Japanese mainland. This was a plum assignment, and Lang sailed across the equator to fun and games in Australia.

On a peaceful, lazy Sunday morning, while on course to Australia, our chief pilot asked my permission to launch our helicopter for a routine test flight. One of Lang's most important weapons systems was its SH-2 helicopter, used primarily for anti-submarine and anti-ship warfare. We carried a detachment of aviation personnel—four naval aviators and eight maintenance crew members.[11] I trusted this pilot's judgment on anything involving flight operations, and the test flight itself was completed uneventfully, or so I thought.

The rest of the day seemed to be rolling by quietly when our peace was shattered by a flash message, directed to us from then Secretary of State Cyrus Vance. A Flash message is the highest priority of message in the navy. It requires the sailor handling the message traffic to bring it to the senior person immediately. The system was a closed teletype: Encrypted messages would be received by machines that would decrypt them. *Wow, how did he even know about our little frigate out in the middle of nowhere?* The answer became very clear when I read his message. Apparently, a U.S. Navy helicopter had

---

9 An official naval vessel of any country has its nation's sovereignty while at sea, like a floating embassy.

10 In the Battle of Coral Sea in 1942, both sides suffered significant human losses from enemy aircraft. The Japanese sank the carrier USS Lexington (CV-16) and severely damaged the USS Yorktown (CV-10), also a carrier. In spite of these losses, in the end, the battle was considered a strategic victory for allied forces.

11 Although the helicopter detachment was administratively assigned to an aircraft squadron back in San Diego, while embarked on Lang, it was an integral part of our team and reported to me.

"violated the sovereignty of an allied nation" by flying low, without permission, over a beach in the nation of the Solomon Islands.[12]

Oh, and that would be us. The pilot and I had looked at the navigation charts before the flight. We were both well aware of and interested in this historic locale, but it never occurred to me to warn him not to overfly land. To be honest, I didn't even know that the Solomons was a sovereign nation. Well, the government of the Solomons was well aware of it! And did not hesitate to wave its flag while filing a diplomatic protest with the U.S. government regarding our overflight. Hence the irate message from Mr. Vance.

The admiral in charge of our task group was copied on the message and the next thing I knew, another helicopter was approaching the ship. It landed and out hopped the admiral's chief of staff, a no-nonsense and crusty captain named Bud Edney. If you looked closely you could see steam coming out of his ears and nostrils. He reminded me—very much—of that army general I'd enraged in Vietnam while trying to help a child. According to him, the USS Lang and its commanding officer had "embarrassed our country and directly insulted the newly sovereign nation of the Solomon Islands."

By that time, of course, I had reviewed the helo pilot's flight path and he did overfly land, but it happened on my ship, and I was responsible, not him. After a rant and a few verbal shots aimed at me, Captain Edney climbed back into his helicopter and returned to his ship to start the process of apologizing to the whole world. I felt relieved. No bullets had been fired, no one got hurt, and I was still in command. The rest of the deployment passed relatively quietly.

In October 1979, Lang made a port call to Busan in the southern part of the Korean peninsula. We had been at sea for several weeks, and the entire crew was looking forward to some down time for a few days. We arrived at the harbor entrance at about six a.m. and requested permission from the local officials to enter port and to proceed to our assigned berth.

---

12 The Solomons were the site of some of the most intense fighting in World War II. The marines had landed in the Japanese stronghold of Guadalcanal and numerous allied and Japanese ships had gone down in the adjacent water, earning the area the name of Iron-Bottom Sound.

"Negative" came the response. "Harbor pilots and tugboats are on strike until, at least, tomorrow, and no one is allowed into the port without a pilot."

This was not the answer we were expecting, nor was it one I was willing to accept. We were not going to waste our cherished liberty time waiting for them. I radioed back that we were "fully capable of maneuvering in confined waters and would be entering without tugs and a pilot."

Angry words came back from the radio, reiterating that we were to remain outside the harbor until the next day. Although I was a fine naval officer and loyal to the service, I didn't always follow the rules when they conflicted with the needs of my crew. We turned the radio volume down and headed in.

It was a tricky passage into the harbor. The Lang was a single propeller ship, which made tight turns a challenge without a tug. After many twists and turns in the channel, we finally approached our berth where we found that the line handlers, who usually received our lines, were also on strike. We launched our twenty-six foot motorboat with a team of sailors who became our line handlers. We tied up safely, and the crew was happy, but I had to face the music.

Within minutes of tying up, an official car—not a helo—drove up to the gangway, and out hopped another steaming officer, the commander of U.S. Naval Forces in Korea, no less. Again, it seemed as though I had caused an international incident, this time by being a strike-breaker and crossing a picket line. I was learning that command of a warship requires knowledge of local customs and political sensitivities and, needless to say, I couldn't *wait* to get back to sea.

To make sure I realized that I'd messed up, the admiral placed me "in hack," meaning that I could not go ashore for two days. However, he did permit me to leave the ship that morning to pay a call on the mayor of Busan, a long-standing custom for navy ships making port visits. I was driven to the mayor's office with a different admiral and the CO from a visiting aircraft carrier where we went through the formality of exchanging mementos and making small talk.

There was a commotion outside when we were leaving, and a motorcade pulled up flying little South Korean flags above the headlights. Drivers and security officers hopped out to open doors. It seemed that the president of South Korea, Park Chung Hee, also had an appointment with the mayor that morning. We were all introduced and then quickly shuttled out the door.

Later that day, I was astonished to learn that the man I briefly met that morning, President Park, was assassinated by one of his bodyguards in Seoul at the Blue House, his official residence, and this was followed by a major coup. Quite a day! Now, *that* was an international incident!

After another few weeks operating at sea, Lang pulled into Subic Bay for a brief rest period. These were my final few days in command and my replacement was on the pier waiting to take over.[13] We spent a few days touring and inspecting the ship with my familiarizing him with the Lang team, and making sure that he was comfortable with taking over. We were in a far-away foreign port with no family or dignitaries to invite, so the change of command ceremony was a simple and quiet affair. I thanked the crew for making the last twenty-seven months a positive experience for me, and for the tremendous effort they had made to keep all our commitments. I urged them to give my successor the same degree of trust and loyalty that they had consistently shown me.

As per navy protocol and tradition, I read my new orders, turned to the new skipper and announced, "Sir, I am ready to be relieved." Clyde read his orders, turned to me, and said, "Sir, I relieve you." At that moment my tour was over. I was about as lame a duck as there can be, but I slept soundly that night for the first time in a long time. I felt a huge weight had been lifted from my shoulders. Although I loved and respected the Lang team, someone else was now responsible for getting them home safely to their families.

The next day, I boarded my flight back to San Diego where I would gather up my own family, then head across the country to take up my new shore duty assignment as director of administration at the Naval Education and Training Center in Newport.

---

13 My replacement was the late Commander Clyde Van Arsdell, and although I didn't know him, I had served under his father.

CHAPTER 16

An Unhappy Time

_6_

NEWPORT, RI, 1980s

OVER THE PAST TWO YEARS, my absence at sea had not been easy on Gwen and the girls, now adolescents. With my feet back on firm ground, I moved the family from San Diego to Newport in early 1980, despite understanding their teen challenges of trying to make friends in a new school. It was some solace knowing that, as girls, they had Gwen as their chief role model.

The navy's education and training center in Newport was where directly commissioned officers from various fields of expertise, such as chaplains, lawyers and medical personnel received military indoctrination.[1] The base included the OCS program where I had received my commission twenty years earlier.

As director of administration, I operated, along with my team of forty sailors and civilians, the non-academic side of the base. We managed buildings and grounds, including recreation facilities, family services and the base police and fire departments. Additionally, we supported the eight naval reserve destroyers and their crews with logistics and supplies. Besides operating the physical plant, we were the ones who made sure people got paid properly, and we prepared orders for next assignments.

For all intents and purposes, I was the base landlord and jailer. My tenants were the sailors who were at the base, awaiting their next assignment. The

---

1 The navy base at Newport, Rhode Island, had once supported the U.S. Atlantic Fleet with thirty-two destroyers and four destroyer repair ships homeported there. In the late 1970s during budget constraints, the ships were relocated elsewhere and the base essentially became a large academic campus.

jailer part was that we managed the brig prisoners and their wardens along with those awaiting courts-martial or even discharge from the service.

I was not happy. The Siren who'd seduced me to sea adventures had turned into a Harpy and would not release her greedy claws from my shoulder. But consider this, anything that followed the ultimate test of leadership—command at sea—and the exhilaration of having done it well, was bound to be a let-down. To make the assignment even less enjoyable, I was the official designated to convene special court-martial proceedings involving sailors and marines assigned to the base and ships in the area.[2] I was frustrated and did not like dealing with this group of sailors. They were not the highly motivated sea-going sailors of the USS Lang, dedicated to their service. Many were misfits who didn't belong in the military. Dealing with them tried my patience.

A case in point: I was making a routine inspection of the brig when I paused after noticing several wooden window shutters on a workbench. They were finely made, brand new and ready to be painted. But since none of the buildings on the base had wooden shutters, and I knew we hadn't used them on our ships since the American Revolution, I decided to investigate.

The brig was equipped with a state-of-the-art woodworking shop where detainees could learn carpentry. Making command plaques for ships was one thing, but shutters? It turned out that the brig officer in charge had recently purchased a Victorian house needing a great deal of work, including—you've got it—new shutters! What better place to do the work than in a government facility, using government material and equipment and, of course, government labor, all paid for by the taxpayer? This guy even had the gall to transport navy prisoners in his personal car on weekends for brush clearing, painting and various other tasks around the house. I convened a court-martial and he was out the door in a hurry. What a way to end your navy career!

Initially, I was impressed by his replacement. He spoke confidently about his purported undercover navy background and he seemed qualified enough for the job. He took over the brig, and, shortly after, the base experienced a

---

2 There are three types of courts-martial depending on the severity of the offense. The lowest is a summary court heard before a single officer with mild punishment options such as loss of pay. The next is a special court heard before a panel of officers with punishments including confinement and bad conduct discharges. Finally, there is the general court with punishment up to death.

series of minor fires, usually at night caused by arson. The fire chief let me know that invariably the first person on the scene was the new brig officer. He claimed credit for responding to the fires and often putting them out even before the firefighters arrived. Of course he was there first on the scene: He was setting the damn fires! The potential for damage and serious injury made his infractions all the more serious and, once again, I had to bring charges against my brig officer. Was this a strange coincidence or was there something about brig officers I needed to know? Fortunately, I transferred to a new assignment before that court-martial, and I never found out what happened. But had I been hearing that case, I would have thrown the book at him.

In general, the assignment lacked command cohesion because most of the individuals were transients awaiting a next assignment or release from prison. Looking after buildings and unmotivated individuals was the least rewarding assignment in my navy career.

My deployment on Lang had lasted a little over two years. For half that time, when the ship was in overhaul, I was able to live with my family. But Gwen had been a single parent for seven of our twenty married years, while I was at sea and in Vietnam. She had taken the girls to school and made sure they did their homework. She helped them through squabbles with each other and at school. She was there for their birthdays, graduations, first jobs, and dates. Although I had a strong bond with my girls, I felt badly leaving them so often for my deployments, but I was doing what I was called to do and supporting my family in the best way I knew how.

Instead of returning and settling into the day-to-day routine of married life and learning to deal with the stressful reality of parenting, I made a poor decision and acted selfishly. I moved out of the house into bachelor quarters on base.

Gwen said she noticed a difference in me when I returned from Vietnam. She would point out that I was less patient, sometimes cranky and irritable at home and at work. I would isolate. It changes you.

Because I had come so close to death, I always felt lucky to be alive. I was quick to heal and recover physically, the loss of an eye was nothing and the lasting physical effects of my wartime injuries were minimal. But, to a degree,

I was suffering the unseen effects of my wartime injuries, the invisible wounds that we seem to acknowledge more easily in our veterans these days, and that I would learn about while helping other vets.

This kind of suffering is about the unavoidable loss of innocence and what happens to one's soul when you experience the most brutal aspects of war. In Vietnam I tried to protect myself from the sight of dead soldiers, ours and theirs, by putting all those thoughts and memories out of my mind.

Killing another human being is unnatural and changes you profoundly. You are forced to look for ways to deal with it, and this means having to deaden yourself emotionally, sometimes with the help of alcohol and drugs, so as not to feel the emotional pain. What is left is a numbness that interferes with your ability to experience joy and feel love. The killing becomes even harder to bear when the moral justification is murky. The devil steps into the conversation when you start second-guessing yourself. *Was I a combatant in a moral war? What did we accomplish? How many innocent people were killed?* You could find yourself in serious difficulty if you survived combat. And let's not forget survivor's guilt. Men standing next to me lost their lives. All I lost was an eye.

As I was now separated from Gwen, I needed to get away, to reflect on my marriage from the outside. That opportunity came in the form of my next assignment followed by promotion to captain (O-6), just below the rank of admiral. Although I'd worked hard for it, the luster of that moment was tarnished by the circumstances. I had been hoping for a major sea command, preferably in charge of a large cruiser or a destroyer squadron. Instead, I was selected for a major shore command in Japan, specifically the Military Sealift Command Far East.

The Japan assignment was an "accompanied tour," meaning Gwen and the girls could relocate there with me, but I chose to go on my own. A small part of me believed that if I had a more satisfying assignment, I'd gain new perspective on the marriage and maybe over time I could figure out how to make it work better. My leaving for Japan was much tougher on all of us than my leaving for a sea deployment had ever been. This time it was like letting go. I would be gone for two years. Our marriage was likely over.

CHAPTER 17

Exotic Adventure

⟶

THE FAR EAST, 1982–1987

MY NEW HOME IN YOKOHAMA had the hustle and bustle of a major international port city. It was 1982, and the smog of any large Asian city was pervasive. But here and there in the historic part of the city you could find little oases of beautiful fragrant gardens and silent temples, as arresting as the work of artist Hokusai, whose famous dramatic landscapes of Mt. Fuji I came to admire. In the commercial areas of the city, the smells of grilling tempura and teriyaki permeated the air. I would often sample the fish, rice cakes, and boiled vegetables, but never grew to like them. The weekends were reserved for when I dined on "local cuisine" at the nearby Denny's and Dunkin Donuts off base.

The foreign land of Japan, the unique logistical mission of the Military Sealift Command, my new command, and the fast-paced demands of the tour itself were an injection of energy for me.[1] I was responsible for contracting with civilian shipyards for the repair, maintenance, and overhaul of the Seventh Fleet's logistics ships and the chartered commercial cargo vessels whose mission was moving military material around the globe and providing at-sea replenishment. Also under my control was a group of seventeen commercial vessels located in Diego Garcia, a British island in the Indian Ocean. These ships were loaded with cargo and supplies and were prepositioned to

---

1 The Military Sealift Command is the ocean transportation arm of the Defense Department. It maintains its own fleet responsible for moving military cargo and personnel around the world. Additionally, the MSC Far East supports the U.S. Seventh Fleet, located in Yokosuka, Japan.

proceed to areas in the Middle East, where and when U.S. forces might be needed.

Even more exotic was travel to my subordinate offices in Guam, Okinawa, Korea, the Philippines, and Singapore, which took up a fair amount of time. Otherwise, living in a military compound and driving to work at a U.S. Army base each day, limited my involvement in the city and interaction with the Japanese. I did not speak the language, although I learned enough to get by in basic conversation. My immediate team of thirty-five individuals was composed of U.S. Navy military personnel and civilians, as well as Japanese nationals, whose polite and proper demeanor impressed me.

Tomiko was one of my Japanese employees. She had worked for the Military Sealift Command for twenty years. One day she asked me if I would like to go to dinner and meet her uncle, who happened to be a member of the Diet, Japan's legislature. I didn't get out much due to work. When I did, it was usually on my own, so I gratefully accepted.

Her uncle, obviously an accomplished individual, brought along an English-speaking aide. We all bowed and he graciously introduced himself.

"I am Minoru Genda," he said

His name was immediately familiar, but I couldn't place it in any context. He noticed my difficulty and quickly turned to his interpreter to rescue me from any awkwardness.

"Commander Genda asks me to tell you—he was a naval commander, too. He served in the Imperial Japanese Navy in World War II."

What followed was nothing short of a few stunned seconds of mental and emotional recalibration. The "Commander Genda" I had read about in history books had been Admiral Yamamoto's main planner for the attack on Pearl Harbor.[2] He was now standing right in front of me, smiling. I harbored no ill feelings to be in the presence of not only a former enemy, but one of its chief architects. Rather, I was more intrigued by his intelligence and felt what

---

2 During World War II the Japanese bombers destroyed many U.S. Pacific Fleet ships that had been docked in Pearl Harbor, Hawaii, on December 7, 1941. It was this attack that brought the U.S. into the war.

I share when in the presence of every person I meet who's ever been in the military—a kinship. He was doing his job, too.

The evening passed too quickly with sea stories going back and forth across the table along with many glasses of sake. The poor interpreter put in overtime and a half! They were pleasant company, but it felt surreal and I could not get used to the idea that I was dining with Commander Genda. I couldn't help but wonder while listening to him, if someone less capable than this man had planned the attack on Pearl Harbor, would America have gone to war against Japan and Germany?

Later, he gave me a parting gift—a replica of the scarf he had worn into battle. He wanted me to understand that although the U.S. and Japan had fought on different sides, we shared the experience of wearing the cloth of our respective nations.

What they say about old habits dying hard is true. A change of location couldn't stop me from causing a bit of a stir among the brass and catching flak from all sides.

My bosses in D.C. had directed me to award a ship repair contract to a certain Korean shipyard. However, my team felt that the shipyard was too inexperienced in repairing aging vessels to meet our standards. I objected and spent several weeks trying to convince D.C. that this was not the right thing to do. Unlike earlier times when I rocked the boat, the stakes were pretty high here, because I was challenging the military-industrial complex at its most senior levels.

For my efforts, Navy Secretary John Lehman summoned me back to the Pentagon and ordered my boss, a navy vice admiral, to make me toe the mark, and give the work to the Korean shipyard. It was a matter of my reading his lips that made the matter clear. To refuse his direction would have resulted in my being fired for insubordination. As predicted by my team, the repair turned out to be a disaster and the ship was delayed. The outcome was that the Navy's Seventh Fleet commander blamed *me* when his ship missed its fleet commitments. I resisted the urge to say, "I told you so."[3]

---

3 The Seventh Fleet's commander was Admiral Jim Hogg.

In 1984, during a tense period of the Cold War, Korean Airlines flight 007 allegedly strayed into Soviet airspace and was shot down by Soviet military aircraft. The plane went down in international waters near one of their islands. The Soviets claimed the aircraft didn't respond to warnings to change course. All onboard were lost and a huge international crisis erupted.

The U.S., Japan, and Korea sent forces to the area to recover remains and wreckage from the plane. I was ordered to a city in the farthest northern reaches of Japan to coordinate the logistics for rescue and salvage forces arriving on the scene. With the help of an interpreter, I set up shop in the local police station, thereby establishing an American presence until a relief team arrived a few days later. Rescue and salvage of the plane's wreckage was a grim operation because of the human remains being delivered ashore to a mortuary, along with parts of the plane's wreckage. This was a stressful and fast-moving crisis but an exciting operation nevertheless, requiring snap decisions. The international spotlight was on us. Luckily, it didn't turn into a shooting war.

My tour in Japan was already winding down in 1985. After a two-year separation I knew I couldn't reconcile my marriage, but my heart was yearning for my daughters, who were now in their early twenties. I visited Korea on business and paid a call to the admiral who commanded the U. S. Naval Forces there. He expressed interest in my next assignment and asked me what I wanted to do. With my hopes as high as a child's balloon bobbing along on his wrist, I tried not to sound desperate. My answer came easily, "I'll do anything that will reunite me with my girls." A few days later, back in Japan, I received my next assignment, compliments of the navy personnel folks in D.C., and my balloon burst.

I was to be the chief of staff for that same admiral in Korea. He had specifically requested me partly because he felt that having a Medal of Honor recipient on his staff would enhance his image. That was my guess, anyway. I was now looking at a total of five years of consecutive overseas commitment at the end of this new assignment. The answer "no" that came so easily from my heart that day was not the answer the admiral had wanted to hear. Nor was he prepared to listen upon further discussion. I had to accept what I had little control over, and there was nothing I could say or do about it. At the very least, I was able to head back to Newport for several days' leave time with the girls over the holidays before traveling back to the Far East for my next stint in Korea.

My marriage separation continued. As I hugged my girls goodbye, the thought that I wouldn't be reunited with them for a couple more years was daunting. More missed birthdays, plus college and career struggles that I couldn't help with. I will say that in spite of my absences and the separation from their mother, my relationship with them was very good. The girls tried not to take sides and understood that no matter what transpired between Gwen and me, each of us loved them as much as we always had and always would.

During the twenty-hour commercial flight from Boston to Seoul in early 1985, holiday images of the past several days with the girls—things like going to the movies and just hanging out—flashed through my mind. I brooded over the choices I had made. But second-guessing was not in my nature. Some decisions were beyond my control. Although I had misgivings, there was no going back.

While I had to leave my real family 7,000 miles behind, I had my navy family. From the moment a member of my new team greeted me at the Seoul airport, the responsibilities of my new job landed on me like a sack of un-opened mail dumped on a desk. My new mission quickly took front seat to any melancholy.

My team of fifty sailors, marines, and civilians (U.S. and Korean) pro-vided logistical and operational support for the U.S. Navy ships and marine units visiting Korea.[4] We also played a substantial role in the overall military picture and served as liaison between these navy and Marine Corps assets and the American army general in charge in Korea. Working in tandem with the Korean forces, we planned joint and allied operations. Some of these opera-tions, such as "Team Spirit," involved a U.S. aircraft carrier task force of a dozen ships along with some 60,000 U.S. forces.

---

4 We were stationed at the U.S. Army Garrison in Yongsan, Seoul. The U.S. Seventh Fleet, headquartered in Yokosuka, Japan, had sixty to seventy ships and could deploy 40,000 navy and Marine Corps personnel. Ships from the large U.S. Seventh Fleet along with our army and air force units operated and trained in Korea and its adjacent waters defending the Korean Peninsula.

As chief of staff, I managed the day-to-day operations of the organization, which meant keeping the command out of trouble with the higher-ups. My department heads briefed me daily on various ship visits and how we were getting along with the operations, logistics, and legal and administrative aspects of their duties. I led a dedicated professional staff and let them work unfettered, which is why my boss's comment one day took me aback.

"You can't teach a marine anything," my boss said.

I smiled, thinking he must be kidding. But his tight lips and red face left a pretty clear impression that he was serious. He did not like marines or enlisted persons. The marine in question, who "couldn't be taught" was Major Cliff Acree, a truly squared-away guy whom the admiral insisted on addressing as "Mr." rather than "Major." The admiral would further demean the officer in front of others by asking him such questions as: "Did you go to college?" This outstanding marine later commanded an aviation squadron and was the first U.S. pilot shot down in Desert Storm. Thankfully, he survived the ordeal in spite of severe beatings by his captors. He must have been toughened by his experiences with the admiral.

The admiral's father and grandfather had been admirals, too. He was a very hard worker, but obviously lacking in people skills. In fact, when I arrived morale was at rock bottom because he had managed to tread on the entire staff. I vowed to turn things around by taking most of the heat by insisting he talk only to me when he had a staff complaint. This way I was able to solve the problem in my own way and no one suffered his abuse.

On one occasion, the admiral went home to the U.S. on leave for a couple of weeks. He left his dog, Mookie, with his enlisted aide who lived off base with his family and his own dog. The morning after the admiral returned to Seoul, I greeted him and asked how the trip had been.

"Fine," he said, "but I am truly concerned about Mookie. He seems to have changed while we were gone. He didn't greet us with his usual enthusiasm and his appetite seems to be off."

The next day, I asked the admiral how Mookie was doing.

"A little better," he answered, "and I've figured out what's wrong with him."

"Oh really, Sir." I responded. "What's wrong with him?"

"Being around that enlisted dog made him out of sorts. He's much better in an officer's household."

The Mookie story quickly made its way around the command, and gave everyone a few laughs. This actually helped boost morale, but the admiral's prejudice was hard to ignore and endure. Ironically, one of his main duties was to meet with representatives of the North Korean military as part of the United Nations Military Armistice Commission, where diplomacy was key.

One time, the Commander of the Korean Navy, a four-star admiral, showed a more than passing interest in acquiring an American weapons system. During the conversation, it became apparent that the Koreans were leaning toward purchasing a similar system from a European nation, rather than from the U.S. My admiral was irate at this news and berated the Korean four-star saying, "Sometimes I feel like a missionary going to darkest Africa to convert the natives." That meeting ended somewhat abruptly. Later, it was no surprise to anyone who was there that the Korean Navy bought the European weapons system.

There were serious moments during my Korean tour, including a skirmish between North Korean and South Korean naval vessels close to the border between both countries. Air raid warnings were a frequent occurrence in Seoul, only thirty miles from that border. They would prove to be nothing, but they were unnerving.[5]

Almost as stressful as dealing with the North Koreans were visits from U.S. Navy and governmental VIPs. Korea was a great shopping destination, known for finely tailored clothing at very reasonable prices. So we were inundated with "official business" visitors from every level of government, all of whom required lodging, transportation, and military escort services.

One high profile visitor, the Reverend Jesse Jackson, was contemplating a run for president. To be briefed on the military situation while visiting the Demilitarized Zone and meeting the troops was one thing, but to buy some

---

5 Although the Korean War resulted in an armistice between the two sides, a peace treaty was never negotiated. Technically they were both still at war. Occasionally there are border skirmishes and posturing, such as when North Korea's current leader Kim Jong-un tests nuclear bombs or uses propaganda against the South.

nice suits and enjoy the Seoul nightlife was another! This sounded like fun, so I volunteered to be his escort. He was a hard guy to keep up with, but he treated me well. From that day on every time I saw him on TV, I would tell anybody within earshot that I picked out that suit for him.

During my limited off-duty time, when I wasn't reading or watching sports, I took up golf at a beautiful course on the U.S. Army base where we lived and worked. My boss, a tennis player, looked down on golfers as ruffians. He would give me a hard time about leaving work to play, and it really bothered him when his boss, the army general, whom I'd met playing golf, took a liking to me and called me to leave work early and meet him at the first tee.

We each had a female Korean caddy as was customary, because it provided employment opportunities for uneducated women. My caddy was most professional, a much better golfer than I, and she regularly provided me with winning advice and golf tips. She also bore a striking resemblance to the heroine of the Popeye cartoons, so I called her Olive Oyl.

One very hot day, with perspiration pouring off my face, I took a giant swing at the ball and my prosthetic eye popped right out! Coincidence? Pop eye? Olive Oyl? Poor Olive Oyl fainted on the spot! Boom! Down she went!

Days would fly by and I'd be happily engaged in keeping my eccentric admiral from driving everyone else crazy. On some evenings, I'd find myself in a favorite chair with a book in my hand and a drink nearby, wondering what my girls were doing. Phone calls were tough because of the twelve-hour time difference and, in the days before email, regular mail was slow.

But fortunately my oldest, Liza, was able to visit me once. "Hey, Dad!" shouted petite Liza, grinning when I picked her up at Seoul airport. She threw her arms around me and I embraced her with complete joy.

Shortly after graduation from Mount Saint Vincent College in New York, she came to visit me for a couple of weeks. As we walked to my car, I kidded her about the Red Sox and Yankees rivalry. Since she'd become a New Yorker, she'd defected to the dark side.

Liza had come courtesy of a program largely funded by the Korean government that provided airfare for military dependents. I had seen very little of her since she graduated from high school, nearly four years earlier, and now she'd grown into a truly mature and lovely young woman. For the first time in our adult lives, we got to spend time with each other travelling around the country, visiting temples and other tourist sites and cooking meals together. During their off time, my staff members spent time with her. I was amazed to see her drinking beer with them, but she had grown up while I was overseas, and I had some catching up to do.

I took pains to reassure her that although her parents' marriage was over, she and her sisters were still the most important part of my life. The joy of seeing Liza, a happy and successful woman, in spite of my absences, eased some of my regrets.

And the regrets could easily be forgotten by comedic distraction. Every time I see the TV show *NCIS*, I laugh. It reminds me of Korea. This is the same outfit I dealt with when my ship was sabotaged while undergoing repairs in Portland, Oregon. NCIS (then just NIS) had a four-person office in Korea that mainly handled investigations of petty crimes committed by sailors and marines. The navy operated a small all-hands club on the base serving drinks and food, staffed by local Korean nationals.

A routine audit of the club's books by my staff revealed that an unusually high volume of mozzarella cheese had been used during the previous quarter. It was determined that while it takes three ounces of cheese to make one pizza, the amount of cheese used was enough to make twice as many pizzas as had been sold. Something did not smell right, and NIS couldn't wait to sink its teeth into this investigation. It set up a sting operation with video cameras and hidden microphones. NIS even had a female agent posing as a waitress and—they caught the culprit.

Sure enough, a Korean cook had been skimming cheese off the top to bring home to his family and they caught the poor soul. The NIS agents acted like they had solved the Boston Gardner Museum's Rembrandt theft. They wanted to bring federal robbery charges against him, but we managed to talk them out of it. The cook kept his job and his family kept its bread-winner/cheese-stealer, and we covered the eighteen dollars in missing cheese revenue.

My two-and-a-half year assignment seemed to pass before it even began. During that time, I was able to arrange a few navy-related trips back to the East Coast to see the girls. One trip involved escorting the head of the Korean Navy on a tour of the U.S. Our navy made an airplane available and we traveled in style to Washington, D.C., New York, San Diego, and Honolulu. In New York City I was able to see Liza and meet her new husband, Bob DuVal. Yes, I felt badly about missing her wedding along with other milestones.

In the summer of 1987, I received a call from the chief of Naval Personnel, Admiral Dudley Carson, to come to D.C. and head up his legislative branch. I had served with him before and was flattered by his offer, so I took the orders willingly and with gratitude. I had enjoyed my five years in Asia, but, at that point, I would have accepted almost any assignment that brought me back to the States. The novelty of living in the Far East had finally worn off and I missed being around ordinary Americans and living an ordinary American life.

My girls were now young women and beginning to make their own lives, and this made it easier for me to permanently leave my marriage. When I finally told Gwen that our marriage was over, she was saddened, but not surprised. I moved to D.C. to assume my new assignment.

CHAPTER 18

Twilight Tour

~&~

WASHINGTON, D.C., AUGUST 1987

YOU MIGHT SAY I WALKED right into it in. I showed up for work on my first day in charge of the legislative office for navy personnel, only to learn that the man who'd recruited me, and with whom I was looking forward to working, was stepping down. It was difficult to see him go, but even more difficult was learning that his replacement was Admiral Bud Edney. The last time I'd seen him was on the deck of Lang with steam coming out of his ears after investigating our helo's over-flight of the Solomon Islands. Suddenly, this assignment seemed a lot less attractive.

Edney made a tour of all the offices and branches in his command to meet the staff. When he got around to calling on my team, I comforted myself thinking that he probably wouldn't remember me. Wrong! I introduced myself as if for the first time, and he replied, "Oh, I do indeed remember you. What have you done recently to screw up?"

Naturally, I thought my fate had been sealed, but I was able to prove myself. We developed a productive and enjoyable working relationship, and Bud Edney became a good friend over time.

My office's primary mission was to draft, submit, and shepherd into law all of the navy's legislation related to types and numbers of personnel needed over the next fiscal years.[1]

---

1 We established close relations within our department, the Bureau of Naval Personnel, particularly with the manpower planning and personnel assignment offices. Outside the bureau, we cultivated a good partnership with the Navy Office of Legislative Affairs, a part of the secretary of the navy's staff.

I had a small team—three military and one civilian—all of whom had been doing this for a long time. While my learning curve was steep, I climbed it with their invaluable help and became very comfortable in my job.

Periodically, a senior navy official would be called upon to testify before a congressional committee on manpower issues. Our job was to prepare written testimony for the record along with briefing materials.

When Bud Edney left, a year later, he was replaced by Admiral Mike Boorda. Of all the navy leaders I have known, this man inspired me the most. He cared about people regardless of their rank or gender. He took the time to learn about the issues affecting sailors and, always thinking outside the box, found ways to improve their lives and those of their families. As a former enlisted sailor and the parent of a special-needs child, he had a perspective on navy life that very few senior officers possessed. Mike's deputy was Admiral Frank Donovan from whom I had learned so much about leadership, years earlier at the school for prospective COs and XOs.

The three of us formed a special relationship based on mutual trust. Being in the highest circle of the personnel command allowed me to serve my fellow sailors beyond my immediate command and some of the changes we made together impacted the entire navy and continue to this day. These changes include expanded career opportunities for women and minorities, as well as initiatives for family support, all of which are factors in attracting and retaining sailors.

Mike Boorda asked me to be part of a team of officers investigating evidence of sexual harassment and cheating at the Naval Academy in 1990. My friend, Commander Ann Rondeau, a bright young naval officer and former White House Fellow, was also on the team. She was about to become the first woman battalion officer at the Academy.[2] We found there indeed had been a breakdown of good order and discipline between the midshipmen and the Academy leadership. Our recommendations resulted in senior enlisted persons—for the first time—training midshipmen in the vital roles that

---

2 This was a big deal because battalion officers were responsible for mentoring all 750 of their assigned midshipmen.

enlisted men and women play. So that, even before their commissioning, they receive a firsthand appreciation for the sailors they'd later lead.

U.S. Senator John McCain from Arizona was one of the members of Congress with whom I fostered close relations.[3] I first got to know the senator when he was on the Senate Armed Services Committee (SASC), a straight shooter then as now. We worked together on increasing the funding for additional manpower billets and bonus incentives to keep people in the service. I respected him for his outspokenness and ability to take on the role of a maverick when he felt his party was wrong on an issue. And I shared a larger bond with him in that he was a former naval officer who had also served in Vietnam where he was shot down and spent several years in a prison camp. I've always admired his ability to move on from that traumatic POW experience.

What a small world, indeed! Another member of SASC was Senator Ted Kennedy, the now deceased brother of the late president, to whom I'd delivered breakfast as a boy. Ted and I established a close bond as fellow Bostonians and veterans.[4] This relationship would continue into my later civilian career as we worked with veterans.

Colonel Barney Barnum, a fellow Medal of Honor recipient, was stationed in my building and was serving as senior aide to the Marine Corps Commandant General Al Gray. When we got to know each other, we quickly realized that we both had a passion for playing golf. The problem was that for lowly O-6s in Washington, it was extremely difficult to play at the Andrews Air Force Base golf course. You had to be an admiral or general officer in order to reserve a starting time on the course. But, as luck would have it, an admiral with my last name (different spelling) had just reported to D.C. and best of all, according to the grapevine, he was not a golfer. This opened a door for Barney and me. Because no one at the golf course knew what Admiral Kelly looked like, I went out to Andrews in civilian clothes, identified myself as him and reserved a 10:20 a.m. tee time every Saturday. I made it a point to call the golf course midweek and confirm.

---

3 As you know, Senator McCain's father, Admiral John McCain, "found" me in the system when I'd been "lost" after my injuries in Vietnam, and expedited my return home.

4 The late Senator Ted Kennedy had served in the army.

"Hello, this is Admiral Kelly confirming my tee time on Saturday."

This went on for over a year until one Saturday, as we stood on the first tee ready to play, we heard a commotion coming from the starter shack. Apparently the admiral's staff had called ahead to reserve playing time and was told that he'd already booked his regular time. A red-faced guy with steam coming out of his ears was gesturing with his hands and pointing towards me. The starter was also pointing our way. He appeared to be defending himself. Yup, the real Admiral Kelly had decided to take advantage of his 10:20 a.m. tee time with some out-of-town visitors, and he was walking my way.

"Who the hell are you?" he demanded.

"Tom Kelley," I answered. That was the end of a very short conversation and my year of Saturday golfing. Fortunately, this was not a violation of the Uniform Code of Military Justice, and I suffered no adverse consequences. It was a reminder, though, that I could push my luck only so far!

But according to other law, I could serve no more than thirty years unless I made admiral, and that was unlikely due to some of my past exploits. This was my final tour. To call it a day and pack away all my uniforms, seldom to be used again, after thirty years was not easy. I resisted, even though I had no choice in the matter. My mandatory retirement date was fast approaching, and I still hadn't taken the required physical exams, or submitted any retirement papers. Mike Boorda called me into his office and ordered me to take the next day off and start the ball rolling.

As much as I wanted to avoid a formal retirement ceremony, my team had other plans.

The date was set for early September, 1990. The event was an elaborate affair held at the Navy Memorial in D.C.—a place very dear to me. The statue there is of an enlisted sailor, not an officer, as the heart and soul of the entire service. And although my time as an enlisted sailor had been brief, to this day I feel an affinity toward enlisted men and women of all services. For me, it had always been about the people for whom I was responsible. I knew that our recommendations in navy personnel would serve its men and women long after I retired and that helped ease the transition.

Liza, Kate, Jane and Gwen came down for the event, along with Liza's two little boys, Tommy and John. I invited Gwen to my retirement, because she had stood behind me all those years, and she came. It seemed like every friend I ever had in D.C. turned out. The Navy Band played, and I was honored by my mentors Mike Boorda and Frank Donovan, who both spoke.[5] Every navy master chief petty officer in the D.C. area attended, and at the end of the ceremony, they bestowed upon me the title of Honorary Master Chief. My eyes welled with tears as I accepted the award with humble thanks.

Finally it was over. What a ride! The navy had been my life from the time my college roommates enlisted and put the bug in my ear. All the goals I had set for myself were accomplished, the most important being command-at-sea. Sure, I had managed to ruffle a few feathers along the way, but for no other reason than I believed I was doing the right thing. The navy was "family" for me, and I felt a real bond with all the men and women with whom I served, but now my beloved navy would have to get along without me and I without them.

When I left that family, I found myself feeling alone and empty at age fifty-one. My girls had careers and lives of their own and my marriage had ended. I could keep up with the friends I served with, but it wasn't the same as working side-by-side with teammates on a daily basis, sharing a common mission and looking out for each other. It's no wonder, then, that I underwent a period of restlessness and rootlessness. I wasn't lonely, but something important was missing in my life.

In the fall of 1990, I moved to Pensacola, Florida, and to this day, I don't know exactly why. A number of retired navy folks lived there, and I thought I would fit in. I volunteered at local veterans' organizations and played golf. Regular trips to New Jersey to visit Liza kept me close to her and my two grandsons.

After eight months of this retirement lifestyle, Frank Donovan called to ask what I was doing. We chatted a few minutes and then he asked if I'd like

---

5 To have served with the egalitarian Mike Boorda—who displayed moral courage in going against the establishment as he pursued inclusive policies toward enlisted minorities and women— was an honor. I still weep for my dear friend and mentor who took his own life in 1995 when he was chief of naval operations. He understood me as no other navy boss had.

to work for him as a civilian at the Military Sealift Command's headquarters in D.C. I came alive again with his offer because I'd thrived on my MSC responsibilities in the Far East, and, more importantly, because I had suspected it was the navy that was missing in my life.

I was sure that once I was back in a routine at work, I'd be fulfilled again. Within a few weeks I moved to Maryland and assumed duties as a senior civil servant. The first few months in 1991 were promising, mostly because I worked directly for Frank, whose leadership I'd tried to emulate. Morale was high due to him. I was responsible for quality improvements in the command's operations, human relations, and worldwide logistics programs. Unfortunately, when Frank retired in 1992, all of this changed. His replacement ruled by intimidation and threats. I left in 1993. I had my navy pension and I didn't need the income. I certainly didn't need the aggravation.

I traveled often during the next five years to visit my children and grandchildren. I thought about returning to my Boston roots, and I still kept my subscription to the *Boston Globe*, while faithfully following my Red Sox.

I was still restless. Maybe such a move would help.

Part Four: Joan

CHAPTER 19

Time to Be Adult

ᘓ

A Profession, Marriage, and a Navy Commission, 1970s

My after-college European trip, especially the Berlin adventure, opened my eyes to a new way of viewing my country and aroused my patriotic spirit. While it was good to be home, now I had to look for a job. Journalism still interested me, but the country was in an economic recession. Professional jobs were harder to find. I had few skills beyond my college editorial ones, so I became a temporary typist. And to add color and balance to my life, I tried dating again.

The fighting that seemed to permeate my relationship with my mother escalated when I told her I was going to move out and rent an apartment. She lost no time in reminding me that only "loose women" live on their own before marriage. Unable to stand up to her, I stayed at home, but got even with the only way I knew how—by sleeping with men I met casually. As soon as I realized my risky behavior was only hurting myself, I stopped.

After a series of temp assignments, my father helped me get an editor's position within a state agency. Being a professional writer made me feel better about myself enough. So much that I embarked on a "makeover," similar to freshman year in high school. This involved shedding twenty-five pounds. As the weight came off, I experimented with using cosmetics and dressing professionally. Buying clothes was fun, actually, since I could now wear almost any style.

And that's when David, a warm-hearted, intelligent man, walked into my life. It was 1972. Our families had known each other and, although I'd heard about him for a while, I'd never met him. I hosted a party, invited him, and he stayed afterward to help me clean up. As we chatted, he put me at ease with his casual attitude, humor, and optimism. He made me feel special.

He was there for me when, early in our relationship, my brother had a mental breakdown and was hospitalized for several weeks, and ultimately diagnosed with schizophrenia. Because Tommy was at risk to himself, my mother, and me, he spent several weeks at a state mental hospital while they tried different medications.[1] My brother's situation was very sad. David offered light and hope and a new normal life that we could turn into our own family.

When David wasn't working or going to law school at night, we went to movies and concerts and hung out with friends. He liked the Irish music that Denise had introduced me to when we visited her Irish uncle. And David was a great reader with a gift of retaining almost everything he read. So if you had a question about history, geography, or current affairs, all you had to do was ask him, kind of a human precursor to *Google*. He had a way with my mother, who could be moody and hold grudges. In fact, both my parents highly approved of this young man who was working his way through night law school.

While David completed school and prepared for the Bar exam in 1973, I had an opportunity to enhance my job prospects by enrolling in a master's degree program in public relations at Boston University, the same program where the navy sent their public information officers, although none were in my class. Yes, I had inquired once about a navy career in college but those days were behind me—or so I thought—I had new roles coming up as wife and, eventually, mother.

When David asked me to marry him, I immediately said yes. His upbeat and nurturing nature helped me grow emotionally and spiritually, and I felt he'd do the same as a father. My own father saw us get married, but passed away soon after from heart disease at sixty. I felt badly that we hadn't been more of a family and vowed to do better with my own family. One of the most

---

1 Although my brother tried different medications, he had other breakdowns requiring hospitalization. These hospital stays would become a pattern for Tommy. He'd improve for a while, then decompensate.

important lessons my dad taught me is that most of the people in the world are good and well-meaning, so long as we give them a chance.

I thought it made sense to postpone our long-planned European honeymoon since we were both unemployed, but David convinced me to seize the moment. He said he'd already paid for most of the trip, we would be working again soon, and so we might not have another opportunity.

It was a great trip. We toured the west coast of Ireland, visited Dublin, and sampled the best of London, Paris, and Rome. Finally, we headed for Naples to visit my relatives. They lived in a small mountain town an hour east of Naples called Venticano, or "twenty dogs." On our daily treks to the mountains, my family members would stop their farm work, embrace us warmly and take us into their homes. Despite the fact that it was usually midmorning, they would offer us beverages, generally alcoholic, and a taste of whatever delicacy—olives, biscotti or Torrone, a regional nougat candy—they had on hand. David didn't know Italian, except what he could interpret from his Latin studies, and my Italian was what I remembered from my grandparents. So we communicated with the ease of two year-olds.

The relatives couldn't understand why this young newlywed couple would insist on staying in the big city of Naples when we could stay with them on the farm. In their opinion the city was full of thieves, and they warned us by making a dialing motion with their fingers that indicated, "Neapolitans will screw you at every opportunity." We weren't sure if they meant by over-charging or by actually taking our wallets, so we were hyper vigilant. We ate and drank whatever they put in front of us to make up for those long silences and experienced most days through the glow of Strega (anisette) or a slight buzz from a sherry-like drink with egg in it. *Yuck.*

One of my great-uncles, who had learned some English while serving in World War I as an Italian soldier, presented me with what became one of my most cherished possessions. One afternoon he placed in my hand his commemorative medallion of that war and said haltingly, "I'm an old, old man, and I want to give you something to remember me by." I was so touched that I put the medallion on a chain, and I wear it frequently. It speaks to me of the man's affection and generosity. Neither of us could know at that time that I would later join his brotherhood.

The honeymoon was over and we started job hunting. Joining the military together seemed like a good idea, but the air force was the only service that would accept us as a couple, meaning they'd find jobs for us at the same location. The navy wouldn't guarantee that we would be stationed together, and the air force didn't interest us, nor did the Marine Corps or the army. For one thing, their uniforms couldn't compete with the dazzling navy blue suits with gold braid, buttons, and stars. Also, they worked on land or in the air and couldn't compete with the navy's mission of keeping the world's sea lanes open. My early brainwashing about the navy had stuck, but the problem of how to stay together remained.

Another series of temporary jobs followed, and then, with Uncle Rudy's help, I went to work for the Cambridge Chamber of Commerce, handling their communications and public relations.

As fate would have it, one day I was at the monthly meeting of a local professional public relations group I'd joined. Sitting at the same table were two journalists, a woman and a man. They were public affairs officers (PAOs) in the local naval reserve unit. Their work was part-time, one weekend a month right in Boston and two weeks of training a year in various U.S. and overseas locations. I learned the navy offered a program called "direct commission" where my master's degree in the field could substitute for prior service, and I could pick up the military training as I went along.

My long-standing interest was being stoked, and the Siren was calling again. I was seriously interested. If I let this opportunity go by, I wasn't sure I'd get another. Panicked, because I thought the cut-off age for applying was thirty, an age I was fast approaching, I raced to get my application in.[2] Here was a part-time opportunity for me to combine my love of the navy with my communication skills, while not uprooting my husband. With David's

---

2 The cut-off age was actually thirty-five at the time. Some of my Uncle Matt's perseverance must have rubbed off on me. He was so determined to get into the Naval Academy that he attempted the effort twice. But when he went to begin at the Academy, a physical exam revealed a heart problem. He had to get a Boston cardiologist to assure the navy that he would be fit to serve before they'd let him matriculate.

encouragement, I applied for a direct commission. The process took several months. The navy required me to submit a lot of information, including every address I'd ever lived at, all my schools, and all the places I'd traveled to outside the U.S. And I needed references, all of which had to be checked. I did all this and, although I was no longer overweight, I lost a few pounds before my physical, just to be sure.

The World War II era building where I underwent my medical exam hadn't changed much. Its halls and offices were hardly occupied. And even though it felt like I was the only one there, I thought I could hear the distant echoes of the excited voices of our greatest generation lining up in these empty hallways, eager to join the fight overseas. I could hear their footsteps and the hustle and bustle of clerks and clinicians trying to get them on their way. Their navy would wrest the sea lanes from German control and carry our troops, who would free occupied Europe. Here I was taking my place in that long line of noble men and women. My father would have been proud. I think he would have approved of a navy career for a *married* woman! I hoped to embark on travel, meet people with many different backgrounds, and learn about other cultures. The Siren was really singing to me now. Later I'd learn how fickle she could be.

I'd worn my glasses and not contact lenses, as the instructions provided. The cranky old doctor who told me that my eyesight was not 20/20 knocked me out of my reverie. Nothing like pointing out the obvious! I was prepared for this and told him that my less than perfect eyesight didn't matter. I explained that I was going to be a *public affairs officer* and that I would be writing press releases, not driving ships. He corrected me saying in his southern drawl that I had applied to be an unrestricted "lie-en" (two syllables) officer, meaning I could go to sea and mumbled something about restricted "lie-en," meaning I couldn't go to sea because of poor eyesight. Frankly, I was a little confused, but before I could engage him he disappeared to talk with someone else. He was still mumbling when he returned, but his body language suggested that I'd won on a technicality. I left his office feeling I could handle this new world once I got the hang of its terminology.

Finally, some seven months later, the navy commissioned me as a lieutenant junior grade (O-2) in the fall of 1979. Not only did the navy credit my

M.S. degree in lieu of prior military service, but allowed me to skip the rank of ensign (O-1). The navy's post-Vietnam troop draw-down had created a shortage of public affairs officers, and that helped in my selection as well.

That dress blue uniform with the gold braid, buttons, and stars was mine now. I smiled in delight at my reflection as I tried it on for the first time. *I've always wanted one of these! Now I have it.* But where to from here?

David and his family were at my commissioning along with Uncle Matt's wife, Angela. They would support me throughout my career. My mother was proud of me, too. I didn't tell her until after I was commissioned. At first she thought I'd gone crazy and joined the regular navy. But I assured her it was a part-time job, leaving out the part about mobilization in emergencies. We were in a period of relative peace and I didn't want to rock the boat. She shared with me how she'd admired the World War II navy women, known as Waves, she'd met during her time as a civilian military contractor.

In the meantime, I was working for a Boston engineering firm in marketing and public relations that laid me off just after I received my commission. And so I, and a couple of fellow officers, who were also victims of the poor job market, requested temporary active duty assignments from the navy.

My first assignment with the Boston Navy Information Office was helping plan and carry out the public relations side of an international parade of tall ships. The navy was bringing the mighty carrier, USS John F. Kennedy (CV-67) to Boston along with several other ships in its task force from Virginia. Named for Boston's native son and the nation's thirty-fourth president, the Kennedy had a huge New England audience of admirers, and we expected extensive media coverage and record crowds during public visiting.

As a protocol officer, my job was to schedule events, itineraries and invitations for VIPs and other invitees. Among the VIPs were the Medal of Honor recipients, and among them was Captain Tom Hudner, a navy pilot.[3] What a rare honor the Medal of Honor is! I was in complete awe of the bravery and

---

3 Thomas J. Hudner, Jr. was awarded the Medal of Honor for crash-landing his plane during the Korean War while attempting to save his wingman, Ensign Jesse Brown, who was shot down at the Chosin Reservoir, Korea, in December 1950. Jesse was the navy's first black aviator and, unfortunately, did not survive. Tom Hudner's biography, *Devotion,* provides an excellent account of this man's heroism.

sacrifices these recipients had made for their fellow men. By tradition, they went to the top of any protocol list.

As a newly commissioned, but as yet untrained, officer I was still trying to figure out how to wear the uniform and address those both junior and senior to me. The first time I saw an admiral in his summer white uniform with the sun reflecting off all the gold braid on his shoulder boards, I nearly fainted. I scrambled to pick up the abbreviations and acronyms fast enough to understand what the heck was going on. Key words like "sitrep" and "fitrep" became part of my vocabulary.[4] Part of the excitement I felt was that I'd joined an exclusive club, and you had to know the right words to fit in.

Fortunately, I reported to a young female officer, who patiently steered me through the steep learning curve of uniform regulations, protocol, customs, and traditions. We both reported to a captain who was demanding, but caring and fair. Once you proved yourself to him, you were part of the greatest team on earth.[5] You would do anything for him, and he was loyal to you. He was my first true leader, and he set an example that I wanted to emulate.

When my captain awarded me and another sailor with a Navy Achievement Medal, I tried to shrug it off as nothing special, but inside I was bursting with joy. I got the medal for my protocol and public affairs work during the Tall Ships in 1980. I felt proud of my service and myself. I may have been formerly unemployed, but now was a decorated LT (junior grade)! I was like a female knight, a warrior, and I could even have an officer's sword if I wanted to go out and buy one. Okay, maybe comparing myself to St. Joan of Arc is going too far—but I felt that the very small role I played was important. I had the privilege and the satisfaction of serving my country.

I was at a meeting between the navy and the mayor's office when I first saw the excitement caused by the USS Kennedy's visit and the public affairs

---

4 "Sitrep" is short for situational report, meaning a report of the current state of affairs in a mission. "Fitrep" is short for fitness report, meaning the written grades you receive for performance and that could make or break your career.

5 The navy for me was like what I imagined life in a religious order to be. You were on a mission, part of a family community and wore uniforms. You often lived with those with whom you worked. You supported one another emotionally. You became part of their lives and they of yours. You were a team 24/7.

challenges that resulted. The two groups were arguing over how many tickets the mayor would receive for the parade of sail event.

"Here's the deal," the police chief said. "The mayor wants 2,000 tickets to view the parade of sail from the aircraft carrier."

"But, we only have room for 1,000 seats on the Kennedy" replied the exasperated navy representative whom I was sitting behind. "The other navy ships can handle the overflow."

"No. We don't want to be on the other ships. We want the Kennedy."

"But we'd have to build bigger bleachers on the flight deck to accommodate all these people."

"Look, I don't care what you have to do—if we don't get our tickets, we're going to shut down every street leading to the harbor, and no one will see the parade of sail!"

My God, can he actually do that? I tried to keep my composure. This was my first exposure to the crassness of strong-arm politics.

Imagine if you will, a floating city with 5,000 crew members onboard coming into Boston Harbor. All morning our operational team had listened to radio chatter describing the ship's entry into the harbor from its position just outside.

"Kennedy, at the Boston Buoy and pilot's aboard," came a disembodied voice.

"Aye, proceed slowly and with extreme caution," was the response.

At the appointed hour, I got into a car with other navy folks and drove to the harbor. From there we watched the Kennedy's enormous gray hull and flight deck fill almost every square inch of water and sky. It was spellbinding. Despite its magnificent size, its equipment and the number of men onboard, it seemed to silently slip by, pushed by tugs. The crew members in their white dress uniforms lining the rails with their hands clasped behind their backs made one proud to be part of the scene.

After the long process of the ship tying up, we went aboard. I was talking with some sailors when a wide section of the steel deck we were standing on suddenly jolted and lifted us very fast to the flight deck. This turned out to be a freight elevator that moved aircraft on and off the flight deck at high speed. Seeing the awesome flight deck from land was one thing, but actually standing on it gave you a sense of the size of the ship on a human scale. Later I would have a nightmare about the great ship.

When Massachusetts became the only state in the union not to vote for Richard Nixon as president in 1972, he closed down the navy shipyards in South Boston and Charlestown. Civilian yards, especially the two in East Boston, picked up the repair and overhaul work. This left the assigned sailors unprotected and vulnerable during their off-duty hours. They could no longer rely on the gated safe refuge of government property with guards to keep others outside the perimeter. Sailors had to venture a bit farther into local neighborhoods to find restaurants and bars. To reach the subway, which would take them into downtown Boston, they had to walk a lonely street, known as Marginal.

The local teens could spot the navy guys in an instant, even out of uniform. With their proper haircuts, Southern accents, and choice of civilian clothes, they not only sounded different, but looked slightly out of place. Black sailors especially stood out because hardly any African-Americans lived in East Boston then. A minority of these youth would taunt and curse the sailors whenever they saw them. Their motive seemed to be resentment because the sailors had careers, money, and a means of traveling, and they didn't.[6]

One night while returning to their ship on foot, a small group of sailors realized they were being followed. First came the verbal abuse. Then, realizing they were being stalked, the sailors broke into a run and skittered over the tall chain-link fence dropping down into the shipyard. One sailor, who was white, fell behind. The locals grabbed him, and that's when one youth bludgeoned him to death with a baseball bat.

The navy needed someone on the scene to improve relations in East Boston, and the local commander asked me if I'd take on the job. Eagerly I accepted. One of the first things I did was form an alliance with the well-connected director of the local YMCA. Together, we brain-stormed with neighborhood opinion leaders: the city hall folks, merchants, religious leaders,

---

6 At one time Italian immigrants, including my own grandmother, Elisa, had made up most of the population of East Boston.

the local judge, the high school administrators along with police and fire representatives. We sought their views on how to improve communication, and mostly we ended up on the same page where it mattered most.

Most East Boston residents felt very badly about what had happened to that sailor and supported our efforts. They genuinely wanted the sailors to feel comfortable in their neighborhood. They also understood how navy contracts brought an economic trickle-down to businesses in the community. We formed a navy-citizen coalition that kept the communications open between the community and the crews whose ships were being overhauled. Essentially, I was doing community-organizing work. And, after one year, our efforts bore fruit. Relations improved.

My work often took me to the shipyards to chat with the sailors about how things were going in the community. The sailors would take me on tours of their ships and proudly explain how the various systems would work once they were out of the yard and underway. They loved their ships the same way you would love a home. I enjoyed being around these proud and dedicated sailors and their great gray ships of the line.

As a female officer, I was a bit of a novelty in the shipyards. There were no women assigned to combat ships then. Sailors rarely encountered navy women except on bases where females typically held administrative or medical positions. Sometimes the shipyard sailors wouldn't salute me, not out of disrespect, but because they were not familiar with a woman in uniform.

One day, I was walking along the pier when a young enlisted man was coming along the other way. I could see him scanning my shoulder boards and recognizing my rank. As we approached, he brought his hand up smartly and saluted me saying, "Good afternoon, Sir!" I just smiled, amused, as I returned the salute and walked past him. He never knew that he had mistaken my gender, but he had properly respected my rank.

Towards the end of my assignment, a fire spread through several three-family homes near the shipyard. My heart swelled with pride when I learned that sailors from a nearby destroyer had rushed to the scene before the local fire department had arrived and helped their neighbors put out the fire. The sailors became instant heroes in the community. My work was done, and when it was time to leave my assignment I felt a sense of pride and satisfaction.

Unfortunately, my navy assignments were only temporary. Going on regular active duty would have meant relocation for me and David, and this didn't seem consistent with our desire to start a family. I had learned that the civilian public relations field wasn't stable during periods of recession. So, I began to think seriously, again, about going to law school.

On one very special day in March 1981, I received three wonderful pieces of news. The crowning piece of news was that I was pregnant! David and I had wanted to start a family and now a little life was forming inside my womb. And, if that wasn't exciting enough, I had been accepted to law school, *and* I'd been promoted to full lieutenant (O-3) in the reserves. That was a great day!

My navy assignment was winding down when I entered the evening division of the New England School of Law. It seemed that being a mother was compatible with being a part time law student and a naval reservist, although there were times when I was definitely in way over my head.

Our beautiful, healthy son Brian was born on December 1, 1981. What a joyful moment! I still remember looking outside at the torrential rain pounding on my hospital window the next day. I was bewildered, because it was sunny, and the birds were singing in my room, especially when I held Brian in my arms. His dark brown eyes sparkled at me whenever I spoke to him. Later when he began smiling at me, I understood that those sparkling eyes were early attempts at smiling. Of course, he was smiling, because he was happy. I would do anything to earn those sparkling eyes. I had never felt a love as deep and powerful as I did for him. Just the smell of his clean laundry would send my spirits soaring.[7]

Fortunately, David was supportive as I juggled law school and my reserve responsibilities. And Brian kept me grounded. The attention he needed made it impossible to obsess over my studies and exams as I may have otherwise done. He napped in the morning, enabling me to prep for class while I was

---

7 Mothering a child is the most creative and wonderful endeavor a woman can undertake. Having the time to do it properly is a challenge when few mothers can stay at home full time. I give great credit to all those mothers who struggle to do it all, especially those who are single parents. Raising a child isn't easy and, unfortunately, they don't come with instruction books.

fresh. When he was awake, we went to parks, playgrounds, and the local play-group, and I didn't miss too many family events or outings or birthdays. At school I had substantive matters to discuss in the classroom and was able to do so without defaulting to baby-talk—as I knew happened to many new moms.

However, not missing much of my family life or classes meant I was missing something somewhere. That something was the navy. When Brian was a few months old, I discovered that I'd been transferred to inactive status in the reserves for missing too many drills. I was puzzled because everyone in my unit knew I was on maternity leave. The reserve center had probably sent me some sort of written notice, and I'd put it aside and forgotten about it.

One day I put on a business suit, packed up Brian with food, diapers, and toys and went to the reserve center. I was going to stay all day until they processed the paperwork to put me back into active drill status. Instead, I was told the decision lay with the commander in Rhode Island. That's when David, Brian, and I went to Newport.

The navy wanted to know who would take care of Brian, if I were to return to active status, and especially if I were called up for active duty. The whole point of having a reserve force was that we could mobilize for war in an emergency.[8] And in 1982, although the U.S. was technically in the Cold War with the Soviet Union, it threatened to heat up at any minute. Once I convinced the officer-in-charge that David was more than ready, willing, and able to do the job, and I signed a statement to that effect, he processed the paperwork, and I was back in drill status.

---

8 During the time I was in the reserves (1979–1999), with the exception of small American incursions into Panama, Grenada, and Lebanon, the U.S. was at peace. During the first Gulf War (1990–1991) I volunteered for regular active duty, but wasn't called. If I'd stayed in service after 2003 when the U.S. invaded Iraq, my chances of being mobilized and sent to the Middle East would have been 100%. I learned this from the admiral in charge of reserve PAO deployments.

CHAPTER 20

Juggling Roles

_____ ᧠ _____

CAMBRIDGE, MA, 1982–1993

BRIAN SLEPT A LOT DURING my first year of law school, allowing me to prep for my night classes. Bundling him up, I'd put him in his car seat, and we'd be off to pick up David from work. David would shift into the driver's seat and drop me at school. They'd go home for dinner, and pick me up after class with Brian asleep, as if he'd never been removed from the car.

David took care of Brian on drill weekends until I returned home each day about five p.m. I was only thirty minutes away, so traveling back and forth wasn't an issue. Eventually we developed a routine, and despite being sleep deprived, I was able to juggle my responsibilities.

My unit's task was, ultimately, to support the navy's mission in training and equipping combat-ready forces capable of winning wars, deterring aggression, and maintaining freedom of the seas. We backed up our active duty counterpart, the Navy Information Office in Boston, with the delivery of press releases, photos and reports to news outlets. On occasion, we produced pieces for navy newspapers and magazines. Among other events, we worked on ships' commissioning ceremonies and navy ship port visits, but could be called upon for contingency and deployed operations anywhere in the world.

Besides our main mission of public affairs, we had collateral duties. Mine were administrative: oversight of attendance, pay, and training records. When paychecks didn't arrive, I took the sad phone calls from unit members wondering how they were going to get by for another month. When I called our higher-ups, I had to temper my fury, with enough begging and pleading to expedite the pay. *It was ridiculous that people shouldn't be paid on time!*

A typical weekend drill would go something like this: muster for attendance on Saturday at 0800 (8:00 a.m.) which actually meant you were at the assigned location, in the proper uniform of the day, at 7:30–7:45 a.m., because, God forbid, you were late and missed the ship's movement (i.e., missed the start of the work day); you could be court-martialed.[1]

The CO would review the plan of the day that we'd already received via mail, make any adjustments and outline what he or she hoped to accomplish over the weekend. We'd spend the morning working in small groups, followed by lunch, usually at a nearby sandwich shop, or we'd eat in. Project work continued until 1630 (4:30 p.m.) at which point we'd "secure" or leave for the day. On Sunday, we'd meet at the same time, as a whole group, and each team would report on where their projects stood, while department heads reported on their responsibilities and problems they faced with suggested fixes. On Sunday afternoons, we'd take our bi-annual physical fitness tests or make the mad scramble to finish projects. Otherwise we'd have to do the work on our own time, often the case.[2]

I learned to shoot a pistol and acquired a license to carry a gun in the reserves. As a PAO, I didn't think I could adequately defend myself with a word processor and paper clips.

In order to impress my reserve bosses, I would organize target practice for my unit at various military bases in the area. The navy gave us the time, training points, and even provided pistols for target practice. But by some quirky regulation, the navy couldn't supply bullets. So, I purchased the ammo and my colleagues reimbursed me.

---

1 I say this in part jest, as PAOs rarely reported aboard a ship about to get under way, but if you were in the *real* navy, they could actually court-martial you for missing a ship's deployment. You certainly wouldn't be flown out on a helicopter. The point is—the military takes being on time *very* seriously.

2 Twice a year, we'd have our body fat measured, and we'd have to do timed push-ups and sit-ups. Those were followed by a timed two-mile run or a lapped swim. All these numbers were combined, and, by some mysterious calculation, it was determined whether you were fit for duty. Passing was not a problem for me, and I rarely saw anyone fail or be drummed out of drilling status for being unfit.

On one of those occasions, in the spring, when the weather could change with the next breeze, we headed to Fort Devens in our summer white uniforms—white slacks, shirts and shoes with black windbreakers—so dressed because of other duties we had that weekend. By the time we reached the base, the temperature had dropped twenty degrees, and intermittent showers had turned the ground into slop, but we carried on with target practice.

After, we trudged miserably through the mud from the canopy-covered firing line towards the dining hall. Our water-filled shoes squeaked and our no longer white slacks were muddied. We looked like we'd shown up to feed the pigs in our Sunday best. We were the butt of a few lame jokes by our army counterparts, who were dressed in camouflage and bivouacking in the rain on tarpaulins. As we passed, we picked up their twitter about our "Good Humor ice cream man" uniforms. We just shook our heads as we slogged by, muttering to one another about "those poor slobs, living like animals and eating in the rain."

While drill weekends gave me a patriotic sense of purpose and extra income, they also provided some hilarity. A couple of guys would play a game called, "What the admiral really said." This involved one person, playing the admiral, droning on about a particular exercise in a very non-public affairs and non-politically correct manner, after which the other, a PAO, would scramble to put the right spin on it. Their repartee was genius and helped keep the atmosphere relaxed and creative.

On Sunday nights, I switched back from public affairs warrior to mother.[3] Those years of child-rearing, school, and reserves required a lot of reordered priorities and organization. And there was also my brother.

One afternoon in 1983, when my brother was in his late twenties, my mother called.

"Your brother has been threatening me. He's very angry and walks around the kitchen with knives talking to himself."

---

3 We found the perfect toddler playgroup in the neighborhood. The mothers enjoyed chatting with one another as much as our children enjoyed the play. We supported each other emotionally, sharing child-rearing tips, and there was one unwritten rule—no gossiping.

"So, he's talking to himself, that's just part of his paranoid schizophrenia. Is he taking his meds?"

"Yes, so far as I can tell. But he's acting very differently from his usual behavior. I found some of my clothing on the closet floor with cigarette burns in them."

"That's not good—let me talk with David, and I'll call you back."

"Okay, but please don't make it too long. I don't even feel safe in my own house, and a couple of times I've had to get in the car and drive somewhere, just to get away from him."

David and I decided the situation was serious enough and advised my mother to call the police. David waited with her while they tried to persuade Tommy to go with them to a mental hospital. My brother refused, and the police took him away in a squad car for an involuntary commitment hearing before a judge. Without appropriate medical care, Tommy would be a risk to himself and to others. Since it was late in the day, the police held him overnight, in jail.

The next morning found David and me in the courtroom waiting for my brother's case to be called. Tommy seemed more disheveled than usual in handcuffs. Even more concerning was how frightening these events were for him. When a person who thinks he's hearing voices, is removed from home by authorities, spends the night in jail, God only knows what delusions play out in his head. This time, Tommy agreed to return to a mental hospital, and the case was dismissed.

I was embarrassed to have a family member brought to court because he was out of control. But the saddest part was that, at age twenty-nine, the best part of my brother's life seemed over before it'd even begun. He'd been fired from a job and had no prospects for another. His few friends had moved on with their lives. He had no hobbies and no physical activities. Watching TV or listening to the radio scared him, because he heard voices beyond what was actually being broadcast. His life was limited to running errands with my mother and helping her around the house. The medications he took resulted in hand tremors, and he became a chain-smoker. Despite medication adjustments and seeing different mental health therapists, he didn't seem to improve.

I was unhappy that I'd "lost" my only sibling. I was resentful that my mother devoted all her spare time to him when she could have been sharing it with me and Brian. I had enough to do with juggling a husband, son, house, law school, and the reserves and I needed some of her attention and support. Regrettably, shortly after this episode, I made a bad choice by holding nothing back in a phone call with my mother. I blamed my brother's condition one hundred percent on her. It was unfair of me. The result was that my mother stopped talking to me altogether.[4]

In the beginning I would call her, and she'd hang up. At least once I showed up at her front door, and she refused to let me in. Through an intermediary I discovered that I was supposed to apologize for the things I'd said. But I was stubborn and felt I would humiliate myself. Several months later, David and I started getting crank calls, usually at night. We'd pick up the phone and there'd just be breathing. When the calls began to unnerve me, we went to the police and it turned out that they originated from my mother's phone, which made me less fearful. I thought she was trying to reach out to me in some strange way, but the effect was the opposite.

During my second year of law school, my mother and brother were taking up too much space in my head. Although I'd try to shrug off my mother's cold treatment, the unfairness continued to needle me like a papercut that wouldn't heal.

I was lost. My concentration was broken and I needed help.

Fortunately, my school had free counselling services. I related well to the psychotherapist who helped me peel back the onion layers and discover just how I'd arrived at this place in my life.

It seemed that if I could muster the courage and work hard enough, things would improve with time. Brian would mature into a good student. I would graduate from law school, pass the Bar, and get a job. Our lives would be less hectic. There was hope on that end.

---

4 Later I learned that no one really knows for sure what causes schizophrenia, but it's believed that something in the brain doesn't develop properly in early adulthood.

But after a few months, I gave up trying to reconcile my relationship with my mother, and our silence continued for several years. I regret not taking the high road and trying again. During that time, my Uncle Matt and Aunt Angela "adopted" us and we spent some holidays with them and others with David's family. But usually every Christmas, I'd get a lump in my throat that we weren't with my mother, and that she was missing the best moments of Brian's childhood. My mother-in-law provided much in the way of childcare and the "congrats, you're doing a good job, keep it up" encouragement that I needed from a mother figure.

My cousin, Elise, called one day to say that my mother had been diagnosed with breast cancer. I called right away and offered to take her for treatment and to doctors' appointments. When we got together nothing was said about our hiatus. We picked up the thread of our lives and carried on. I'd missed her healthy years as an older woman, but I was happy for the reconciliation and what the future held.

Unfortunately, the immediate future held some discouragement. As I opened the thin envelope from the Board of Bar Overseers, I held my breath, hoping I'd passed. Nope, I'd failed the Bar exam! Overcome by a sense of hopelessness, my head bowed, I crumpled into the nearest chair. All that time and money: attending classes, analyzing cases, passing course examinations, and now this. I shook my head. It was only by a few points that I'd missed the mark. And it was on the multiple choice part, not the essay part. How frustrating! I'd graduated from law school, but without passing the exam, there would be no admission to the Bar, and with no admission to the Bar, none of it mattered. I couldn't practice law.

I'd taken a part-time job as a law clerk at a local law firm after graduation in 1986. This gave me practical experience, plus additional household income. Brian was already going to nursery school nearly full time, so I wasn't feeling too guilty about working. I enjoyed my reserve duty and planned my time around that commitment.[5] All of these competing interests took the energy

---

[5] I could have left the reserves by resigning my commission, but it was my goal to serve for twenty years, entitling me to a pension and health benefits.

I'd otherwise use to study again for the Bar exam, and drastic measures were now necessary.

I knew I had it in me, like Uncle Matt, to persevere and succeed, and I was determined to pass. I sought the advice of my favorite law professor and broke down crying in his office. The professor pushed a tissue box at me and waited while I composed myself. He'd obviously been down this road before with others. He suggested that I find a prep course that focused on multiple choice questions.

"You may have been over-analyzing these questions in choosing your answers," he pointed out. "Obviously, you know the law, as you showed in your essays."

"Prepping for the Bar exam," he said, "is like training for a road race. You plan to run so many miles a day. You establish a set time and place. You do a couple of practice runs. You take a day off each week and the day off just before the exam. And when the exam day arrives—you're ready."

So, I took a one-month leave from my job and devoted myself to studying.

Six months later, I received another thin envelope from the Board of Bar Overseers. Opened it. Scanned it. And danced around the house with the letter in my hand, grinning. Determination had paid off. I had passed! Passing the first time around would not have meant as much to me.[6] This was a glorious moment. Brian, then five years old, sensed that something big had happened and told people that I had "won the Bar!"

I became a lawyer at the same law firm, but left a year later to start my own practice closer to home. This arrangement gave me more flexibility to balance work, look after Brian, and fulfill my increasing reserve responsibilities, which were now spilling over into the work week. Life was hectic and full in so many ways. Brian and David came with me on some drill weekends and annual training exercises, especially to places like Newport and Washington, D.C. There were plenty of attractions and amusements for them during the day, and at night I would join them for dinner.

---

6 Having worked so hard for this goal made me appreciate the great privilege I had earned to practice law. I hoped never to do anything that would jeopardize that privilege. How fortunate I now felt to uphold the laws of the country as both a naval officer and an attorney.

When continually bumping into the only other woman officer in my unit on Sunday nights at the photocopier with piles of paper, it occurred to me that the guys had better assignments. They created, planned, and executed our projects, while she and I were stuck with keeping a river of administrative paperwork flowing. While important, such work wasn't career enhancing and didn't necessarily lead to promotion.

I asked my commanding officer why I had been passed over for a department head's job in favor of the male who received it. He explained that he didn't think I could handle the time commitment because I was a mother. I challenged him with two words: "Try me," and he reluctantly assigned me as the training officer.

That's when I became familiar with the concept of setting someone up to fail. He assigned me too much work and no staff. Once he became overly critical for insignificant and even nonexistent errors, I realized I needed to leave. I transferred to another unit in New York City, to which I traveled on weekends and where I was accepted as a peer and given more responsibility.

At the same time, in 1993, I gladly accepted an offer as a part-time solicitor in the next city. It was becoming difficult to keep my single practice going, because I had no one to cover for me when I'd leave for my navy training assignments. Just a couple of years earlier, people from my unit were mobilized to active duty for the Gulf War. If I were mobilized too, I'd have to give up my clients. There was more security in public service. Over the next few years, I would have the privilege of working in the public sector, while helping Brian develop into a well-rounded, generous kid who was near the top of his classes.

There was glamour in many of my two-week reserve assignments, not to mention exotic locales. Working with big name journalists and reporters provided a few short-lived exciting moments. Wolf Blitzer of CNN, Pete Williams of NBC (when he was with the defense department), and Eric Schmitt of the *New York Times* were all at the top of their game. Our job was to pitch positive stories and theirs to get the necessary details while trying to meet their deadlines. In some ways we were on opposing teams, but there was no denying the professionalism and respect between the members of the media and military spokespersons.

And there were moments of humor. Despite high heat, humidity, and an extra supply of bugs, in August of 1996, I had my annual training at the Marine Corps Base, Camp Lejeune.[7] More than one thousand troops from the U.S. and NATO nations (Canada and the Netherlands) and some sixteen partner republics (including former Soviet bloc nations such as Uzbekistan, Kyrgyzstan, and Kazakhstan), sweated through peacekeeping exercises.

It was especially sweaty for me. As an officer, I had to buy my own camouflaged uniform, including boots. And after tramping around in the summer heat in my camos and nearly melting, I discovered I'd bought the winter weight, not the summer weight uniform.

While traveling in a truck on the enormous base with a dozen partners to a helo landing zone to view air operations, our senior American officer got separated from us. Suddenly, I realized *I* was the senior officer. I sensed "my" troops were as greatly relieved as I was when the officer returned before I had to make any command decisions.

During another operation, pinpoints on the sea horizon gradually became bigger and bigger, then the noise of their engines went from a purr to a growl, as tracked vehicles emerged from the water and drove up onto the sand. I was standing awestruck on the beach as the mighty amphibious landing craft rolled right up onto it, from which the partner nations launched their "assault."

Another operation involved small groups of soldiers with automatic weapons who slithered along house perimeters, and stealthily peeked into open doors in house-to-house searches of a mock Middle Eastern village. It was like watching a play unfold, and I wished it never had to be more than a play. I declined a ride in the enclosed spaces of an LCAC (landing craft, air cushion) commonly known as a hovercraft, because I was so hot in my winter uniform I was afraid I'd pass out.

One afternoon, we were given time off at the beach, and I waded into the cool water (in my bathing suit, of course) and stayed there for two hours. I can't begin to imagine how difficult it is to be deployed to Afghanistan or Iraq where the scorching temperatures soar during the summer and sandstorms

---

7 Camp Lejeune is a Marine Corps training site in Jacksonville, North Carolina, comprising 265 acres, some of which are on the Atlantic Ocean.

make life barely tolerable. I'm in awe of anyone just serving in that environment, let alone doing so while performing their missions and getting shot at.

There were foreign locations as well. My two-week assignment in November 1997 was another NATO exercise in the Mediterranean (where the Sirens supposedly operated) aboard the USS La Salle (AGF-3), an amphibious transport that had become the command ship for the U.S. Sixth Fleet, homeported in Gaeta, Italy. The first morning in that port on my way to breakfast, I glanced out a porthole and stopped when I saw the rosy-golden light rising over the azure water, framed by a line of pastel houses. Off-hours would find me walking the deserted beach and admiring the Victorian-era buildings, landscaped with elegant palm trees. I couldn't believe it was November and vowed to return one day during the high season.[8]

I was assigned to the active duty public affairs staff onboard for this sea-based exercise involving a handful of western European nations—France, Italy, and the Netherlands. We steamed from Gaeta to Naples, where the operation began, and then transited to Marseille (I know!), where I was a media escort for domestic and international press such as *Agenzia Giornalistica Italia* and *Agence France Presse*. My job was to accompany them, explain certain aspects of the exercise, and answer their questions or find answers for their questions.[9]

When we arrived in Marseille, we hosted a reception onboard for a delegation of city officials and ex-patriot Americans. I tried to converse in my rusty high school French, but was thrilled and relieved to meet my counterpart (a French navy PAO) who was as beautiful as that first female recruiter I met. Her superb English meant I no longer had to struggle to keep up the conversation. The next day, French government officials hosted us at a reception in Marseille's beautifully appointed and historic hall, at which they served champagne, of course, to toast our arrival as NATO allies.

---

8 When I last visited Gaeta, it was summer and even more beautiful than I remembered, but, alas, the Sixth Fleet had moved to Naples.

9 After I became an attorney, I looked at transferring from public affairs to the JAG corps (judge advocate general—or military lawyer) in the reserves. But I was more than halfway through my career, so I would not have been competitive with my peers. Plus, military lawyering seemed boring compared to the amazing movie-set like experiences I had as a PAO.

Upon returning from a particularly enjoyable weekend or a two-week assignment, I would have to admit to myself that real life isn't always as exciting and rewarding as doing work in the nation's vital interests and pursuing it with a rare kind of energy and eagerness.

Part Five: Tom and Joan

CHAPTER 21

Joan's Dream Job

~6~

THE RECEPTION AREA WAS NICELY furnished, and every office of this tenth floor department had a magnificent view of Beacon Hill and the Charles River beyond. *This wouldn't be a bad place to work.*

The offices of the state veterans' department (the agency) located at 100 Cambridge Street in Boston's Government Center had a prime downtown location. It was in close proximity to other state buildings for meetings and near the Downtown Crossing area, great for shopping!

I'd been seriously looking for a full-time and more stable job for several months in early 1996. My part-time assistant city solicitor's position, which I'd taken on three years earlier, wasn't paying enough. With Brian about to enter a local prep school, I needed the security and benefits of a full-time position to help pay the tuition.

I'd heard something about veterans' preference in hiring for state jobs, and I wanted to know if I qualified. The state's war records division, where I'd gone to collect my military discharge papers showing my active duty in 1980 and 1981, referred me to the veterans' offices next door to see if I qualified as a veteran for a state position.

A friendly gentleman in the reception area took one look at my military discharge papers and pronounced that I was a "veteran for purposes of state employment!" "Oh, that's great!" I said enthusiastically, resisting the urge to pirouette on the spot, which might have been a career breaker.

"Do you have any openings for attorneys?" I asked my new best friend.

"Well, I wouldn't know about that, but let me see if our general counsel is available. Hang on."

I waited, feeling hopeful that I would be working here, and confident about the legal skills I could bring to anything the agency would offer me.

A few minutes later, Jack ambled into the reception area with his hands in his pockets. We introduced ourselves and he invited me into his office. Stacks of files were on his desk and floor, rising like stalagmites. On his cluttered table, a huge glass ashtray, overflowing with cigarette butts, seemed to indicate the center of the room. I found a chair, Jack sat behind his desk and we had a good conversation.

He explained that the agency oversaw a public assistance program for needy veterans that was administered in every city and town throughout the state by local agents. These agents determined who was eligible based on income, and issued a monthly stipend to those who qualified. The agency audited and authorized the local payments and reimbursed the cities and towns for seventy-five percent of the stipend. If the veteran disagreed with the agent's decision to deny benefits, then he or she could appeal to the agency. The program had been around since the Civil War, and I had no idea that it even existed.[1]

"Most people don't." Jack said.

It was my turn to talk about my legal background, and after I'd finished, he leaned forward over his desk, pointed at one of the stalagmites, and said he could definitely use the help.

I glanced around his office again and nodded.

"See," he said, "those are appeal hearings we held months ago, but I've had no time to write the decisions."

As if convincing himself that a second attorney would be a great idea, he said he had a young son who could use more face time with his dad, and then he revealed that Commissioner Tom Hudner had wanted to do something meaningful for women veterans, but did not have the staff.

---

1 The public assistance program that had been started with private funds after the Civil War for returning veterans who were unable to work, for one reason or another, became a publically funded program when the legislature enacted Mass. General Laws, chapter 115.

"Soooo, maybe—" he started again. As Jack rambled on about the responsibilities of the position, my synapses were firing like mad. *God, I could do all of that!* This sounded like the very regular, full-time legal position I'd been looking for. And working side-by-side with veterans to help other veterans was definitely something I would enjoy.

And then it struck me: *Tom Hudner? Navy Captain Tom Hudner? The Medal of Honor recipient, Tom Hudner?* I'd met him doing protocol work for the navy in Boston in 1980! This interview was definitely moving in the right direction, and Jack seemed as pleased as I was.

"That's great!" Jack said, eyes dancing. He suggested that I write the commissioner, tell him about this meeting, and get an appointment with him.

When that day came, Jack joined us at the conference table and we talked about individuals in the navy whom we knew in common. The commissioner, a Naval Academy graduate and an impeccably dressed old-school gentleman with a courtly manner, was interested in my reserve assignments, and we talked about that, too.

Then he went off on a tangent, talking about how the governor's office never wanted to greet any ships, U.S. or foreign navies, when they made port calls to Boston.

"You know," the commissioner said, "the governor is a really good guy, and I don't know how many times I've called them and tried to persuade someone from their office to come out for ships' visits, but they always say they're too busy. It gets me so g-darned mad! I usually go myself, because someone should acknowledge their presence and pay them respect."

My heart sank. *This is not going well. I've been here twenty minutes, and there's been no discussion of a job. But how can I steer the conversation the right way without sounding too pushy?*

Jack must have been thinking along the same lines, because he interjected, saying that I'd come to discuss how my legal and navy skills could help the agency.

This did the trick. The commissioner was back on track, and after more discussion about my qualifications, I could sense he already considered me a strong candidate. He told me to be patient that it would take him a few months to get the position approved by the administration and posted.

I didn't want to appear impatient, but neither did I want to create the impression that I didn't care. I called the commissioner's office from time to time and stopped by to see him when I was in the neighborhood, especially when wearing my navy uniform.

It was around this time that I faced the greatest challenge in my reserve career: struggling to be promoted to full commander (O-5) rank. I'd been passed over for promotion *four* times. Not surprisingly, it was also around this time when I had the nightmare about the massive USS John F. Kennedy sailing out of the harbor, while I stood on the shore in civilian clothes shouting, throwing pebbles and trying to get someone's attention, as the stern faded away. No one even turned a head. I was left onshore, a not-so-veiled metaphor for feeling as if my career was beached.

I consulted with a fellow reservist and lawyer who referred me to a little known statute providing that women who had entered the navy when I did could still complete twenty years of service and achieve federal veteran's status, regardless of how many times they were passed over for O-5.

One of my mentors along the route to becoming a commander was the former dean of students at Boston University, Admiral Norm Johnson. As one of the first African-American flag officers, he too encountered difficulties in promotion. Later in his career, he developed cancer and had to fight to stay in the navy. His advice to me was, "the navy likes a fighter."

Whenever the reserve center personnel started making noises about people who were passed over having to resign their commissions, I quoted that statute and let them know I intended to try for promotion as long as I had breath in me; I wasn't giving up. This challenge had turned me into a fighter. I updated my record by chasing down some missing fitness reports. And that's also when I went to D.C. to talk with the navy commander who had actually been a recorder, but not a decision-maker, on my review board.

He told me there was nothing bad in my record, and I asked him the obvious question, "Why didn't I get promoted?" All he could say was that the PAO community is highly competitive and somewhat political.

He gave me a few tips on how to make my record shine and, with the zeal of the fighter I had now become, I followed this advice to the last detail. My struggle was worth it. In August 1996 I was promoted, and this time I did allow myself to do pirouettes—in the privacy of my own home. Not only did this promotion put me into the ranks of senior officers, it meant I would have a chance of further promotion to captain (O-6) rank. More importantly, I could now go out and buy a new uniform hat with that row of gold braided embroidery that I'd been coveting for a long time. Without mentioning my focus on a new hat, I immediately shared this great news with the commissioner, hoping it would help move my application along. Finally, in November 1996, I was hired.

Like any job, there were a few obstacles blocking success. One was a bully named Wally. Wally threatened me at a staff meeting, because I'd supported Jack's position that instead of cubicles, attorneys needed offices for privacy.

Wally passed me a note that read, "If you cross me, I will ### you," with a word scratched out. My eyes boggled. Somewhat shaken after the meeting, I showed the note to Jack. He was red-faced and furious, and with the note in hand he sought out Wally, stood two inches from him, and shouted, "Don't *ever* do that again!" They nearly came to blows, but Wally was a bully and, thus, a coward. He backed down.

Another downside was that Jack didn't get along well with the agency's operations people. He felt that they couldn't or wouldn't understand the law. They found him condescending and inflexible. Jack held his legal views very passionately. He would ask me to back him up with the operations people, explaining that they sometimes ordered agents to cut off public benefits from veterans without a fair hearing first. This was a violation of civil rights that would end up with the state being sued.[2] I felt loyal to him and would readily back him up, but I also had to get along with operations in order to be effective. Sometimes it felt like I walked a tightrope between two warring factions.

After sitting in with Jack on a number of appeal hearings, I began conducting them myself. I would read the veterans' files in advance and wonder, *how did they get into these messes? What systems had failed them? What could we*

---

2 The U.S. Supreme Court held that before public assistance benefits could be cut off, there had to be adequate notice and due process procedure, *Goldberg v. Kelly*, 397 U.S. 254 (1970).

do to get them back on their feet, at least temporarily, or could we refer them to another organization? Their stories were unique, but drug and alcohol addiction were a common thread. Whenever I could help the veterans, I did. Some had suffered physical disabilities. Some were mentally and emotionally damaged. Almost all had left family members, civilian jobs, and the comforts of home to live and fight in foreign and hostile environments. We should be forever grateful to them. The agency's mission of assisting those who have made sacrifices for the rest of us is a noble one.

The commissioner wanted the agency to pay more than lip service to women veterans. Military women were somewhat marginalized when they became veterans. Many, especially the World War II women, did not even know they were veterans, because it was only in 1948 that Congress recognized them as such.[3] They were unable to access their benefits in the same way men were, because they did not join veterans' organizations. They needed their own program to fully access the benefits they had earned, and I began championing women's issues.

In general, things were going well in both of my major work areas. While it was a headache to travel to Atlanta, Georgia, (my new reserve duty unit) once a month—especially in the winter—I had complete flexibility to take off early Friday afternoons and attend drills[4]. My reserve responsibilities increased dramatically when I became the XO of my new unit. As the number two person, my job was making the unit operate smoothly in accordance with the mission as envisioned by the CO.

One weekend, I actually became the CO for a day when the captain was delayed, unbeknownst to me. As I had to make it up on the spot, I called an all-hands meeting and asked folks to update where they were on their projects. It didn't take me long to realize I was better suited for the number two job—better to help the leader achieve his or her goals—than lead myself. This realization played into my decision not to compete for the rank of captain.

Unfortunately, just when things seemed to be sailing along, a major obstacle from an unforeseen source loomed on the horizon.

---

3 President Harry Truman signed the Women's Armed Services Integration Act into law on June 12, 1948, giving women the same federal veterans' benefits as men.

4 Of course, I had to make up the missed time, but at my own choosing.

CHAPTER 22

Tom's Chance to Serve Again

⎯⎯ɕ⎯⎯

A CIVILIAN JOB HELPING VETERANS had been foremost in my mind for some time. In the navy, I'd traveled to diverse places and lived for that adrenaline jolt every time my team completed a successful mission. All that was behind me now, but I'd also worked alongside the finest individuals I could ever know. Maybe I could recapture in my civilian life some of the joy of teamwork toward a common goal. What better way to continue my service than by helping those who'd made sacrifices for their country?

In early 1998, I contacted Tom Lyons, a Vietnam veteran who had become a leader in the Boston veterans' community.[1] He referred me to Tom Hudner, a fellow retired navy captain and Medal of Honor recipient, whom I knew, and who happened to be commissioner of the state veterans' agency. Tom seemed interested that I was looking for a suitable position on his staff, and suggested I consider the deputy commissioner's job that was available. A short time later, he called back to say that the position had been filled and that the director of administration and finance position was about to become available.

"Interested?" he asked

"Naturally!" I responded with enthusiasm, wondering why the number two job had been filled without my having had a chance to apply. Tom had a reputation for keeping promises, so I assumed that higher-up political considerations played a role.

---

1 Tom Lyons continues to advocate for veterans, and his reputation is both statewide and national.

"I know you'd be good in this position, Tom." His encouragement led me to believe that my prospects were good. He had studied my resume and, being a navy man, he knew that my assignments had given me the managerial experience and personnel and budgetary skills for the position. My legislative assignment at navy personnel had put me in a good position to work with the state legislature.

That summer, all the appropriate administrative procedures were completed and my candidacy for the job was approved by the governor's office. In August 1998, I accepted Tom's offer. I had never worked in state government and had no idea what to expect. I figured I'd just take it one day at a time, and focus on learning my job.[2]

In the navy, there was a definite hierarchy, and you knew where you stood in the chain of command. This was different. In state government the chain of command wasn't always followed, and the power structure could be difficult to discern. It was important to learn whom I could trust.[3] It took a while to learn.

Union employees had rights that military personnel lacked, and their grievances could tie up a lot of agency time and resources. Bad apples were difficult to eliminate, and, ironically, managers could be fired at will, despite a stellar record. More about this later. I felt welcomed as a member of the team. Overall, the staff was supportive and it was a pleasure being around my long-time friend Tom. We had weekly senior staff meetings during which Tom had a habit of leaning back in his chair and balancing on two legs. The day he almost went over, we all vowed that next time, one of us would spot him. There were disagreements and although some staffers became frustrated with his deliberative management style, he was beloved.

---

2 Among my responsibilities were overseeing the budget, human resources, and public relations. I had to get up to speed on state and federal veterans' programs. Besides public assistance, we offered annuities for the disabled, and educational and employment benefits. Not to mention the state's two veterans' cemeteries and grants to non-profit veterans' shelters I had to manage.

3 Navy people are moved to new assignments every two to three years to enhance their experiences, but also to avoid grudges, personal alliances, and petty jealousies that arise when people become entrenched in their jobs and there's little upward mobility.

I had a favorable impression of the general counsel, Jack, who was actually responsible for providing the impetus for expanding the state's definition of veteran to include those who had only served during peacetime.[4] Once the bill was enacted, the new definition opened the door to all who'd served honorably to receive benefits.

As I got to know Jack better, I could see that his temper made him difficult to deal with. And some of his radical ideas to help veterans placed too much demand on our staff resources. As much as I wanted to encourage his creative legal thinking, I had to temper his well-meaning impulses.

On the other hand, our associate general counsel, Joan O'Connor, was quiet and reserved and seemed better organized. Initially, because I spent more time working with Jack and because my work experience in the navy with women was sparse, I felt uncomfortable around Joan. Small talk? I might have made an effort to know her that way, but I was preoccupied with learning my job and adjusting to work life in a state agency.

Tom had told me that Joan was in the naval reserve, but frankly my overall impression of naval reservists was not too favorable. As for those who were public affairs officers? Well, no one outside their own community really knew what they did.

Joan and I worked together for the first time when she was trying to find the keynote woman speaker for the annual Veterans' Day ceremony at the State House.[5] And even without knowing her, I could sense her dedication to the women veterans' program. From my days at navy personnel, I understood how service women were side-lined.

Around this time, some of the state's veterans' agents had generated a media storm over the appointment of a woman agent who was technically not a veteran, under Massachusetts law, at the time because she'd served during

---

4 Jack argued that the distinction between peacetime veterans (those not eligible for benefits) and wartime veterans (those who were eligible for benefits) was arbitrary. A service member could serve in a safe zone during a war and *vice versa*. I agreed with Jack that the distinction was without merit, and it didn't fit with my sense of fairness and inclusiveness. Jack was influential in ultimately helping us pass the Peacetime Bill.

5 I suggested we invite Admiral Pat Tracey. I'd served with her in D.C. and admired her leadership that successfully inspired her team to excellence. Joan was enthusiastic about this because Pat was the highest-ranking woman in the navy at the time, and a role model.

peacetime.[6] It didn't matter that her Air Force occupation was guarding missile silos. The agents' association accused the commissioner of bending the law to have her appointed, which was not true. She was forced to resign, but was reinstated when the law was changed.

The association's leadership circulated rumors that Tom didn't deserve the Medal. They said he crash landed his plane in Korea because he was a poor pilot, not a hero for rescuing his wing mate. I would have my own challenges with the association too, as it turned out.

---

6 The Massachusetts Veterans' Services Agents' Association represented the veterans' agents in the cities and towns and worked to protect their jobs. It also lobbied the legislature when favorable veterans' bills were under consideration and provided some training for new agents.

CHAPTER 23

They Meet-Joan's View

⤚

I ENTERED A DARK PERIOD in my life in the spring of 1998 with persistent back problems resulting in severe, sciatic pain. The pain would be light in the morning but by noon, it was so bad, that I couldn't sit or stand. For five months, while struggling to work and perform my navy drills, I saw specialists. I did physical therapy. I took anti-inflammatories and was given a cortisone shot. I'd always enjoyed running along the river or diving to return a tennis ball. Staying in shape had been a joy, but now even walking was difficult. With every step I was haunted by the image of my mother's withered legs after she was confined to bed with back pain. Finally, the only remaining course for me was surgery to decompress the nerve root.

I was frantic at work, trying not to let on how much pain I was in, afraid of losing my job. Jack was extremely kind and understanding and allowed me to work from home when I had to. The thought of having to leave the reserves unnerved me. I had only a couple years left to make twenty, and that would entitle me to a retirement pension and practically free healthcare in the veterans' system.

At that very moment, big personnel changes shifted like tectonic plates under my feet at the agency. Tom Kelley, another retired navy captain and Medal of Honor recipient, had reported aboard as the new director of administration and finance. According to the rumor mill, Commissioner Hudner had brought him on to evaluate his potential as his successor. The commissioner hadn't yet announced his retirement, but we all knew that it was just a matter of time.

I was in the midst of the worst back pain and working only half days in the office when I spoke to Tom for the first time. Surgery was still in my future. I worried that my physical state might impact Tom's impression of me.

"Hi, Captain Kelley," I said brightly as I entered his office. "I'm Joan O'Connor, the associate general counsel."

"Nice to meet you," he responded, as he stood up to shake my extended hand. His face was blank. I could tell something was wrong with his right eye. The right side of his face was less expressive, contributing to his impassive look.

"We share an interest in the navy," I said, plowing ahead and telling him about my Uncle Matt graduating from the Naval Academy and serving in the Korean War.

"Oh, really?"

I paused, giving him the chance to join in. I told him about discovering the naval reserve and then pursuing my law degree, my commission, and my first assignment.

Nothing.

I plunged into conversation about a two-week reserve duty during which I was assigned to the public affairs office of the Naval Support Activity in Manama, Bahrain. I went on about how exotic and scary it was to be working in the Middle East and having our quarters guarded by armed locals—still nothing. His expression was inscrutable.

Name recognition might spark a response.

I mentioned certain public affairs officers I figured he might know—

Hello! His expression was still inscrutable.

The sound of my own voice was beginning to tire me and Tom was making me self-conscious. For all I could tell, he might have decided that I was a raving lunatic. I walked away with absolutely no clue of what kind of impression I had made on my prospective boss.

I was feeling vulnerable because of my back. I also worried that if Tom were insecure, he might view my loyalty to Commissioner Hudner as a threat. I decided then and there to make it my mission to demonstrate to Tom that I could do my job well, and that I would be loyal to him when he became commissioner. The problem was that I had very little interaction with Tom, because Jack was the lead lawyer.

A month after the surgery, I returned to work still in pain, worried and depressed. It would be another several months before I would fully regain my stamina and return to work full-time. Physically and emotionally, I had fallen into a black hole. David was worried about me, as were my friends. With their encouragement, I sought professional help and relief in the use of anti-depressants.

During that challenging period I re-read *Learned Optimism*—a book I strongly recommend that I first read for inspiration while fighting for my reserve promotion and looking for my dream job.[1]

Jack had his eye on the deputy commissioner's position and he wanted me to replace him as general counsel when the deputy retired, which was rumored to be soon. I thanked him for the offer, adding that I wasn't sure I wanted the job. I liked doing the appeal hearings and especially enjoyed the women's project.

"I won't give up working with the women veterans, even if they hire an associate for me."

"Think about it, will you?" said Jack.

I was grateful for his confidence in my abilities. However, as time went on, I became less convinced that Jack was ready for the deputy's job. I saw how his disorganization resulted in missed deadlines and incomplete work.

My mother passed away a few months later in February 1999. After failing rapidly from Parkinson's, she was admitted to the hospital, barely conscious. Within a day or so of my telling her that she'd been a good mother, she passed away. And she had been a good mother under the circumstances. She did the best she could with my brother, and he'd taken care of her almost until the end. When she died, he started to unravel.

---

1 *Learned Optimism* by Martin Seligman uses empirical data to support its thesis that even those who are born as pessimists can turn into optimists, with practice.

Tom, Jack, and another gentleman from work, Frank, came to the wake. Respectful, yet, purposely cheerful, the trio hit the perfect balance. I was touched that they came at the end of the workday, on their own time. I wanted so much to work as well with Tom as I had with Commissioner Hudner. Maybe this unexpected gesture was a sign?

Initially, I wasn't happy with the office move to a lower rent industrial area of Boston, but it was necessary due to budget constraints and asbestos throughout the building. It was the winter of 1999, not the best time of year to move. We lost our breathtaking views of Beacon Hill and the river and said goodbye to lunch-hour shopping downtown. But the new location slowly began to declare its advantages, from the mouthwatering Italian restaurants and pastry shops of the North End to St. Leonard's, the Franciscan church, where I would sometimes go to pray at lunchtime. The key advantage turned out to be our proximity to a branch of the great Boston Public Library.

Knowing that Tom was an avid reader who frequented that branch, I began reading more myself. Office politics had taught me that it was good to mirror the interests of your boss, whenever it seemed natural. My son needed less of my time and reading was a good pastime.

I started leaving my library books in a conspicuous place in my office so that if Tom popped in, he would see serious works by local authors like Roland Merullo and Richard Russo on display. Maybe this would spark a relaxed conversation?

CHAPTER 24

Tom's First Challenges

~~~

TRANSITIONS AND I WERE BEST buds, so I wasn't unnerved when, early in 1999, Tom Hudner called me into his spacious office. He was surrounded by plaques and other memorabilia of his service, and there was a faint tobacco aroma. He indulged in a pipe at day's end, as this was still in the days when you could smoke in your office.

"Have a seat," he gestured to the chair nearest him.

He explained that he was, indeed, thinking of retirement. He wanted to leave the agency in good hands, and would I be interested in his position?

I was stunned. I had only been there for six months and had barely learned my job, let alone had time to consider my next career move.

I told him I'd be delighted. He thought that was a good answer.

"Good, I was hoping you'd say that. I'll start the wheels in motion." His next step was to recommend me to Governor Paul Cellucci.[1]

Although I was fully qualified to lead the agency, I had no political connections, and this worried me until I remembered that Tom, an ardent Republican, had originally been appointed by a Democratic governor, which goes to show that sometimes qualifications trump political connections. I knew virtually nothing about Massachusetts politics. I had never even voted in the state, because I left for the navy when I was twenty-one. Since I now

---

1 The late Paul Cellucci was governor of Massachusetts from 1997 to 2001, when President George W. Bush appointed him as U.S. ambassador to Canada.

lived in South Boston, I contacted my congressman, Joe Moakley, and asked him to make a call to the governor on my behalf. He did.[2]

Tom arranged my meeting with the governor, which was actually my second meeting with him, but my very first job interview since I had been a teenager.[3] I wasn't used to applying for jobs, or requesting interviews; the navy always told me where to go. So I decided to just be myself. If that had been good enough for the navy, well then—

Lieutenant Governor Jane Swift joined the governor, and they had obviously done their homework. Not only were they familiar with my background, they asked me pointed questions about how I would meet the agency's challenges. I guess my answers struck a chord because even before the interview ended, the governor shook my hand and welcomed me to his team.

The navy had prepared me well for change. This promotion to commissioner of the agency was just another such assignment, one that I knew I could handle very well.

There were a half-million veterans and their families living in the state when I took over in 1999, but most civilians weren't thinking about veterans then. The agency had been operating the same programs for a generation since the end of the Vietnam War. The short conflicts that followed in Panama, Grenada, Lebanon, and even the Persian Gulf War in 1991 had not produced many new veterans.[4] In a sense, despite an expansion of the mission to include annuities, educational benefits, and tax abatements, I had inherited an agency without an evolving mission and without a lot of visibility. But on 9/11, all of that would change. And I would face the towering challenges of addressing the unique needs of a new generation of veterans.

Stepping back a bit, I knew that my great-grandfather had died in the Civil War in 1864. But what I didn't realize before taking this job was that

2 Congressman John Joseph Moakley (deceased) was a World War II navy veteran and served as the U.S. Representative from South Boston from 1973 to 2001.

3 I had met the governor once at a navy social event when I intercepted him on his way to the men's room to introduce myself and tell him how privileged I felt in helping the administration serve veterans.

4 Vietnam veterans mainly comprised the agency's public assistance clients. Few new veterans were being added to the rolls because the U.S. had not been engaged in a significant war since Vietnam. More significantly, Congress ended the draft in 1972.

his widow and son, my grandfather, survived on this very program. The Civil War produced the same veterans' assistance program I administered. Its purpose—then as now—is to aid those veterans and their surviving dependents who have no other means of support. During the Civil War there were limited federal veterans' benefits and no Social Security or other government-provided help for disabled veterans or for their surviving dependents. Instead the state provided assistance.[5]

It was business as usual in a pre-9/11 environment, but I sought to expand our scope and level of services. The agents and the department had traditionally focused on the public assistance benefits. In my tenure, we refocused our efforts toward greater access to federal disability compensation and pensions. In this way we'd shift some of the financial burden from the Commonwealth to the federal government. For this initiative, I needed the support, backing, and active participation of my staff, the local veterans' agents, and the agents' association.[6] The veterans they served deserved their best efforts, and my team set out to help them achieve this.

Another of my goals was to improve outreach to veterans themselves, advising them of the benefits that their service had earned them. Again, I needed the support of the veterans' agents who were the tip of the spear when it came to outreach.[7] They were well-connected within their communities and had various networks to locate needy veterans.

The majority of agents were conscientious and dedicated. In my efforts to build a good relationship with all of them, including the association's leadership, one of my first steps was to re-brand the veterans' agents, calling them

---

5 The U.S. Veterans' Administration was not established until 1930, and Social Security for the disabled and elderly did not come along until 1935.

6 By and large, the agents needed to become fluent in the details of federal programs. Some agents were already astute and creative in finding federal benefits. My staff set out to improve their knowledge and commitment. We instituted training programs and gave them the informational tools they needed to access them. Since the agents worked for the cities and not for me, I couldn't mandate their attendance.

7 I encouraged the agents to submit frequent local news articles and to appear on local access TV shows. Many times I went on local shows myself with the city agents, and we held town meetings state-wide to get the word out about the whole panoply of benefits.

"veterans' services officers." This would emphasize the all-inclusive services they were expected to provide and accord them additional prestige as officers.

I began regular meetings with the association's leadership, but after a two-month honeymoon period, Paul, the association's president, began attacking the agency. His most vigorous attacks were usually saved for the biggest audience of agents. And he became increasingly skilled at humiliating the agency in a public setting, when I wasn't present. It would have been more productive and reasonable to bring up contentious issues at our regular leadership meetings, but that was not the way Paul operated. I heard that he had referred to me as the "medal boy" and accused me of "hiding" behind my medal.

As bad as our relationship with the association was during those early days, at least they weren't writing the governor for my job—yet. We continued to operate without missing a beat. We expanded the mission while improving outreach. My spirits were as high as the day I took the USS Lang out of San Diego and that translated into good morale among my staff.

CHAPTER 25
Joan's Bad Vibes

—c—

TOM MADE IT UNCOMFORTABLE FOR me to be in his office longer than two minutes. He would get up from his desk and usher me to the door while I was still talking. The fact that he'd shoot the breeze about anything with others, both male and female, heightened my sense of insecurity. I learned to edit myself, but it was still frustrating and worrisome. *After all, If I can't Interact with my boss, how can I develop a good relationship with him?* Even though Jack was my direct supervisor, it was smart to have buy-in from the boss in case you needed him in your corner farther down the road.

My progress was slow. Tom's dealings with legal were mainly with Jack, and I had little direct interaction with him. So I created reasons to see him regarding the women's project. One day, when Jack was out of the office, a legal issue arose that couldn't wait. I was anxious to give Tom my two-minute summary, but it didn't come out right.

"Excuse me, Tom. If you have just a minute—I just need to let you know that one of the towns we've had trouble with has cut off benefits to a veteran—who's appealed to us. The city is supposed to continue paying until we—decide the case—but the veteran has gotten himself an attorney. And—if we can't come up with a solution pretty quickly, they're talking about suing us—"

"Well, what I am supposed to do about it?" came his curt reply.

"Well, I don't know—I mean—I haven't given it much thought. Jack's not here today, and—I just thought you'd want to know—"

"Look, we're paying you an awful lot of money to work here. I would hope you could figure this out for yourself or at least give me a set of options and recommendations!"

I was devastated, but determined not to cry in front of him. Instead, I headed for the door. The tears waited until I closed my office door, and then spilled down my cheeks. But to my surprise, while I was in mid-sob, Tom came in and apologized.

Although pleased that he had made this effort, I was embarrassed that he caught me in an emotional state, indecisive and lacking assertiveness. I wanted to be like those squared-away commanders who had reported to him when he was on active duty, who would coolly analyze a situation and present a set of options.

It wasn't that I had a bad relationship with him or that we butted heads on issues, we simply had no relationship. I was stumped by how to relate to him. No, I didn't think he was a chauvinist. I knew he had daughters whom he appeared to treat well. I thought he hadn't much experience working with women, but I knew he'd worked with women later in his career. Maybe he was trying to figure me out? Maybe he was protecting himself from something I represented?

Since Maria, our director of administration and finance, seemed to have a better handle on how to deal with Tom, I asked her to share her secret. She told me she started dropping by his office over her morning coffee. An informal chat would usually lead him to talk about his priorities from which she'd take her direction for the day. She suggested I continue interacting with him a few times a week on women's issues or hearings, and I did. She even offered to tell me what kind of mood he was in before I entered his office on any given day. It was like having my own personal meteorologist to forecast Tom's weather.

Around that time, I was reading the *Rascal King*, the story of former governor and Boston mayor James Michael Curley. He grew up in South Boston, home to mostly poor Irish immigrants, when he lived there in the late 1800s.[1]

---

1 The *Rascal King: The Life and Times of James Michael Curley* by Jack Beatty, Perseus Books, 1992. Curley was a powerful Boston Irish politician who went to jail for felonious fraud. Some viewed him as a Robin Hood character who stole from the rich to give to the poor.

As a child, Curley sold newspapers before school to help support his family, because his father had died prematurely in a work accident. When Curley's shoes wore out, he outfitted them with newspapers to keep his feet warm and dry. Tom was living in South Boston, and I knew that he'd transferred to the agency to "come home," so I assumed he also was from a rough-and-tumble childhood. I hoped the book would give me some insight.

One day Tom dropped by my office and saw the book on my desk.

"What are you reading that for?" he smiled as he picked it up and flipped through a few pages.

"Well, I'm interested in that period of Boston politics, and I know you're from South Boston so I thought I'd learn more about the area."

"What, you think I grew up in Southie?"

"Yeah, didn't you?"

"No, I grew up in West Roxbury."

"Oh, sorry!"

He'd grown up in a leafy area of Boston, similar to my old neighborhood. Why couldn't we relate better to each other? With Maria's advice in mind, I spent more time talking comfortably to Tom about my women's project than about legal issues. I acted more decisively and assertively, using buzzwords and acronyms like "ETA" in place of "estimated time of arrival" and "OBE" rather than "overtaken by events." And wouldn't you know, after a while Tom was no longer abruptly ushering me out of his office in mid-sentence. In fact, at times, he seemed genuinely interested in what I had to say.

In a surprise move, although others saw it coming, Tom fired his deputy commissioner, for cause. I had never worked in an office before where someone was actually fired. To save face for the man, Tom called it a voluntary resignation. Apparently the deputy had pressured his subordinates into helping him campaign for political office while on the job. Tom's decisive action sent a clear message throughout the agency that he expected people to measure up. Although my relationship with him was improving, *Was I doing enough to keep on his good side?*

Around that time, Dick, our new director of operations, reported aboard. He was an attorney and retired from the National Guard. Soon, it was clear that Dick and Jack were vying for the deputy's position. Tom must have thought that it was more trouble than it was worth, because he put out the word that he was going to leave it vacant for a while. Better to keep the two potential competitors for your own job further away as rivals between themselves. I watched Tom's maneuvers, always hoping to gain understanding. I concluded that he was politically astute.

On the personal side in 2000, I worried about Brian. As a high school senior, he was driving the family car and staying out late on weeknights, with little notice as to where he was going, who he was going with and when he was coming home. All I got were monosyllabic answers, and these nightly escapades were leaving me sleep deprived. But my real anxiety came with his apparent indifference towards getting his college applications done on time. He'd always been an excellent student.

During a car ride to a training session with Tom and a co-worker, I brought up the subject of parenting. I knew Tom's daughters were older than Brian, and I'd heard that he'd experienced challenges.

"Is this normal, and when do they outgrow it?" I asked.

Tom replied, "Well, be patient with him and keep the lines of communication open. Don't alienate him and make sure he knows that you love him, even if his behavior isn't always what you'd like it to be."

Tom's words reassured me that Brian would be okay, and I felt, for the first time, that Tom and I had bonded over something important. It wasn't just books or neighborhoods.

It had taken a year and a half, but things between us were improving. I convinced him to come to our annual women's workshop. Even though I had a superb helper, Heidi, I put many hours myself into planning and coordinating, and I wanted him to see what we'd done.

The culmination of the event was a luncheon with a special guest speaker, the first woman commandant of Boston's coast guard district and a helicopter pilot.[2] Tom agreed to introduce her. I knew he would be uncomfortable in this crowd of mostly women, as well as with public speaking. But I watched

---

2 Vivien Crea later became the first woman to hold the second highest position in the U.S. Coast Guard.

and saw him pleasantly surprised to find a few males he knew. He relaxed as he chatted during lunch with the admiral and comfortably rose to introduce her.[3] The next day he congratulated me for an effort well done, and I floated for a while like a dust mote in a sunbeam. *Finally, he appreciates my work!*

Things started well enough between Dick and me. But when insecurity overwhelmed him, he tried to make other people look bad, hoping to make himself appear better.

I'd been conducting hearings concerning a veteran who failed to report that he was collecting federal and state benefits at the same time. His testimony that he thought he was entitled to both wasn't credible since he was a former veterans' agent himself and should have known better. He was working toward a master's using his federal benefits. He drove a newish car and lived in an upscale community. Yet, he maintained that he was too impaired to work.

Midway through the hearing, Dick asked for a recess and left the room to have a conversation with the veterans' agent. When the hearing resumed, Dick proposed a settlement that would have mistakenly rewarded the veteran. I was aghast at Dick's selling out the department and the taxpayers. I ordered the hearing continued to another day, so I could brief Tom on this absurd turn of events. I wasn't sure what Dick's motive was, and the mutually respectful relationship I'd hoped for was becoming an obstacle in the way of performing my job. Tom supported my decision to deny benefits. *Phew!*

When our executive office mandated sexual harassment prevention training, Jack ignored the requirement. This alarmed Maria, who, as our head of human resources, was responsible for training. She asked me for help. I was familiar with this area because the navy had been in the news for sexual harassment of women and the navy was now expert in its prevention.

Maria and I met ahead of time and developed a few lighthearted skits on the same themes as the handout material. We enlisted the help of a co-worker to play the harasser, a courtly man, who'd be the last person to sexually harass anyone, which added to the humor. Maria's gift for comedy brought out the best in me, and we delivered our difficult message in a palatable way, but Jack

---

3 Later Tom would develop into a fine extemporaneous speaker.

and Dick were furious and complained to Tom. They said the training was inadequate and incorrect. He ignored them.

My worst dealing with Dick was when we revised our regulations. I coordinated with Dick's team, and knowing how tedious the task would be, I tried to make it entertaining. One of our group was a master of mimicry. I encouraged her to do impersonations of office personalities. She made us so hysterical with laughter that we had to take time to settle down, that is, until Tom began sitting in to see how much progress we were making and we decided to cancel the impersonations.

In the end, I gave Dick a set of professional revisions shortly before I was to leave for my vacation, with a mutual promise to discuss when I got back. When I returned, there was a note from Tom asking me to see him. Dick had gone to Tom behind my back with many criticisms and objections. Tom, in a slightly irritated state, called us to a meeting. He couldn't understand why he had to referee two well-paid professionals who couldn't seem to resolve their differences. I answered each of Dick's objections, point by point, and it didn't take Tom long to side with me. When he asked Dick why he couldn't have talked to me before reporting his criticisms, Dick had no answer.

From this single event, I began to feel that Tom valued and appreciated my legal work as much as my women's work.

CHAPTER 26

Tom's House of Cards

―᷉―

Demanding my deputy's resignation had not come easy. I hated the task of having to fire anyone, even in the navy. Of course, the deputy chose to resign, and I stuck to my word by keeping the reasons confidential. But within a day, he spread gossip that I'd fired him for backing a Democratic candidate against the Republican governor. *That's putting a creative spin on it!* I chuckled to myself. Although it may have worked outside the office, I don't think many of the staff believed his story. Petty complaints stopped for a while. People seemed to work more efficiently, and I earned the respect of those who may have doubted my strength as a leader. Getting rid of a bad apple always worked out for the good of the team, lest one person ruin it for the others.

Dick had deployed to the Middle East during the Gulf War and, although I respected his service, I found him a bit overbearing. In the beginning he seemed to be doing a good job, but as I learned more about Dick, I questioned his fitness for leading the operations' department.

I was already aware of his questionable judgment regarding a series of hearings about a veteran who was double dipping. Dick had an irritating tendency to deny veterans their benefits, whenever possible. This was totally contrary to my view that veterans should be aided whenever possible. He could be harsh on his staff. And he had numerous health issues that resulted in an unusually high number of absences. In November 2003, after an early retirement program was introduced, I decided it was time to move Dick out of the agency, and I did.

Jack had a mercurial nature. He was cranky and argumentative, yet he was a soft-hearted champion of the underdog. He did a lot of good work and helped many individuals in need. But sometimes his passion for serving the underdog went too far—like the time he brought a lawsuit against the Commonwealth, his employer! I suspected he had an anti-authoritarian streak.[1] His recalcitrant nature meant that he disregarded department rules and office protocol. He would show up late, and not report his whereabouts. And sticking to priorities meant little to him.

He spent a lot of time at the attorney general's office, initially with my approval, successfully tracking down individuals who ran veterans' charities, but were enriching themselves while allegedly raising money for veterans. But he was frequently absent and his agency work suffered.

I knew I had to do something drastic to rein Jack in. Formal discipline would have almost certainly meant litigation. So the best solution for all was to get him out of the office. I felt I'd been as patient and understanding as possible, but his erratic behavior continued to alienate staff, disrupt work and embarrass the administration. He had to go. But when?

The answer to that question declared itself when Maria said she had to see me right away. Apparently Jack had left Joan an inappropriately hostile voicemail about her work that she forwarded to Maria. She told Maria that she hadn't minded covering for Jack in his absences, and that she enjoyed picking up some of the work he procrastinated in doing, but she didn't want to take the abuse. That was the last straw. Within a day, I transferred Jack to our other office across town. From that day Joan would report directly to me.

It was important to watch how we conducted ourselves outside state government, too. Since I instituted regular meetings with the agents' association leadership, I witnessed the outrageous statements their leader Paul made. Eventually these would trigger Jack to fly off the handle. Joan was usually silent when a shouting match would end the meeting shortly thereafter. The shouting upset anyone who'd witnessed it, and it disrupted our work flow, because I'd overhear staff discussing it all afternoon.

---

1 I received a phone call from the soldiers' home, another state agency, telling me that Jack had filed a lawsuit against the home on behalf of a resident, a conflict of interest.

At our next meeting, Paul began with a degree of civility but soon turned bombastic. Jack held his fire. I could see Joan shifting in her seat. I let Paul have the floor, and in a very short time, he turned from attacking the department to attacking me. From the corner of my eye, I saw Joan put her hand over her mouth.

I slouched back in my chair with my head bowed, arms folded against my chest, until Paul finished his rant. I had already decided to end the meeting when Paul stopped. The next thing I knew Joan was sitting forward on her chair, arms on the table, unleashing a verbal torrent. She was angry, and now Paul was silent.

"Paul, how dare you twist the facts that way? That's the most ridiculous, disingenuous version of what happened! You made that up on the spot because you couldn't be bothered to actually check the facts!"

With Paul paused in his bluster, I stood up announcing the meeting was over, and there'd be no more meetings until further notice.

Joan apologized to me in my office after the meeting. She was embarrassed.

"I can't believe I lost it," she said. "After all my advice to Jack about having a reasoned discussion and not reacting, I stooped to Paul's level. I'm so sorry, but I saw what he was doing to you, how helpless you looked and how he was really getting to you, and…"

"I was trying not to take the bait. That's all you can do in those situations. Clearly after he finished his attack, the meeting was over."

She paused for a second. "Oh, so you took the abuse on purpose?"

"Of course," I said. "I was so angry, I couldn't even speak. I knew if I said something at that point I was going to regret it, and it wouldn't have reflected well on the agency."

"But that was the worst bullying I've ever seen. Where did you find the willpower to resist responding in kind?"

"Well, I survived a rocket-propelled grenade attack in Vietnam, so I figured I could withstand a few personal remarks."

"Oh," she said leaving meekly. "That's a very good thing you did, then. I guess I swallowed the bait."

For a few seconds, I pondered Joan's strong emotional reaction while I was being attacked, and wondered why she felt she had to jump to my defense. *Maybe she was having an off day?* I turned back to our budget reports. We had to increase our appropriations.

As time went on, Joan demonstrated her competence in the legal arena. Her analytical and writing skills were strong. If she made a mistake, she'd quickly let me know about it and fix it.

I was especially impressed with her compassion for veterans who'd fallen on hard times. Usually she was able to sort out disagreements with the operations department about whether individual veterans should remain on benefits. On one occasion she came to me and argued that even though a veteran, rendered unemployable by alcohol addiction, had been on benefits for a long while, we should keep him on. She saw a fragile man, whose unfortunate childhood led to his dropping out of school and being drafted. He was further damaged by the horrors of duty in Vietnam. Upon discharge he had multiple issues that prevented him from holding steady jobs. All the support systems had failed him. He had lost his family, housing, and education. Chapter 115 had become his last hope. Of course I supported her position. It was directly in line with my philosophy.

Joan seemed more relaxed around me and I was growing more comfortable around her. I made it a point to get to know her better, as I did with other staff. This had been my pattern in the navy. Not only is it easier to work with people you understand, but it also makes conditions more pleasant. And happy people work better together.

CHAPTER 27

Joan's Good Vibes

~⟡~

I STILL CAN'T BELIEVE I got paid to do some of the things I did in the reserves. I flew on helicopters, including one actually landing on a moving ship. I had been at sea on an amphibious command and control ship, ridden a destroyer into dry dock, traveled in Humvees and trucks, and become an expert marksman.

In my unit, I was fortunate to work with those whose weekday jobs were as gifted journalists and editors at the *Boston Globe* and *Boston Herald*, along with the producer of a local network television show. They taught me a lot about their craft.

During my initial year and a half of active duty and the subsequent two-week yearly assignments, I worked with the very best line officers and enlisted personnel from all military branches. Their idea of teamwork was to foster a family relationship where each member has a special job, but depends upon the others for success.

I learned how to market and promote our news and events by being politely persistent, but not pushy—following up on every request until "no" came. Giving up was not an option. I learned to check and recheck my work. I learned that collaboration produced the best results.

Even mundane assignments, like making training videos for reservists and writing hometown news releases were opportunities to stretch my abilities and sharpen my skills. I was challenged with doing my best every time I put on the uniform, and I was working for an organization I loved.

By far my NATO assignments were the best because they represented the ultimate in teamwork: international cooperation. My more adventuresome two-week duties included service in Bodo, Norway, during a naval exercise in the North Atlantic in which I helped run the media center 24/7, as we cranked out press releases and photos, answered calls for more information, and fielded journalists into the operations.

I served on the Navy News Desk at the Pentagon during Desert Storm for two weeks. I was there at the lull between massing our troops in Kuwait and our invasion of Iraq. I volunteered for mobilization when I could have backfilled in the U.S. for an active duty person sent overseas, but I wasn't recalled. And I've told you about training duty in Europe, Camp Lejeune, and Bahrain.

My last drill weekend in the naval reserve was by accident. I needed twenty years' service. Because I'd been commissioned in October 1979, I'd expected to retire in November of 1999. But when I checked with my reserve center folks, they pointed out that I actually had enough points to retire after my August drills that year. I hadn't given much thought to a date, but on the way home that warm Sunday I thought, *Gee, I could retire today. What's the point of additional drills, since I've made my goal? Why prolong this cutting of the cord? Why not move on to the next phase of my life now?*

Neither David nor Brian was around when I arrived home. Only the dog, Elizabeth, was there to greet me. Still in my summer white uniform, I took off my hat and put down my bag. Then I sat on the living room couch and began sobbing. Elizabeth rose from the floor where she'd been resting, came over to me and licked all of the tears off my face. I had never seen this depth of empathy from the poor dumb animal, but she'd never seen me in such an emotional state either. The dog's comfort had the opposite effect, making me cry harder. It had been a joy and an honor to serve my country, but now it was over.

David wanted me to have some type of ceremony to celebrate my retirement. Unsure how I wanted to mark the event, I didn't. Maybe I thought that by not observing it, I could pretend it hadn't happened. Then Karen, my office colleague and a naval reservist herself, came up with the idea of having my retirement at work during lunch time. We would invite my family and the whole office to share in the event. Karen and I would wear our summer white uniforms. She would explain the rich tradition of the ceremony as it was happening. And I would ask Tom to be the principal speaker.

The day of the event, my co-workers turned our hearing room into a ceremonial venue with additional chairs, posters and plants from their offices. At one point, I noticed that Tom had brought his model of the "Lone Sailor," which was normally on his desk. As I watched the seriousness of purpose with which he placed the statue onto the dais, I was touched. Tom's own navy retirement had been at the real Navy Memorial in Washington, of which I knew he was fond.

I explained to the assembled group how I came to be in the naval reserve. I went through the family history of my Uncle Matt's career, my experiences in East Berlin, and finally what the navy did for me.

I told the audience how the navy helped me develop a type of discipline I lacked. Just the basics of being sure my uniforms were ready and that I was on time (early) for drills influenced me. I stayed in shape because of the semi-annual physical fitness test and to be sure my uniforms fit.[1] The navy instilled some of a fighter's mentality in me. Whenever I felt beaten down, I remembered I was a naval officer, a senior one at that. I had achieved rank and others had confidence in me, so why didn't I? That reminder would cause me to hold my head a little higher.

But, more importantly, the navy had given me a lens through which to view the world that complemented and enhanced my legal career. In both, I had taken an oath to support the Constitution of the United States. As an attorney, I researched and interpreted the law. As a naval officer, I trained for what happened when the rule of law no longer functioned to hold society together and when diplomacy and negotiations fell apart. War is like litigation. It is what happens when the legal and diplomatic constructs break down and fail. Both are risky and unpredictable with unforeseen human costs, and

---

1 I still have most of my uniforms in the unlikely chance I get called off the retired list to active duty. Mostly it's because I can't bear to part with them, and the last time I wore my dress uniform was to Uncle Matt's funeral.

often no clear exit strategy. So much in the way of human treasure, monetary resources, and time are used that both sides eventually wonder if it was worth it. In war and litigation, compromise is important to avoid complete devastation, but always hard to achieve.

Working with people of different nations, I developed an understanding of how the rest of the world viewed the United States, in its quest for world stability by its deployment of far-flung military forces. I learned that the Europeans found the nuclear arms race between the U.S. and the USSR terrifying. After all, they were perfectly situated between the two.

And if I had to choose the single best element of my service, it was serving as a team with people of varying backgrounds, people whom I never would have otherwise met. I became acquainted with those from combat veterans to women commanders—those from outside New England and from all economic and ethnic origins. I served with those who could build a forward deployed base almost overnight, and those trained in diplomacy and international relations. With a couple of exceptions, the people I met were ones with whom "I'd share a foxhole," as the saying goes: those to whom you'd trust your life.

Next, Tom spoke.

"Joan's commitment to the agency's mission of serving veterans shows through her careful sifting, weighing of the facts, and written decisions."

He alluded to an earlier case I'd been to see him about.

"All of the support systems had failed him. He had lost his family, housing, jobs, and education. Chapter 115 assistance had become his last hope. Even though this man had been on benefits for a while, partly because of his addiction, Joan argued that an exception should be made in this case. Those who are fighting such demons are not willfully unemployed, but fighting a disease, from which recovery is marked by many false starts. I agreed with her. Part of our mission is to be patient with these individuals while they struggle to overcome substance dependence. We look for ways to help the veteran whenever we can."

Wow! Tom made the effort to tailor-make his remarks about me, personalizing them to my understanding and compassion for veterans. He didn't regurgitate the usual platitudes about service and patriotism, or even talk about his own career. I had been expecting something more generic.

Tom's public acknowledgment of me put wind in my sails that would take me in a new direction towards independence. I felt like I did that beach day as a child, when I let go of the sand under my feet, moved my arms and kicked to swim.

CHAPTER 28

Tom's Team Saves the Agency

~~⸏~~

WHEN MITT ROMNEY WAS ELECTED governor of Massachusetts in November 2002, I wrote to congratulate him and offered to continue serving on his team. Reappointment with a new governor wasn't automatic. I hadn't been involved in his campaign, but others had, and now they were aggressively lobbying for my job.

A few weeks earlier, one of the governor's inaugural team members had asked me to round up a group of veterans to attend the state house inaugural ceremony. I worked hard over the Christmas holidays, contacting fifty influential veterans from all over the state and inviting them to the January ceremony on the new governor's behalf, all the while keeping Romney's people informed.

No sooner had we gathered in a state house room, waiting to be called upstairs to the Hall of Flags where the inauguration would take place, when another Romney aide told me there had been a change of plan. Only three veterans would be allowed to attend the swearing-in ceremony, and they were already seated inside with Romney. What's more, I was not invited. Stunned and embarrassed, I had to tell the fifty veterans that they'd also been uninvited. I was also furious. After I broke the news to them, I left and returned to my office so hot with anger that I could barely speak.

Joan, who'd been watching at the state house with a couple of other staffers, came into my office as I hung my coat on the rack and flung my briefcase onto the table.

"What happened at the state house today?" she asked. "I saw you get upset with someone and then you were gone."

"I was asked to leave."

"What? By whom?"

"The people organizing the receiving line. They told me I wasn't on the list, and that I had to go. But that's when I saw what's-his-name there, who's been lobbying for my job, and they didn't ask him to leave. I'm seriously concerned about my job," I said, sitting at my desk.

Joan tried to assure me that it was just an oversight by an inaugural staff volunteer who was not the governor's permanent staff, and that the governor was probably too preoccupied with his transition to even know who was invited.

"Even in the unlikely event that Romney didn't want you at his inauguration," she said, "it doesn't mean he doesn't want you on his team. You can't assume the worst!"

Joan's words helped, and I was touched by her attempt to boost my spirits. She was trying to protect her boss, as she would have done for a superior in the navy.

By then the Global War on Terror had resulted in the deaths of 121 Massachusetts service men and women, all of whose funerals I tried to attend. Their families needed other forms of state assistance, and the veterans returning from this war had a unique set of needs. My new priorities became greater outreach to these veterans and more professional training of the veterans' agents. We were so well positioned to take on these new veterans' challenges that the department became a model for other states. We were leading other states with a proactive team that identified, reached out to, and met the unique needs (including suicide prevention) of veterans returning from war in the twenty-first century.[1] Our new thrust put the agency into the spotlight, and I wanted to stay on and keep the momentum going.

---

1 We'd made the whole array of local, state, and federal benefits known to this new cadre of veterans and their families. As time went on, I also saw the need for and helped create new benefits. I was concerned about Guard and Reserve members losing their civilian employment while away on deployment, even though there was federal law to protect them.

The road to re-appointment was not only challenging, it was rocky and treacherous. Agency heads had to offer their resignations and wait to see if they were reappointed by the new governor. I tried to stay apolitical in order to maintain the integrity of the agency. Old what's-his-name shot out any rumor that came to mind: I was an alcoholic, citing an episode where I had been observed stumbling out of a local bar at ten in the morning. Another rumor was that I was closely aligned with our then U.S. Senator John Kerry, a Democrat, who was running for president at the time. Allegedly, I had also been campaigning in Georgia on behalf of Democratic U.S. Senator Max Cleland's re-election campaign. All unproven, unjustifiable and, most importantly, one hundred percent false.

One evening, this same rumor-monger came to my home, unannounced, to tell me that the "White House was upset" with me. He said I was undermining President George W. Bush's administration and re-election prospects by working on behalf of John Kerry, and he offered to protect me from "White House reprisals." I seriously thought he had become mentally unhinged. Perhaps it was the stress of trying to get my job. Whatever it was, I had to ask him to leave my home.

Ultimately, Joan was right. My fears were unfounded. There was a groundswell of support for my re-appointment from Democratic and Republican state legislators, mayors, and veterans' organizations. My staff observed with amusement as a parade of characters visited me in my office, including a couple of casually dressed "Irish-looking" guys, one with a gun in a holster. They didn't even want to ask—about my off-duty police friends.

Two events pushed things in my favor and led to my re-appointment. The first related to Romney's plan to reorganize the state government. By the time he took office, we had still not experienced large numbers of veterans returning from the Global War on Terror. Not many people outside the veterans' community even knew the agency existed.

Romney's people proposed merging our agency with the elder affairs department. This merger plan had been buried with other provisions to consolidate certain key administrative functions such as human relations, public relations, and legal matters.

Fortunately, Joan flagged the hidden merger plan while reviewing the legislative proposal. The deadline for responding to the administration about the proposed legislation was fast approaching, but we moved even faster. I started calling my fellow veterans' advocates and friends in the legislature. The veterans' community did not want to see the agency's unique identity, which had existed for 140 years, buried with elder affairs. A betting man would have put his money on me, Joan, Maria and a few other key staff members losing our jobs.[2]

What followed was a highly orchestrated (not by me) letter and phone campaign to the governor and key legislators in support of the agency. Veterans' agents and individual members of various veterans' organizations such as the Veterans of Foreign Wars, American Legion, Disabled American Vets, Jewish War Veterans, and Vietnam Veterans of America all voiced their displeasure to the governor's office.[3] Several public hearings later, the administration had to accept that its merger idea had little merit. It also helped that the governor viewed veterans with great respect and as a constituency whose vote he could count on.

The second event leading to my reappointment involved the electric company servicing the veterans' shelter headed by what's-his-name. The agency funded part of the shelter's housing program and one day I received a call from a utility executive who revealed that the shelter was $100,000 in arrears. Astonishing! We'd been reimbursing the shelter for its electric bill every month for the past year. Apparently the shelter was using the money for something else, a case of mismanagement. I immediately warned the Romney administration of potential media fallout and, over the next few days, we worked out a repayment plan between the shelter and the utility.

The situation forced more interaction with the new administration, and as my regular contacts with them increased, I demonstrated the type of successful agency management and leadership that appealed to the Romney people. I had earned the administration's trust and confidence.

---

2 By this point I had made Maria my deputy. She was competent, especially in personnel issues, trustworthy, and loyal.

3 It was a highly orchestrated protest and moved so quickly because these organizations are made up of veterans, individuals used to operating in the military as teammates.

Instead of burying us with elders, in August 2003 Romney proposed that the agency be elevated to a secretariat, meaning the commissioner's position would also be elevated—to that of a secretary. The governor wasn't required to make this decision by statute, but he chose to make my position part of his cabinet. For veterans, this meant they now had direct access to the governor and his administration through me. The added visibility and increased stature of veterans in the Commonwealth made a world of difference in having their voices heard and, ultimately, in having their programs funded and implemented.

The agency had been reborn, and my position as its head was secure, but staff members still worried about losing their jobs because Romney's business reputation had been made by helping failing businesses to succeed partly by laying off employees. The question on a lot of state employees' minds then was—How much of this model is Romney planning to use in state government? There was talk of economies that would be made, including layoffs, in order to balance the budget. An early retirement incentive was offered that would move older and better paid workers out while replacing them with younger, lower paid ones. Either of these programs was enough to strike terror in the heart of any state worker.[4]

One state worker who worried about her position was Joan. Early in 2003 the governor's chief legal counsel scared all the lawyers by announcing there were too many such positions in state government, and he hoped to cut a significant number. Even though Joan had union protection, she was so concerned about losing her job that she even came to work during snow emergencies when non-essential personnel were designated to stay at home.

I knew she was trying to impress me with this level of dedication, and that she didn't want to be considered non-essential. During one particularly

---

4 I really enjoyed working with Governor Romney and his team of professionals. They were smart, polite, creative, and dedicated, and they didn't take themselves too seriously. One of their crowning achievements, although the governor later diminished its importance when he ran for president in 2008 and 2012, was the requirement that every Massachusetts resident have health insurance. Many of the provisions of the current health care system, known as Obamacare, were derived from the Massachusetts program. When Romney left office he gave us, his cabinet members, Windsor chairs with the state seal on it, a nice touch and I felt privileged to serve in his administration.

bad storm—two feet of snow on the ground, still falling, gusting winds and mini-whiteouts—I was the only person who showed up, and I didn't expect to see anyone else. Next thing I knew—Joan had arrived, dressed like a kid in ski clothing, and toting a very large lunch, correctly anticipating that every coffee shop and sandwich place would be closed. We worked for an hour, and after I sent her home I left myself.

CHAPTER 29

Joan Becomes General Counsel

I CHEERED WITH THE REST of the staff when Tom was sworn in as secretary by Governor Romney. What looked like our darkest moment had turned into our finest hour. Instead of losing our agency's identity and our jobs, we were now being elevated and distinguished from other departments. Optimism permeated the air like fragrant spring flowers on a warm breeze.

With Jack now retired, I experienced relatively little increase in my workload, since I'd been doing the majority of his duties anyway. My output actually increased, because I didn't have to put up with Jack's moods and the fallout from his antics. This set a precedent on which Tom based his decision not to hire a second attorney. While I previously hadn't any interest in being the general counsel for a variety of reasons—now I did! No second attorney in the agency meant no job for me!

The hiring of a new general counsel would be a joint decision between Tom and the executive counsel of our branch. First the position would have to be posted and advertised, followed by a series of finalists' interviews with Tom and the counsel. I assumed Tom's preference would be respected, but stranger things have happened in state government, and although I was among the top three finalists, my latent insecurity got the better of me.

Minutes before my final interview, I passed a young female applicant just leaving and went into a slight panic:

Oh God, they'll hire a young woman lawyer. I'm in my fifties; they'll want someone younger. Wait a minute! You're the incumbent with the experience; for all intents and purposes, you've been the general counsel all these months, and you're a veteran, so start feeling confident!

During the interview, I made all the points I had planned to, but the counsel seemed distant all the way through, and I couldn't tell if I'd impressed her. I worried that maybe Tom wouldn't have the last word after all.

When Tom walked into my office and told me the job was mine, my worries evaporated, and I floated like a seed pod on the wind.

Because we were a small agency, I was filling a dual role: I was the general counsel and also the legislative director, so I was invited to two sets of executive meetings. My favorites were with the governor's legislative staff where I would learn about the major issues facing other executive agencies—transportation, education, and economic development. This kept me in the know about important state issues. The latest personnel gossip was interesting, too. I was definitely an insider.

For entertainment, there was no one better than the whip-smart individual who ran these meetings, when he and another witty legislative director with a similar irreverence for the legislature riffed off each like a comedy duo. They let fly phrases like "hacks in hackarama-land," or "hack it up, baby," or "the hacks are always on hack holidays," and "have a hacky day." Everyone would dissolve into laughter. It was always amusing, and I got to be one of the *cognoscenti* as well!

While not as entertaining, the meetings for our branch counsels let me see the big legal picture in the Commonwealth. Regular topics included proposed legislation, major agency problems, as well other issues that didn't make it into the press. Of great interest to all was which agencies were being sued over what issues and by whom. Although only the attorney general's office could represent agencies in court, litigation required heavy participation by us. We were called to help draft and review pleadings, and to research and produce discovery documents. I eagerly absorbed everything and briefed Tom when I returned.

Another new responsibility came along when Tom asked me to moderate a panel discussion on veterans' issues that was open to the public. I was leery of taking on this task, as I'd not done anything like it before. About halfway into it, I noticed Tom sitting in the audience with that inscrutable look that made it difficult to know what he was thinking.

I sensed he was okay with what I was doing, and in that instant, while observing him, I realized that I no longer felt awkward, but was truly enjoying the moment. I was developing a skill I didn't even know I had. By making me his general counsel, Tom had empowered me to exceed my own expectations. I felt I had earned a place on his team. I felt that I could do almost anything he asked of me. I continued to float.

CHAPTER 30

Joan's Shifting Marriage and Dating

_6_

SHORTLY AFTER I BECAME GENERAL counsel, I felt a shift in my marriage. David and I had been to a marriage counselor, but we continued to differ on important issues. Brian had taken a break from college, and I was concerned that he wouldn't return. Financial pressures didn't help. After many hours of individual therapy and learning to be truthful with myself, I understood that I was responsible for taking some of my unhappy past into my marriage. I had married David because I loved him and because I felt he truly loved me, and, in contrast to my sometimes rocky situation at home, he was secure and stable. Despite the fact that David was a good man, and we had a wonderful son, our twenty-seven year marriage was now unraveling.

Coincidental with my marriage coming undone, Massachusetts became the first state in the nation to recognize same-sex marriage.[1] Now gay and lesbian couples could be legally married and receive all the same benefits as married straight couples. The irony was that while I was thinking about getting out of my own marriage—there was a whole cadre of the population who wanted to get into marriage.

Tom dropped by my office one morning and proclaimed brightly, "This is a great day for gay and lesbian persons. They deserve the equality they've been denied for years."

---

1 In _Goodridge v. Department of Public Health_, 440 Mass. 309 (2003), Massachusetts became the first state to recognize same sex marriages.

"Yes," I agreed. "It's an historic moment!"

I was so wrapped up in the state of my own marriage that I hadn't closely followed the landmark case. I discovered that despite the fact that same sex marriages were now being recognized in our state, there was a disconnect on the federal level. At this point, federal law didn't recognize same-sex marriages, and continued to deny benefits to those lawfully joined here. So while a veteran in a same-sex marriage was entitled to *state* chapter 115 public assistance benefits, he or she wasn't entitled to the *federal* benefits we administered in the agency's two state veterans' cemeteries. The reason was that although the state had provided the land, the cemeteries were constructed and equipped with federal funds, and the VA helped defray the cost of each funeral.

Our immediate problem was that we had a burial application pending from a same-sex married couple. Under state law, when the veteran died, the non-veteran spouse had the right to be buried with him or her. But under federal law, the non-veteran gay spouse had no right to be buried with the veteran. As I told Tom, whenever there's a conflict between state and federal law in cases like these, federal law always preempts state law, and must be followed.

I contacted the VA's general counsel in D.C., whose response was that the VA had authority to recoup all federal monies—in other words, the $19 million already granted to the agency for construction of the cemeteries—for failure to follow federal law. In addition, the feds could withhold future funding for individual burials. Despite our best efforts, the Romney administration put the issue on the back burner, and Tom and I prayed that our veteran's spouse would not pass away before the issue was resolved. Fortunately, the issue became moot.[2]

Tom and I worked hand-in-glove on this and other issues, and we learned how to accurately anticipate each other's next move. We hummed on the same frequency now, but even this could not distract me from the profound unhappiness in my own marriage. Although counseling had opened communications between David and me, it didn't bridge the gaps. We were continuously running into dead ends.

---

2 Since this time, the U.S. Supreme Court has overturned the federal law that had restricted marriage only to persons of the opposite sex.

That December, Tom and I were walking up Beacon Hill to a meeting as the frigid wind sliced through our coats, hats, and gloves.

"So have you started your Christmas shopping yet?" I asked.

"No," he said. "I don't have much to do."

"We're giving ourselves a gift, a new TV. We've had the same one for twenty-seven years. While there's nothing wrong with our set, we want a bigger screen." Naturally, our conversations went to how much TV we watched and our favorite shows. I said David and I both loved to watch British shows, especially reruns of *Fawlty Towers*.

"John Cleese is amazing."

"Isn't he?" Tom agreed. "He was great in *A Fish Called Wanda*. I loved Jamie Lee Curtis in that movie," he said.

"That's funny; my husband really liked her too. I don't think she's that attractive. What is it with her?"

"She's a sexy woman," he said.

I couldn't think of anything else to say for a few beats. Then I changed the subject.

In March, I decided to attend the governor's birthday party. It was a good opportunity to be seen and to network. Tom had mentioned he'd probably be there with his grandson, but he didn't know that I was going, and he was surprised to see me. He introduced me to his grandson, Tommy, a polite, quiet teenager with a curly head of hair. I hardly knew anyone else, so I stuck with them and felt comfortable as we flitted from one person Tom knew to another. At one point, while talking with one of Tom's friends, I gushed about how great a boss Tom was, and how he had saved the agency.

"A lesser man would have fallen apart or backed down under the same pressures. Tom not only persevered, he flourished under the strain," I said, suddenly becoming self-conscious about the tone of admiration in my voice. I hesitated, flustered, *Had I just crossed a line? Does Tom's friend think we're having an affair?* Then Tom picked up the conversation and we were onto something else. *Did Tom even hear it? Was he covering for me?*

After the three of us had met everyone Tom knew, it was time to call it a night and go our separate ways. Now I was feeling a bit uncomfortable. And it was beginning to dawn on me that my admiration for Tom had progressed to something else. I had to admit to myself that I was developing a full-fledged crush on him. I had even begun wondering what a future would be like with him.

Not long after, I began to think about what it would be like to move out of the house and have a month's separation from my marriage. I talked this over with my therapist.

In April, I took the painful step of moving out of the house. David hoped this was only temporary madness, and that I'd eventually come to my senses.

What am I doing? I loaded the car in the pelting rain that seemed to reflect my melancholy. *None of my close friends have left a long-term marriage. There's no abuse or neglect. David's nurturing and supportive love has helped me grow into an independent woman, and he gave me a wonderful son. But I don't love him the way I should.*

I unpacked, settled in, and then collapsed on the hotel room bed. I didn't know what to expect, but I realized that I felt physically and emotionally secure as I drifted to sleep, comforted by the sound of the rain against the windows. This was my own place, a safe place with a roof over my head, where I could think about whether I wanted to continue my marriage. The place felt soothing and calming.

I wasn't sure how I'd survive the month, but I planned to take it one day at a time and there was always the option of going home. I tried to see my separation as just another temporary duty assignment. But it *wasn't* temporary duty. If I proved happier single, it meant the permanent end of a long-term commitment that was supposed to last. Although Brian was in his early twenties, it also meant the end of our family unit, something I'd missed in my own childhood. I kept telling myself that the coping skills I'd developed in the reserves would get me through. I tried to convince myself that I would be okay.

Tom and Maria knew what I was doing, but not where I was staying. I didn't want Tom to know in case he'd try to find me, which was unlikely. The day I told Tom about my separation, we were sitting at a table in his office, facing each other as usual. He told me he'd been through a painful separation and gave my foot a slight kick, as if to add, "Good for you that you're doing this. It takes a lot of courage!" I desperately needed him to think well of me, and I took comfort from this small gesture.

However, my therapist wasn't so happy when I told him that Tom knew. That was a problem, he said, even though he understood how much I admired Tom. He thought I was revealing too much personal information to the boss. I couldn't accept this and broke down crying.

"You don't understand," I said. "I've told almost no one, just my closest girlfriends. I had to tell a man—someone besides you—who believes in me!"

I felt badly about myself, about failing in my marriage and about the pain I was causing David and Brian. My desperate need for Tom's support was partly to make up for my failings. I needed to have him think well of me, not just as a co-worker, but as a person I cared about. I was becoming emotionally dependent on him. I needed Tom to reaffirm me as a good person.

I explained. "He's been *through* this. This is so very, very hard." I couldn't stop crying. The therapist knew to let it go.

Everything else in my life I tried to keep the same: my work schedule, art classes, church on Sunday. Brian would come by most weekends for a visit. I'd have talks with my friend Judy. And Linda and I would go regularly for dinner and a movie. I progressed from surviving to thriving and at the end of my hotel stay, I realized that I was happier on my own. The marriage was over. When I broke the news to David, he took it hard and I was ridden with guilt and failure. But, ultimately, there would be less family stress if David and I went our separate ways.

Gradually I began to feel better about myself. I loved my new freedom and when friends asked how I was doing, I gave them the answer one rarely expects to hear in this situation. I told them I was fine, and that leaving had been the right move. They were pleased.

Early that summer during a women veterans' meeting in D.C., I confided in a colleague, a highly decorated female army colonel. In a brave moment, while feeling like I was twenty-one years old instead of fifty-five, I asked her for dating advice.

"How did you meet your husband?" I asked over a cup of coffee.

With a playful grin, she said, "Poker."

I wrinkled my brow. "Okay, you don't have to tell me."

"I'm being serious," she said. "I love poker. I used to host poker parties. The day he sat down at the table was the day I was dealt the best hand I have ever had."

I laughed. "I don't like poker. Guess I'll be single forever."

"Oh, come on, Joan. What do you like? Sailing? Traveling? There's a group for everything nowadays. Join one with lots of men."

I decided to give it a whirl. I signed up for sailing lessons. Sailing was a metaphor for my life then. To do it properly one had to be independent and confident enough to accurately gauge the wind and steer out of harm's way. I could find the wind direction, and I knew how to steer the tiller. I could work the sails and control my speed and direction, but I'd never sailed alone before. *How hard can this be?* I hoped that it wouldn't prove too difficult. It was a challenge.

I joined a women's book club, because I needed a social life that didn't solely revolve around looking for a mate. I signed up for a divorced Catholics group because having some spiritual help wasn't a bad idea either. During this time I saw Brian regularly as he alternated between staying with David and with me according to his schedule at a local garden nursery.

Plotting a way to get to know a recently divorced man at the office, I discussed my plans with Tom and Maria. Tom suggested that the three of us go out to lunch. He would arrange to have someone call him to an "emergency meeting," and leave the man and me alone. This was too contrived for my tastes, so I offered to host a party for one of our coworkers, who'd just married. I would invite the divorced man, and we'd have the opportunity to socialize.

The divorced man was a no-show at the party and I felt stood up. Feeling sorry for myself, I looked around for a distraction and started playing catch with a kid who had been dragged to the party.

It was the summer of 2004. *That makes ten.* I dragged the last of the jumbo black garbage bags to the curb and plopped it on top of the pile. Sweat covered my forehead, but I had a smile on my face. I spent my free time cleaning and making minor repairs to the downstairs apartment in my two-family house—the apartment I needed to rent if I were going to support myself.

With the last bag of trash finally piled on the curb, it was now clean and ready for new occupants.

To help pay bills and give me some company, I took into my upstairs apartment a boarder—a lovely young Korean woman named Jinny. A college graduate, she came to the U.S. to study English, and I enjoyed her companionship. As her "American mother," I enjoyed helping her with English colloquialisms and customs. We went to the local rowing regatta in the fall, handed out candy at Halloween, and made apple pie for Thanksgiving. Brian, now twenty-two, also helped Jinny learn about American popular culture.

Although not yet legally divorced, I considered myself a divorcée—rare among my group of friends, despite the statistics on marriage in the country. I was worried about how they would accept me, my dating, and possibly another marriage down the line, but I had to stay strong, healthy, and resilient. Self-doubt and panic were not options. My new mantra became: "How hard can this be?" or "I'll figure it out."

Along with Brian's unconditional love, my burgeoning independence kept my adrenaline going and I forged ahead into online dating. I was a bit leery at first. Wasn't this an impersonal and strange way to meet someone whom you hoped to spend your life with? But it had worked for others I knew of, and nobody told stories about meeting ax murderers. Unless it was that nobody survived to tell? Seriously, once I became familiar with the system and its safety features, I would work on my profile at night, on my home computer.

Working my way through the likes and dislikes, I learned a lot about myself. I got to the part about describing my ideal mate. *Why don't I just describe Tom? Even though he's not available, he has all the qualities I admire. He's confident, forceful and humble at the same time. When he's not being serious, he acts boyish and slightly mischievous. He's not someone to deceive or mislead. He talks in a straightforward manner without offending people, but still gets his points across. Also, I love the way he dresses for work in those elegant wool suits with the pleated pants. And because he's a real person, I wouldn't be creating a paragon of virtue to which no man could ever measure up.*

My online description of an ideal mate took the following form:

"I would like to meet someone of high moral character who takes good care of himself with a healthy lifestyle. He doesn't have to look like a movie star, but should take pride and care in his dress and grooming. It's important that he's done something in his life for others, whether it is in government, military service, teaching, or charitable/religious work. I am also looking for a man whom I find attractive and exciting and who finds me equally attractive and exciting. I prefer one who is separated or divorced and has children. A good sense of humor is vital along with a survivor's mentality and intelligence. Someone who is well-educated and likes to read would be great. Looking for an active man who wants a mate and a partner. A leader and a good team player who thinks the team is more important than he would be my ideal. I am also looking for a long-term and stable relationship."

I showed this description of my prospective mate to Maria and Tom. Maria thought everything looked good. Tom had no clue that my requirements stemmed from him or that I may have been looking for his approval. Even after I specifically asked him,

"Should I include my navy experience? Would this put a man off as too—I don't know—aggressive or unwomanly?"

"Of course, you should include your navy experience," he said. "It's such a big part of your life. It's something to be proud of. If a man doesn't appreciate your naval service, you shouldn't be dating him anyway."

"Okay, but what about these photos. Here's one with glasses and one without."

"No, use the eyeglasses. That's who you are. There's nothing wrong with a woman wearing eyeglasses. In fact, on the right person it's attractive," he offered. "I hope you find this mythical character you've concocted," he looked up with a grin as he passed back the photos.

Oddly, Tom had gone from being my inscrutable boss, to my go-to "girl-friend" for dating advice.

One night after several failed attempts to get my online dating system working, I cried myself to sleep in frustration. I was desperate to meet the right person. I badly wanted to be in love and not alone. I was learning that it takes courage to find someone to truly love in a committed relationship. You put everything into loving someone and face the possibility that it may not work out over time. Unlike the love between parents and children, the love between a man and a woman is a gamble. You risk rejection and being hurt, and it doesn't matter how old you are.

For some, the risk is too high, so they avoid it. Other people and interests fulfill their lives. But I didn't have other people to take the place of a mate—no parents or siblings as my brother's mental condition was only worsening. My son was a young man with his own life. While I loved my work, it wasn't as complete and fulfilling as a mature loving relationship with a man. I had to find a mate; my survival and future happiness required it. And that's what drove me during the darkest hours. Although the course I was embarked on felt like the emotional equivalent of jumping off a cliff, I also felt an undercurrent of excitement and hope. Maybe I *would* find my perfect soulmate?

On a date, a conversation should be like a tennis match, right? One person says something, then waits for the other to respond, then says something again. One of my first dates was with a man who dominated the conversation. After a while, I got so confused about which topic we were on that I couldn't remember what I was going to say next, even when there was a pause. Although he'd had a long career in the National Guard and I liked the fact that he took responsibility for his marriage break-up, the conversation was strictly one-way. I decided to keep quiet for the rest of the date. Apparently he knew things hadn't gone well. When he asked me if we would see each other again, he didn't seem surprised when I said no.

I continued with my extra-curricular activities hoping they would put me in situations where I'd meet men who shared my interests. When I described my sailing adventures to Tom—leaving out the part about how I once deliberately ran aground and walked ashore—he told me he loved sailing and that he used to teach it summers up in Maine where his family went. I changed the subject, because it was around that time that I realized my infatuation for Tom had turned into genuine love.

I'm already so in love with you that I've described you as my ideal mate, which you don't even know because you're so modest and have no idea what a special man you are. Now you're going to tell me you have all these other interests we share that I knew nothing about, so I'll be even more in love with you?

I found it hard to stop thinking about Tom, and I was angry at myself for lacking the discipline. But he was with me day and night, a phantom companion, except when I'd see him at work, of course. In my non-work hours, I often felt I'd suffered the loss of a long-time mate or friend and carried him spiritually. Tom wasn't gone from this earth. As my boss, he was unavailable to me.

I wasn't interested in a casual affair. I cared for him too much to hurt him, I didn't want to get hurt myself and I didn't want to hurt others. Instead, I pushed my thoughts aside and kidded and joked with him in the usual relaxed way he called "shucking and jiving." Whenever I spoke with him, I thought I saw a gleam in his eye that I'd not noticed before. The light that was there when he was smiling felt like the sun shining on me, full of warmth and cheer. When it wasn't there, I felt cold and dejected.

Sometimes when passing his office from the street, I would stop in his window and make faces at him, if he wasn't on the phone, until he laughed. One day I went by and found the blinds drawn. My world went gray. *Was he trying to shut me out? Did he feel our relationship had become too personal?*

CHAPTER 31
Tom on Joan

⟿

HAVING BEEN THROUGH THE END of a long-term marriage myself, I worried about Joan during this time. Although she was a subordinate, she was closer to me than other staff because of the special naval bond we shared. We'd each been drawn by the Siren's call to adventure. We'd each assumed greater responsibility at a young age than many in the civilian world. We'd experienced similar struggles in getting promoted, but also the joy of working with the greatest team on earth.

Although I had more service time, and actual combat duty, we'd been cast in the same crucible. I'd think of what President John F. Kennedy once said, "I can imagine no more rewarding a career. And any man who may be asked in this century what he did to make his life worthwhile, I think, can respond with a good deal of pride and satisfaction, 'I served in the United States Navy.'" Considering that we'd both served in the same place at the same time (Newport, RI, and Norfolk, VA), and that we were both nurtured in the same Boston culture, it's amazing we didn't meet sooner.

I empathized with Joan as I remembered how I anguished over whether my separation had been the right decision and how it would affect the family. And I knew how painful the divorce had been for Gwen and especially for the girls. The feelings of guilt and failure could be overwhelming. Not to mention the loneliness.

Joan was taking on a daunting task in trying to find the man of her dreams. She looked great. She was an attractive woman who stayed in shape, kept her looks up, and dressed well, but she was, after all, middle-aged. Her problem was a matter of numbers. There weren't that many suitable men available. Yet, she seemed at peace with her decision and optimistic that Mr. Right would come along. I thought she was either delusional or extremely courageous. I liked this newly independent side of her I was seeing.

Time went on and I heard more about her dates. One was with someone who'd been in the navy about the same time as I. He'd gone to college later, but she didn't feel that they had much in common. Still, she remained hopeful that she'd find her soulmate out there. I became more interested in hearing about her dates, secretly hoping they'd fail and, on some level, trying to compete against them.

"Don't wait too long to find someone. Time's running out," I admonished her once. But was I really speaking to myself?

Away from work, I found myself thinking about Joan. *Was she all right? What was she doing for supper? Was she lonely?*

I worried about the kind of person she'd meet. There could be an ax murderer out there.

CHAPTER 32

Together

—↶—

EVENTUALLY TOM AND I FOUND our way to one another. We married in 2005. I moved to another agency. Temporarily, Tom moved into my house, but we both yearned for our own single-family home. Cambridge was too expensive, so after our marriage, we looked next door in Somerville and found a lovingly cared for Victorian that needed a little work. It's where we live today.

We have great neighbors, and the gentrification that's taking place ensures a happy future with more young families moving in.

Not even a winning lottery ticket could take the place of the life Tom and I now lived. Home, marriage, even my new job were blessings. We were a team. We thought alike in many ways, yet respected each other's differences. We were determined that nothing would get in the way of our new happiness. We planned to keep the stress out of our lives by realizing certain events were beyond our control, looking for silver linings, keeping a sense of humor, and focusing on the gift of our great love.

Unfortunately, large dark clouds were gathering that would negatively impact us both. But life never stays the same. Nothing is forever. Change is constant and all we can do is adapt.

CHAPTER 33

A Thousand Cuts

⟶⟵

WE SAILED ON AN EVEN keel into and throughout 2006. Governor Romney left at the end of his first term, in January 2007, to run as a Republican candidate for President. He said he'd appreciated my efforts in leading veterans' programs for the Commonwealth. I had built an excellent team by allowing good people to do their best without getting in their way. I was responsible for major decisions, and, best of all, the governor's office didn't interfere with or try to set the course for our actions. He was my type of leader.

Under Romney, veterans' issues were truly non-partisan with most of our initiatives strongly supported by the Republican administration and the Democratic legislature. Unfortunately, all that would change when a new governor took office in 2007.

My initial reaction to the new governor was that he didn't have a solid grasp on state veterans' programs. Though he'd been educated in Massachusetts, he'd lived elsewhere for many years. On the plus side, I had formed a good relationship over time with his lieutenant governor. We'd worked together on building a memorial for Vietnam veterans and pushing the VA to open another outpatient clinic. I counted on him as a reliable friend and strong advocate for veterans. And so, when early in the new administration, the lieutenant governor was given the task of overseeing veterans' programs, I felt it was a good sign.

My team had developed an agency recognized for doing more for its veterans, including the new generation, than almost any other state.

A call from a worried parent whose son had been seriously injured in Iraq led me to a young marine named James. I saw something of myself in James:

his wounds, the mystery of his whereabouts, and then having to deal with his wartime injuries. I monitored his progress closely as he recuperated.

When James was better, I reached out to him on numerous occasions and eventually convinced him to join the agency. We needed new blood. He was smart, very personable, and I knew the younger veterans would relate well to him. I put him in charge of the suicide prevention program (SAVE) and watched his rapid transformation from a frail and angry young man into a dedicated team leader who produced good results. He told me he felt motivated and fulfilled each day to do his personal best to help his peers.

I wrote to the incoming governor describing the agency's work and formally asked him for the privilege of continuing to lead the agency under his administration. I waited for a reply—and kept waiting.

I thought I might hear something about my status after the inauguration. But January came and went and there was still no word. The first clue that things were going to be different was when I went to the governor's initial cabinet meeting. Before I even got into the room, a functionary asked me who I was and then told me that I was no longer in the cabinet. A call would have saved me a trip up the hill, but I attributed it to early days and organizational growing pains.

Some of my friends, associates, and veteran colleagues began a campaign on my behalf and sent letters to the governor's office, pointing out our successes and recommending that he reappoint me. But a strange occurrence was unfolding the likes of which had not been seen in recent administrations. Not only were agency heads rolling with virtually no notice, even middle managers were being replaced by new political hires. Experience, qualifications, or competence didn't always stand. The new hires were being rewarded with government jobs often solely for their work on the election campaign.

Predictably, this administration would fire someone on a Friday, knowing it would be in the Saturday newspapers with a small, weekend readership. It got so that Joan and I would wake up after the Saturday paper thudded against the front door, and head downstairs to find out who'd been fired that week. When *my* name didn't appear, we toasted each other with our coffee mugs.

Finally, a year later, the governor's chief of staff told me that the administration was pleased with my performance as secretary. I suggested they end the uncertainty and suspense and strengthen the agency's position by officially appointing me as secretary, which they agreed to do.

I continued to enjoy my work for the veterans of Massachusetts despite an attractive job offer in the spring of 2009 from the new VA secretary, Rick Shinseki, a highly decorated Vietnam veteran and a person of integrity.[1] I notified the governor of this offer and assured him that I would remain serving Massachusetts veterans.

Even though I was seemingly secure in my position, I began to sense a change in my relationship with the governor's office and with my immediate boss. This change seemed coincidental to the arrival of an individual who'd worked on the campaign, and whom the administration directed me to hire. I was gradually and increasingly being left out of decisions regarding veterans. Many times my bosses were by-passing me and dealing with the person I'd been directed to hire, and also, with a few of my staff. This was embarrassing and counter-productive.

When my team realized that I was being marginalized, morale in the agency dropped like a brick tossed into the sea. It was clear to them that the person I'd been directed to hire was trying to take over. On any given day, staff wasn't sure who was in charge. No servant can serve two masters. He will either hate one and love the other, or be devoted to one and despise the other.[2] In the navy, politics of this sort could jeopardize the mission, which is why it rarely happened.

In early 2010, the re-election campaign swung into high gear. I refused to be dragged into a political contest, knowing that caring for veterans was and had always been a non-partisan effort in Massachusetts. This year was different. Under intense pressure from the campaign, the agency was directed to produce a video podcast—using public funds—highlighting the veterans' programs in the state. What resulted was, in effect, a campaign ad touting not

---

1 General Shinseki stood up to former Defense Secretary Rumsfeld in President George W. Bush's administration in urging that more forces be used in the initial invasion of Iraq, in 2003, to guarantee success. Shortly after, the White House side-lined him.
2 The Gospel according to Luke, Chapter 16, verses 1–13.

the long history we enjoyed caring for veterans, but rather what had been accomplished since the new administration took control. It smelled of electioneering and cost thousands to produce. Predictably, it was used at campaign stops around the state, and it made me physically ill, but at least I could look myself in the mirror each day, having had nothing to do with it.

There were other instances of the administration's politics in the workplace. I even went to my immediate boss with my concerns, but was told there was nothing they could do about it.

My dilemma was: did I expose the malfeasance to the public, which would have led to my dismissal, or did I stay and try to look after veterans and the people who worked in the agency?

At home, Joan and I tried to stay centered on the positive. But the thought of what would happen to veterans if I lost control of the agency was as difficult to shed as a nagging headache. It was so disturbing that we made a pact not to discuss it after dinner.

Meanwhile, many happy personal events occurred such as Brian's and my grandson Tommy's college graduations. We traveled to Naples and southern Italy for a couple of weeks, where the hospitality of Joan's relatives was equally matched by the hospitality our navy family provided when we stayed at Capodichino. We had grand visits with the top navy commanders in Europe and their sailors and marines.[3] I had a lump in my throat and tears pricked my eyes when one commander greeted us at his headquarters and rendered full military honors to me, including the Sixth Fleet band playing the national anthems of Italy and the United States.

No matter how troublesome my days were at work, I reminded myself that I wasn't getting shot at, not literally, anyway, and the ship wasn't sinking. And so it went, death by a thousand cuts. But the final cut was yet to come.

Just after Christmas of 2010, my boss called me in to explain that, although the administration valued my services, it had decided to go in a new direction and replace me with the individual I'd been told to hire. My

---

3 At the time, Admiral Mark Fitzgerald was commander U.S. Naval Forces and Admiral Harry Harris was Commander, Sixth Fleet.

employment would end in three weeks. It was like being punched in the face and pushed in front of a Mack truck.

Whereas in Vietnam, I'd lost an eye, I didn't lose anything physical as a result of the political practices of the administration. Rather, my survivor's instincts taught me to pick myself up after being knocked down, and move on. So I took the high road.

Sure, I had mixed emotions. Although leaving wasn't due to any failure on my part, it was still hard for me to accept that I'd been let go.[4] How nice reinstatement would have been—or at least reinstatement until I could find something else. I'd fantasize that outrage in the veterans' community and the extensive media coverage that was on-going would prompt the administration to reconsider its decision.[5] Clearly, this was a pipe dream.

Eventually reality had a calming effect on me. There was nothing further I could do. I had no control over the situation. I served at the governor's pleasure, and I accepted the inevitable. At least the uncertainty was over. What helped me the most was looking back over the past twelve years and taking a good deal of pride in the many achievements of the agency that I'd been privileged to lead and serve. Now my sleep improved.

But Joan was not sleeping well. She struggled with the way in which I was let go. "It's as if they tossed you out like a stale loaf of bread! You are respected and beloved among the veterans' community and even beyond."

I worried about her getting up before dawn to read laws and regulations and compose legal arguments meant to reverse the course. But her hard work was to no avail. In the end, she helped organize a rally for me outside the State House on a bitterly cold day. My closest supporters were there, and while the event made us feel better at the time, it only heightened our sadness once it was over. We both took some consolation in learning that even people who didn't know me could easily surmise from what they read in the papers that I was treated badly.

---

4 As I said, although of course there were politics in the navy, people were generally "let go" for cause, or for the good of the service because the individual was not measuring up. Firing someone for purely political reasons was not the practice.

5 A series of articles in the *Boston Globe, Boston Herald*, and *Patriot Ledger* revealed the administration's political shenanigans and my shoddy treatment.

One morning in February 2011, out of the blue, Charlie Baker, who had just lost the bid for governor as the Republican challenger, called me.[6] While I had known Charlie through a mutual friend, when Charlie was head of a healthcare insurance company, I hadn't seen him in years, so the call was a surprise.

"Who was that?" Joan asked after I hung up.

"Charlie Baker," I said. "He wanted to know if anyone was doing anything for me in the way of my retirement. I said no, not really, and he asked if he could do something."

"What did you say?"

"I said I wasn't sure and I wanted to think about it."

"If someone wants to do something nice for you, why don't you let them?" she said. "I don't think we'd be reliving the trauma of what happened. This would be something positive. It would honor you and celebrate your years of public service."

"I know this is supposed to be my retirement," I told her, "but I don't feel comfortable being the center of attention. If it could be a fund-raiser for a worthy charity, I would be okay with that."

Certainly that phone call from Charlie helped me see things in a more positive light but, admittedly, at some point we both questioned Charlie's intentions. It now seems strange that we were actually looking for negatives in his very thoughtful offer, but politics had made us overly cautious and gun shy.

Sanity prevailed, and we knew Charlie's offer was heartfelt and genuine. With his gentle persistence and Joan's encouragement, I finally agreed that my retirement party would be a fundraiser for the Massachusetts Soldiers' Legacy Fund. One hundred percent of the money raised would go to the charity.

Joan jumped in, hands and feet, and after our first meeting with Charlie that winter, her eyes were wide with excitement.

---

6 As it turned out, Charlie Baker would run a successful bid in 2014 and became governor in 2015. His hard work and excellent bi-partisan effort have earned him a high degree of favorability to date.

"Tom," she said, "this is going to be great! I was totally impressed with Charlie and his people."

I started to pick up on her enthusiasm. I liked the idea of a "classy, dignified, nonpartisan, happy celebration," as Joan put it, which would also help fallen veterans' children.

Soon we were working side by side with Charlie and his young and talented team making the fund-raiser happen. For three months, all worked for *gratis* under Charlie's leadership. His six-foot, four-inch presence was both physically and symbolically large in the room and we grew to admire him.

The big day was fast approaching. Joan and I grew slightly more nervous as sponsors and featured guests lined up and the event took shape. *Would we raise enough money to cover our expenses and have a decent sized donation to the charity?* The tables sold out, which was great, but the sponsors had more seats than they could fill. We didn't want the empty chairs to look like no-shows. Soon my days were consumed with filling empty seats by calling my contacts at the local ROTC units, the VA, the Massachusetts National Guard, a couple of local navy units, my high school and college, the University of Massachusetts veterans' association, and the state soldiers' homes.

Joan was busy with her own special assignment. I suggested we could get away with a rotating slide show of photos highlighting my forty-year public service career, but she had bigger plans—and produced a full-fledged video. She wrote a script, found a narrator, located film and video footage of me, along with photos, and put it all to music. She worked with professional film editors to complete it, and it turned out great.

Little by little, with every phone call, with every completed preparation, we felt ourselves being lifted to a higher place. Bitterness was taking a back seat to building excitement about what was looking to be a tremendous night.

⁓

And almost before we know it, the main event is over and we are going home—

Charlie closes the event at 9:30 p.m. by announcing we'd raised $300,000 and thanking the volunteers. He tells the audience that I didn't want an event just *for myself, that I had to be talked into it and convinced it was going to support a good cause. He adds, "Tom even bought his own tickets!" I publicly express my gratitude that he humbly accepts.*

Joan and I round up our kids and cross the street to meet Charlie and some others for the after party at a pub. As we're walking hand-in-hand Joan says, "You did a great job tonight. I was so proud of you."

I smile as I put my arm around her waist, hold her close and tell her, "All because you were there supporting me."

⁓๑

A May 11, 2011, piece by the *Boston Globe*'s Adrian Walker highlighted what I regard as a most important value: perseverance. In this case, it took the form of putting aside the past and moving on to new challenges.

He wrote: "Kelley had no interest in reigniting the controversy that broke out after he was replaced, saying diplomatically, 'I really had a wonderful experience working for the state and was able to get a lot of good things done. I feel very good about my life.'" The article also quoted Charlie as saying that my career called for an appropriate send-off. "Anyone I talked to had nothing but great things to say about him, and twelve years is a long time to advocate for veterans, anywhere, including Massachusetts. He got a lot of important things done."

Later in the article, Charlie modestly minimized his own efforts by saying, "I didn't give Tom a great night; he earned it, one act and one day at a time. I was just able to take advantage of all the good work he had done over the years."

Much of the good will generated that night lives on. I still run into people who tell me how much they enjoyed it. As for Joan and me, the afterglow has stayed with us and even now when we pass the photo of us from that night that lives in our bookshelf, we can't help but smile.

CHAPTER 34

Moving On and Looking Ahead

⁓ɕ⁓

AFTER A FEW JOB INTERVIEWS in veterans-related areas, I decided I relished setting my own priorities and being master of my own time. I had little interest in returning to a full-time position.

Soon, I was asked to serve on the leadership board of the VA's New England healthcare system. The VA's Secretary Shinseki appointed me as his representative on the Army's Arlington National Cemetery Advisory Commission, on which I still proudly serve.[1] My friend Andy Bacevich, military historian and author, recommended me for an honorary doctor of laws degree from Boston University that I received. For my work with veterans suffering from the hidden wounds of war, I was awarded an honorary doctoral degree from the Massachusetts School of Professional Psychology, and I now serve on their veterans' advocacy team.[2]

My Medal of Honor colleagues elected me to a two-year term as president of the Congressional Medal of Honor Society. I enjoy being responsible for the health and welfare of our nearly eighty recipients and their spouses. It's almost like being the skipper of a ship again. It's a pleasure working with and

---

1 After the misplacement and misidentification of certain remains became an issue, Congress mandated this group to review and report on the improvements.

2 The school is now called the William James College.

just hanging around some of our youngest recipients, who served during the Global War on Terror, and who are able to reach our youth on a special level.[3]

Our Character Development Program in middle, high, and now elementary schools draws lessons from the recipients' lives on courage, commitment, citizenship, sacrifice, patriotism and integrity. As a director of the Congressional Medal of Honor Foundation, I make sure the best interests of our recipients are represented before this group of highly accomplished and dedicated men and women.

I remain close to Holy Cross and serve on its O'Callahan Society that supports NROTC there.[4] From time to time, I mentor students at B.C. High, and I'm active in alumni events.

In my spare time, I provide meals to the local homeless shelter, and I assist in running the veterans' ministry at my church. Always an avid reader, I now have time for books on history and biography, as well as by my favorite fiction writers.

Joan retired as an attorney from the state with twenty plus years of service. Among her activities are volunteering at our church, weekly walking with her lady friends, gardening, and reading. Influenced by two of her favorite humorists (author Dave Barry and local comedian Jimmy Tingle), she keeps promising to take a comedy-improv class, and I might join her.

Oh, and we've both put many hours into this memoir. It's taken three years to get to this state (because we didn't know what we were doing), and the slow process has nearly driven us mad, as we're both so results-oriented. But it's kept us from hanging on street corners and stealing hubcaps—neither of which young people do any more. Seriously, we've learned a lot about good writing, the editing process (it's never done), and the agent-publisher business (difficult). We've read a good many books we might not have, learned new words, and looked up the meanings of ones we thought we knew pretty well.

---

3 Ed Byers, Kyle Carpenter, Ty Carter, Sal Giunta, Flo Groberg, Dakota Meyer, Leroy Petry, Ryan Pitts, Clint Romesha, Will Swenson, and Kyle White.

4 Commander Joseph O'Callahan, a Jesuit priest and navy chaplain, lost his life organizing damage control to put out the inferno caused by a kamikaze attack, while also tending to the dying, during World War II in the Pacific.

It's reassuring that we can write coherent sentences and organize material in an interesting and logical way: we haven't lost our minds yet!

I don't pretend to have all the answers. I'm just an ordinary man who, when facing the biggest challenge of his life, acted in a way he was trained to. The fact that others found my action extraordinary doesn't diminish my belief that they would have acted similarly under the same circumstances. We've written this book to explore the values we've lived and to share our strong belief that a life lived for others and with courage, especially courage to take an unpopular, but morally right stance, is a fully satisfying one. A life lived without courage is only half a life.

And to use an old saw: "if at first you don't succeed, try, try, again!" Life offers second chances, sometimes more, as we personally discovered. If you keep hopeful, you'll recognize them when they come again, sometimes disguised as something else—maybe not exactly your first choice, but close enough! When people say they are "lucky," they generally mean they were in the position to take advantage of opportunities that came their way. Not that they were struck with a thunderbolt of luck out of nowhere. Usually and thankfully, many of us get our share of second chances.

For us, finding true love in mid-life was a rare blessing, but worth every moment of waiting. We were cast in the same crucible of service, which helped us develop courage and perseverance. We traveled parallel paths that intersected at the right moment. Had they intersected earlier, we might not have been mutually attracted to each other. Had they intersected later, it might have been too late. Divine fate intervened with our decisions about careers, family and what matters most in life.

Things happen for a reason.

ACKNOWLEDGMENTS

WE'D LIKE TO THANK THE following people who helped make this book possible: First, our children for loving us and having faith in us all these years. Next: our grandson-artist John DuVal who created an original painting for the book cover, and his Emily for promotion help.

Appreciation goes to our sharp editor and author in her own right, Lori Goldstein, for her exacting eye, painstaking and conscientious editing that is always on deadline, as well as her guidance in the publishing process, and encouragement through numerous rejections. Plus she gave us the book title, *The Siren's Call*. We also appreciate our excellent proofreader, Daniel Barks, who fine-tuned our story in a very short time.

The following individuals, some of whom took the time to read our manuscript, made helpful suggestions, and eventually led us to the self-publishing world, deserve credit. They are authors Bill Albracht, Joe Callo, Dick Couch, Tom Cutler, George Daughan, Carl Higbie, Adam Makos, Alex Quade, and John Timmins; publishers Tom Colgan, Bruce Bortz, and Erika DiPasquale; and agents Dan Pollack, John Silbersack, Timothy Strabbing, and Vinny Viola.

My gratitude goes to my Medal of Honor colleagues who graciously shared their editing and publishing knowledge and contacts with us: Sammy and Dixie Davis, Wes Fox, Sal Giunta, Tom Hudner, Jack Jacobs, Jim Livingston, Tommy Norris and Mike Thornton, Leo Thorsness, and Clint Romesha.

To our friends who listened sympathetically while we griped about the state of modern publishing, but also helped keep our spirits afloat along the way, goes our appreciation: Bob Ahern, Kevin Ainsworth, Andy Bacevich, Charlie and Lauren Baker, Linda and Mark Burke, Gerry Byrne, Mario and Mary Conway, Denise Farrell, Anita Hampl, Georgea Hudner, Lucine Kasbarian, Judy Kamm, Nancy and Rick Kelleher, *the amazing* Tiffany Kovaleski, Moira Linehan, Tom Lyons, Sally McElwreath, Grace McMann, Marie Schappert, Perry Smith, Bob Ticehurst, David Warsh, and anyone else we may have forgotten.

Finally, we want to thank each other for staying the course in this three-year project, when we sometimes felt like throwing it out the window, literally and figuratively. Yes, we had 150 rejections, but we learned from each one. In the end, we told the story we wanted, in the way we wanted.

In the process, we learned more about each other as we probed our family histories, childhoods, and formative years. And as we read each word aloud to one another day after day, through early drafts and numerous revisions, it was like falling in love all over again, if such a thing is possible.

Fortune has shined on us, because we've been able to share this project, while also enjoying the luxury of good health and the leisure time in which to do it. Beyond our great bond, we're grateful for the many blessings we enjoy: loving children, grandchildren and their spouses, great friends, exciting careers, and, now, a comfortable retirement.

We're proud of the final results and hope we'll inspire others to hold onto their dreams and hopes, even in the darkest moments.

PHOTOGRAPHS FROM
AUTHORS' COLLECTION

Tom on Beach, Maine, 1941

Tom and John Boating, Maine, 1944

Basil and Elizabeth Kelley, Maine, 1959

President Richard Nixon awarding Tom the Medal of Honor. Daughters Liza,
Kate, and Jane in foreground with wife Gwen. Standing right is Bob Kerrey,
MOH recipient; former governor and U.S. senator from Nebraska, 1970

Elisa and Carmine Antonio Russo

Rudy and Gemma Russo with Tony and Elisa, 1939

Tom and Gemma Chiara, 1947

Gemma, Ensign Uncle Matt, and Tom, U.S. Naval Academy, 1948

Joan Chiara, 1953

Joan and Ballet, 1959

Tom's Retirement, 1990

Tom and Admiral Mike Booda

Kate, Liza and Jane Kelley

Tom Hudner, Joan and Mary Jane Hillery, Women's Memorial, D.C., 1997

Tom and Joan, N.Y. Stock Exchange

Tom and Governor Mitt Romney, 2006

Andrea Young and Brian O'Connor

Dina and Tom DuVal, Emily Petrick, and John DuVal

THE AUTHORS

Tom and Joan Kelley

TOM KELLEY SERVED FOR THIRTY years in the U.S. Navy, after which he took care of Massachusetts veterans as the secretary of veterans' services for the Commonwealth. He was awarded the Congressional Medal of Honor in 1970. A graduate of Boston College High School and the College of the Holy Cross, Tom is the father of three daughters and he has two grandsons.

Joan (Chiara) Kelley served in the Naval Reserve for twenty years and was an attorney for various government agencies. She received her B.A. in English from Emmanuel College, an M.S. degree in public relations from Boston University, and her J.D. from New England School of Law. She is the mother of one son.

Tom and Joan live in Somerville, Massachusetts, and travel through-out the country for the Congressional Medal of Honor Society, of which he's currently president.

To reach Tom and Joan, email: elisadchiara@gmail.com.